Running the Trans America Footrace

Running the Trans America Footrace

Trials and Triumphs of Life on the Road

Barry Lewis

Foreword by Ted Corbitt

Stackpole Books

Copyright © 1994 by Stackpole Books

Published by
STACKPOLE BOOKS
5067 Ritter Road
Mechanicsburg, PA 17055

Printed in the United States of America

Cover photo by Barry Lewis
Cover design by Tina Lloyd

First Edition

10 9 8 7 6 5 4 3 2 1

Library of Congress Cataloging-in-Publication Data

Lewis, Barry, 1959–
    Running the Trans America Footrace: trials and triumphs of life on the road/ by Barry Lewis; foreword by Ted Corbitt.—1st ed.
        p. cm.
    ISBN 0-8117-2582-0
    1. Trans America Footrace, 1992. I. Title.
GV1062.5.T73L49 1994
796.42'4'0973—dc20   94-26474
                                                                                          CIP

For Lisa—
With all my love

Contents

Foreword

As the 1992 inaugural Trans America Footrace contestants neared their "Holy Grail," the finish line in New York City's beautiful Central Park, two runner friends reminded me that the race was about to come to an end. The years of false starts in getting a coast-to-coast running event off the ground appeared to be over. A race was alive at last.

As the weary runners drifted across the finish line, I studied their running forms and speculated that I could have done well in such a race when I had my best running skills. I was reminded that man's spirit of adventure knows no bounds. If he can think of a stunt, more often than not he can eventually do it. Man has long been a wanderer, both out of curiosity and out of necessity, reenacting symbolically a need to explore, or to find new homes and sources of food.

Many years earlier, I had watched a woman from Great Britain finish a walk across the United States. She walked into the famed Times Square area in New York City, during the height of evening rush-hour traffic, after the most publicized solo crossing to date.

I also watched Don Shepherd of South Africa, Bruce Tulloh of Great Britain, Mavis Hutchison of South Africa, Jay Birmingham of Florida, and James Shapiro of New York finish their solo cross-America runs. They all started in California and finished in New York City. I saw one other runner take off from New York, heading for the West Coast. There are other solo runners who have slipped into or out of New York City underpublicized, barely noticed, completely unsung.

I seriously thought of making a solo run across the United States myself after reading about the professional transcontinental runs held in 1928 and 1929. In 1968, my appetite for such a run was whetted when Tulloh ran across the country in a record sixty-four days, covering 2,800 miles. During the same period of time that Tulloh was making his run, I ran 2,000 miles in training, while working a full-time job. I reasoned that if I could avoid injury and accidents, I could cross in a faster time.

I made preliminary plans for such a run after conferring with Bill Wiklund, a long-distance runner from Clifton, New Jersey. He had been a handler for John Salo, a Finnish American who lived in New Jersey and who had won the 1929 Transcontinental Race. I had previously read Wiklund's unpublished book about Salo's winning race.

In the summer of 1974, I got permission from my employer, the ICD (International Center for the Disabled), where I worked as a physical therapist, to take two weeks of unpaid leave and add it to my month's vacation to run from California to New York City. My target was an all-out charge for home in forty-two days. I planned to start each day with a brisk 2-mile walk to loosen up and end each day with a 4-mile walk to facilitate recovery and rehydration of the body. I planned to do extra-long days as my energy level permitted or when I woke up early. Success would depend on getting good, flexible handler help and staying relatively injury-free.

I was already physically fit after twenty-three years as a marathoner and ultramarathoner, and from numerous exploratory training run stunts. My feet were so toughened that it was impossible to penetrate the skin with a needle to drain a blister.

A "fast run" seemed doable. In late 1974, however, I developed bronchial asthma, which stopped me from starting off for my targeted goal. I never again got fit enough to run well. I was fifty-four and had waited too long to make the effort.

Annually, thousands of runners do more than the 3,000 miles needed to cover the distance across the United States, but compressing that mileage into less than two months puts one in a different world.

Many trans-America runs have been done just as personal stunts, with time not a crucial factor. Other solo runs have been done with the clock as the prime competitor. In 1985 a modern race across the United States took place, with New Jersey's Marvin Skagerberg defeating Malcolm Campbell of Great Britain in a two-man event.

The enthusiasts lured by the challenge of crossing our vast nation have included adventuresome health seekers, skaters, bicyclists, pedestrians (including race walkers), retirees who wanted to see some of the country, handicapped athletes, plus all kinds of runners: novices, former record holders, veteran track men, marathoners, and ultramarathoners.

The time of year selected to run across America is an important consideration affecting survival and success. Besides weather, hazards include snakes, scorpions, dogs, vehicles, people under the influence of substances or in bad moods, and the possibility of developing either crippling or run-ending soft tissue or joint injuries en route.

Those who strive to run across the country in a fast time need a great deal of good luck and some special preparations to toughen the body. They must be prepared to deal with a lot of intermittent pain and to survive deep fatigue symptoms that affect everyone differently and await all who run for very long periods of time. There is no way to know about the demoralizing physical and emotionally destabilizing feelings until a sustained effort produces them. The runner finds out then if he or she has the will to endure a lot of suffering and the stomach to get the job done.

Some successful runners like Tulloh have done this run with minimal extra running preparations. He had assistance, and during one breakdown period, he was moving East with the aid of a walking cane. Shepherd also ran solo, unassisted, at one point having to deal with flood waters. Shapiro ran solo, with occasional handler assistance. Birmingham had no handler help. Prior extensive training and racing experience at long distances does not guarantee success.

It is hoped that there will be a permanent annual or biennial Trans America Footrace, either as a "Go as You Please" event or the safer, more manageable stage format, and that sponsorship dollars will arrive to meet expenses and provide meaningful prize money as the athletes' reward.

Besides trophies and possible money for those taking on a Trans America Footrace, there are personal rewards—mainly experiencing the kingly, uplifting sense of conquering and savoring the achievement of the quest. The finishers bank physical and emotional booty.

The observing populace and the race supporters share in the run experience through vicarious means, all getting energized, entertained, and buoyed up by a successful event. Hail to those who endure, who never completely give up!

Ted Corbitt, New York City
September 28, 1993

Acknowledgments

Twenty-eight athletes had the courage to join a pair of dreamers on a beach in California to embark on a journey that would change them forever. This is their story. To them, and to the two who had the audacity to believe that they could orchestrate a running race across the country, I am in debt. To Dale Beam, John Surdyk, and Tom Rogozinski go special thanks for helping me see through the darkness and recapture the light.

To the many people who knew of the race and took time out of their lives specifically to help, we are all thankful. Most notably, they are Gutdayzke, Oliver Volk, Michael Hansmann, Bob Wise, Thelma Porter, Lori Walker, Sharyne Herbert, Lorraine Harrison, Don Choi, Bill Shultz, Al Cruzado, Bob and Sara Risser, Stan Baker, and Patrick Cooper.

You meet many people when you take a journey. This journey, like most, became more about them than about the places we saw. Of the hundreds who coordinated stopovers, encouraged, fed, and put roofs over the heads of the Trans America group, special thanks go to Erv Nicholls, Harry Drew, Dick Devlin, Jim and Sue Ellison, Carla Ely, Carey Horton, Julie Westland-Litus, Marshall Ulrich, Jerry Dunn, Janet Bruce, Yola-Bee Strobel, Linda-Rex Dobson, Terri Carroll, Julie Clark, Richard Lutovsky, Jeanne Carmody, Kevin O'Grady, Ron Hart, Bonnie Busch, Sam Berthenthal, Mike Witter, William Campbell, Rich Innamorato, Tom McGrath, and Fred Lebow. Kudos, of course, to all the rest.

The medical team was a wondrous conglomeration of students and professionals who gave freely of themselves, their time, and their supplies to keep the runners moving forward. Without Mark McKeigue, D.O., Andrew Lovy, D.O., and student doctor Jordan Ross, the number of finishers would surely have been halved. The network they pulled together on extremely short notice included Kathryn Calabria, Larry Copeland, John Doran, Erik Emaus, Edward Hoffman, Martin Levine, Robert Luberto, Kenneth Maynard, Sydney Ross, Richard Walsh, Phillip Zinni III, Ben Booher, Robert Dempsey, Jr., Cheryl Cavalli, Theron Tilgner, Eric Filbiger, and Bill Moore.

Of the companies that supplied product, service, financial, and in-kind support, *Runner's World* magazine did more than anyone will ever know to make the event a success. Amby Burfoot had the vision to get them involved; Jane Serues suffered along with us, from her office, every day of the race; Mike Greehan and George Hirsch had the courage to stick with the dream when things looked to be going off the rails.

Bill Serues came to the race to help his wife out of a jam and became an essential fiber that kept the fragile fabric from falling apart. He also became a true friend.

Media interest was as crucial to the mental health of the athletes as on-course support was to their physical health. Patrick Taylor guided the publicity effort; Susan Campbell and Maria Farnon put theory into practice and made it all work. Special thanks go to Dave Weisenfeld at *USA Today*, Anne-Marie Parr at *CBS This Morning*, and Mike Maltas from *ABC Weekend News*. Gatorade and PowerBar provided more product than we could possibly use, while Blimpies, Mrs. T's Pierogies, and Mahatma Rice also donated goods at various points in the race.

Without my editor, Duane Gerlach, this story would not have been told. He believed, and he guided me from a sketchy outline to this published result. Of those who read and commented on early drafts, Karen Straub offered an honest, unbiased eye, as well as reassurance when I needed it most. Having Ted Corbitt bless my effort with his opening is a dream come true.

This collection of words has been an ultramarathon in the true sense of the word, and like all sustained efforts, it began slowly, a long time ago. For guiding me through the early years and letting me run when I began to find the path, I thank my family from the bottom of my heart.

For her encouragement at the start, the enthusiasm with which she shared the high points, and her ability to redirect my energies during the all-too-frequent lows, I thank my wife, Lisa. She gave up her dining room when my desk could no longer contain my notes, and set aside a good chunk of her life to help me do what I felt had to be done. Her understanding, patience, and unwavering support through the many months she found herself without a husband made this project possible. This book is for her.

1

Down to the Beach

I shall be telling this with a sigh
Somewhere ages and ages hence:
Two roads diverged in a wood, and I—
I took the one less traveled by,
And that has made all the difference.
—Robert Frost

The surf crashed somewhere off in the distance, well within earshot,
but in the predawn darkness it was too far away for anyone to see. An air of expectancy
hung over the parking lot. You could feel it. After a year of planning, hundreds of hours
of dedicated training, and weeks of anticipation, the representatives of seven countries
and thirteen states were more than ready. They were primed.

Some rustled through duffel bags. Others spent tender moments with family or
friends. Photographers scrambled to capture the passion that hung in the air, while the
public-relations director barked at the man with the videocamera. Emotions ran high and
tears flowed easily as everyone in the group struggled to comprehend the difficulty of
the task they would soon undertake.

The youngest of the athletes stretched nervously, away from the rest. The red
bandanna over his head made him look older than his twenty-four years, but his constant
movement and glowing eyes gave the impression of a hyperactive child preparing for a
first outing at school.

The Scotsman stood under the glare of the video lights, carefully knotting a gaudy
tie. After removing the black nose guard from his tinted glasses, he spoke to the
interviewer, stroking his beard thoughtfully and spitting out answers in a thick brogue.
His long, blond hair was knotted into a ponytail and hung down to the middle of his back.

On the far side of the parking lot, the veteran from New Jersey spoke quietly with
his girlfriend about the most sensible strategy for the very first day. The hometown favorite
drank steaming coffee nearby. He adjusted his hip pack and discussed pacing with his
coach.

The sky began to brighten as the interviews ended. The nervous athletes fidgeted
and checked their watches. It was 6 A.M. Saturday, June 20, 1992.

The first open running race across the United States in sixty-three years would begin on a California beach on June 20, 1992. Twenty-eight athletes from around the world prepare to begin the journey, from which, said one, they would never return: "Life will never, ever, be exactly the same."

Most of the group had arrived and checked in with plenty of time to spare, but the three-ton Ryder truck that would carry their personal gear and supplies was far from prepared. The scene was one of total bedlam: Boxes, coolers, buckets, and tents lay strewn across the parking lot, from one end to the other. The race manager, who should have been loading and organizing the supplies, was instead flipping through maps, trying to write a new set of instructions for the volunteer driver of the van that was to bring up the rear.

The title sponsor's head of marketing struggled with bags of equipment, hurrying to load them aboard. Her friend stood inside the truck. Unable to find order in what had already been started, he tossed the luggage haphazardly inside.

I was down on the beach, struggling to secure the gleaming new banner between a pair of wavering ladders in the gusting wind, when I heard a sudden roar of laughter. The race director was slowly pushing his bike up the path toward where I was setting up the start. Oblivious of the pandemonium, he was sharing a private joke with a friend.

The Europeans talked among themselves, choosing German as the most comfortable tongue. They looked past the flurry of activity and out toward the Pacific Ocean. For many, it was the first time in America. What a trip it promised to be, I thought to myself, still amazed that we were there at all, getting ready to embark on a journey that would take every ounce of our physical energy—and tax us to the limit of our emotional souls. The 3,000-mile running race between Huntington Beach, California, and New York City was about to begin.

It had actually started with a letter to the editors of *Ultrarunning*, a publication that acted as a voice for members of the little-known ultramarathon community.

"Spring is just around the corner," wrote Michael Kenney from his home in Eugene, Oregon, "and with it comes that familiar longing for the open road. For many of us, this manifests itself in the hope that we will see an ad in this month's *Ultrarunning* for the ultimate open road experience—a transcontinental stage race. . . .Maybe the time has come to take matters into our own hands. In the tradition of other great ultra-endurance events, maybe we should get things started by just setting a date, picking a course, and, as the Nike ads say, JUST DO IT . . ."

The heartfelt appeal struck a chord deep inside many of the magazine's followers when it was printed in April 1991. The instant Jesse Riley, a dishwasher from Key West, Florida, finished reading the words, he scrambled for the phone. He hung up ninety minutes later, feeling somewhat taller than his 6-foot-2. Although they had never met and lived at opposite ends of the country, Riley and Kenney reached an agreement: They would do everything in their power to help a race from one end of the country to the other make the leap from dreamy concept to actual fact.

The idea of a running race across America had been a fantasy to many over the years, but like the first successful ascent of Mount Everest, the event that drew the group to the West Coast on a breezy morning in June was not merely the work of the few who were there—it was part of a legacy that had been handed through the ages, and those of us present felt privileged to reignite the embers of discovery that had smoldered in daring hearts from the beginning of time.

Looking far back in recorded history, we find tales of men who traveled great distances on foot. The legend of Pheidippides, who ran between Sparta and Athens to proclaim the Greeks victorious in the Battle of Marathon, began in 490 B.C. Explorers, adventurers, conquerors, and pioneers walked to their glory more often than not. Adversity was a foe to be faced; privation and hardship were challenges, not reasons for retreat.

Though it was said that men had performed the feat before, it wasn't until 1788 that an Englishman was certified as covering 100 miles in less than 24 hours. In the late 1800s the movement known as ultrarunning truly began.

Edward Payson Weston was working as an office boy for the *New York Herald* when he first demonstrated his athletic ability, as he ran errands in a literal sense. Later, as a reporter, swiftness of foot helped him gather many a scoop. His initial foray to be considered truly extreme came in 1861, when he walked from Boston to Washington, D.C., for Abraham Lincoln's inauguration. Six years later, he walked from Portland, Maine, to Chicago, covering the 1,326 miles in twenty-five days and winning a $10,000 bet. He was declared the walking champion of the world and became a household name. The Golden Age of Pedestrianism was about to be born.

Within a decade, long-distance footraces were booming. In 1879 alone, there were more than one hundred contests in the United States and England, varying from 12 hours to 2,500 miles. The most popular were the six-day events, races in which competitors fought to accumulate as many miles as possible in 144 hours, stopping only for food, brief rests, stimulants, or massage. Thousands of spectators from all classes of society paid admission fees and packed smoke-filled arenas to watch the heroic performances of Weston and his peers. Betting was rampant, prize money was exceptional, and media attention was extraordinarily high.

Weston broke the magical 500-mile barrier in 1874, and as pedestrians added running to their races, the world record for six days was pushed ever upward, eventually reaching more than 623 miles. By the mid-1880s, however, the fickle public's fascination with the sport had come to an end, and the athletic pioneers became all but ignored.

Chicago's John Ennis was a seasoned pedestrian by the time he set out to prove that a determined soul could walk almost any distance. In 1890, he walked from Coney Island, New York, to San Francisco in eighty days. Marathon racing over a distance of 26 miles, 385 yards began with the advent of the modern Olympics in 1896 to commemorate Pheidippides' reputed run; the famous Boston Marathon commenced its unbroken annual existence the following year. Two decades after Ennis's crossing, at the age of seventy-two, Weston completed a journey across the country, covering the 3,611 miles between Santa Monica, California, and New York City in less than seventy-seven days. It was the second transcontinental adventure for the renowned walker.

The East Coast lifestyle of the Roaring Twenties may not have been conducive to an old man who espoused the virtues of walking, but it was receptive to the most outrageous of ideas. While Weston's exploits slipped out of the public eye and the aging pedestrian fell into poverty, a new form of marathon mania took the country by storm. Hero worship suddenly became a national pastime, and bizarre feats of daring and endurance attracted enormous crowds.

Flagpole sitting, nonstop dancing, and pie eating were common venues for the ordinary man. Amid the record-setting madness, the aggressive son of a Methodist Episcopal clergyman rose to prominence as a professional sports promoter. Charles C. Pyle saw opportunity where others saw dust, but when a highway from Chicago to Los Angeles was commissioned in 1926, even he had little idea it would become the venue for the biggest venture of his life.

While the interstate was still on the drawing board, Pyle had come to realize that he would rather promote boxing than pursue a life in the ministry or face bodily harm inside of a ring. With the theatrical skill he had developed while running a string of nickelodeons in Champaign, Illinois, Pyle moved from turn-of-the-century Don King to the P. T. Barnum of sports. Along the way, he turned indoor tennis and professional football from regional novelties into national news.

At about the same time he heard about the plan for the highway that was to be promoted as the Main Street of America, Pyle learned of the popularity of a bicycle race known as the Tour de France. The combination sent the money-hungry entrepreneur's mind spinning, and he devised an ambitious new plan. The Tour de France, he felt, was like a license to print money, but cycling as a sport was still relatively new in America. The event he envisioned would be similar to the Tour, but with a significant twist.

When Pyle called a news conference in the early part of 1927, he set typewriters to chattering all over the globe. He announced the ultimate marathon, a contest that would pit man's strength against his grandiose land: the First Transcontinental Footrace, a running race from Los Angeles to New York.

Every trained marathon man in the world debated the merits of vying for Pyle's $25,000 first prize against a chance at glory as an amateur in the Paris Olympic Games. Press reports claimed that the race was too extreme a test for the human body and that it would never begin, yet 199 entrants toed the line for the start at the Ascot Speedway on March 4, 1928. The field lacked the world's best marathoners, but it did contain the international flavor Pyle had promised: a bedraggled conglomerate consisting of accomplished athletes, hobos, unemployed laborers, and various others looking to cash in on their luck. Few had ever covered 26.2 miles on foot, let alone ventured into the world of ultrarunning. None knew what lay ahead.

Though distance running was a novelty that fit into the mindset of the Twenties it wasn't long before it lost its commercial appeal. It took four decades and a gold medal in the Olympics for the American public to view the sport seriously again.

"Winning the marathon in Munich made my running, in the eyes of others, legitimate," said marathoner Frank Shorter after his win in the 1972 Munich Games. "Suddenly it was okay to be a runner, to train for 2 or 3 hours a day. There was purpose behind it, something to be gained. My running had been looked upon as a diversion, as a peculiar habit for a grown man. After all, it was not done on behalf of a university team. It was not earning me a living. It was not even making me look manly, skinny guy that I was."

Knowing how Shorter felt makes it all the more difficult to comprehend what Ted Corbitt must have gone through twenty years earlier. It was in 1952, as a black member of the U.S. Olympic Marathon Team, that the New Yorker first tried to promote ultradistance running as a legitimate sport.

Corbitt found that after running a standard marathon, he still had energy, so he started to experiment, running beyond. Training up to 40 miles a day on a regular basis, he found, opened a whole new world; he entered an unusual arena where few since Pyle's day had ventured to go. A true pioneer in the sport, Corbitt set numerous records in 50-mile, 100-mile, and 24-hour races throughout an incredible career.

At the same time that Corbitt was discovering new limits of human possibility, ultramarathon races were taking place in other parts of the world. South Africa's Comrades Marathon, a 56-mile race between Durban and Pietermaritzburg, was first staged in 1921 as a tribute to soldiers who had lost their lives in World War I. It was the proving ground for the great Arthur Newton, one of the first athletes to develop a set of true training principles, many of which form the basis for techniques still in use today. Besides being a multiple record holder, Newton was a strong favorite going into Pyle's transcontinental race.

The Comrades draws close to twenty thousand runners and hundreds of thousands of spectators annually, carrying on the tradition that started with thirty-four brave entrants more than seven decades ago. In America, one of the most well known of the hundreds of modern ultra events is the Western States Endurance Run, a 100-mile race through California's Sierra Nevada. It owes its inspiration to an annual horse race. In 1974, a competitor took to the trail on foot when his steed became ill, and finished in less than 24 hours, 10 hours behind the number one rider.

Still, ultradistance events didn't come into vogue until after the Ironman Triathlon first appeared on television, shattering all preconceived notions about what the human body could do. Initiated as a beer-induced challenge by a navy commander after discussions about whether cyclists, runners, or swimmers were the toughest athletes, this single race made up of a 2.4-mile swim, 112-mile bicycle ride, and 26.2-mile run was televised as a novelty event on *ABC's Wide World of Sports*.

Something unexpected happened: People dubbed the Ironman the ultimate endurance event. They recognized that it required multidisciplinary training and a sustained mental fortitude rarely seen in athletic competition, and gave those who challenged it the utmost respect. It didn't take long for endurance to become a mantra to the image-conscious generation that was coming of age.

Aerobic exercise soon became an essential element in the average person's routine, and outdoor sports like hiking, biking, and running prospered as never before. The athletes who competed in the Ironman Triathlon or the Tour de France bicycle race were no longer scorned for their obsessive behavior; instead, they were embraced as heroes for having fine-tuned mind and body to the highest possible peak.

In the decade following Shorter's medal, the Running Boom began. Schoolteacher

Bill Rodgers won the Boston Marathon with an everyman's attitude that captured the hearts of many involved in the fitness craze. Marathoning regained its reputation as the supreme test of a runner's ability, and 26.2 miles became the ultimate goal for millions of recreational joggers, while on mountain trails, city streets, and tartan tracks, a handful of ultrarunners followed the footsteps of Corbitt. They weren't talked about much. They were misunderstood and considered part of the lunatic fringe.

The spirit of adventure continued to lure individuals to challenge the vast expanse of the nation, and numerous successful transcontinental crossings were recorded over the years, but it wasn't until the publication of *Flanagan's Run* in 1983 that serious talk of an organized event really began.

Based on Pyle's Transcontinental Footrace, Tom McNab's novel depicted a bygone era, a time when heroism was epitomized by character and self-sacrifice, not monetary worth. A dramatic tale of competition and camaraderie, the book looked into the minds of athletes as they struggled against the odds to run across the country, a seemingly incredible goal. Whether it was the popularity of the novel or just a matter of timing, more than one American promoter attempted to re-create the legendary event.

The first effort was shelved when the race director couldn't pull together the multimillion-dollar sponsorship and media package he had hoped for. Less than a year later, a similar scheme appeared. While most athletes were skeptical, talk of a million-dollar purse encouraged several to pay a $1,000 entry fee for an event known as the Sea to Shining Sea. Like its predecessor, the race relied on major funding from outside sources and never made it off the ground.

For a pair of ultradistance runners, however, the transcontinental dream actually came true. Forty-seven-year-old Marvin Skagerberg vocalized his visions of such a race whenever he could. The notion reached the offices of the National Amyotrophic Lateral Sclerosis Foundation and intrigued the executive director. She approached Skagerberg, and together they designed a race as a fund-raiser for ALS. Named the Lou Gehrig Race for Life after the great Yankees baseman who died of the disease, it was to be a two-man competition to test the idea. If it worked, the plan was to expand the field and make it an annual event.

When the Ford Motor Company and Coca-Cola USA offered financial and in-kind support, the plan became a reality. By the time the race got under way in April 1985, a New Jersey–based event-management company had planned the logistics to the last detail.

Skagerberg chose England's Malcolm Campbell as his rival. Both were veteran ultramarathon runners who had competed in hundreds of events, from 100-mile to six-day races, all over the world.

The 3,560-mile Tour de France–style stage race started with a ceremonial running of the bases at Anaheim Stadium before a baseball game between the Angels and the Twins. Although the runners exchanged friendly conversation at the starting line each day and had dinner together on three nights out of four, they almost always ran apart. The race was fiercely competitive, but incredibly, neither athlete suffered a major injury nor opened a decisive gap on the other. From the time they left California to the finish in Manhattan's Riverside Park, the lead changed hands eleven times.

The pair had only six rest days during their three-month ordeal, and after averaging 41 miles a day, Skagerberg won the $25,000 first prize, beating Campbell by exactly 16 minutes.

Athletically, the Lou Gehrig Race for Life was a wonderful success, but as a fundraiser, it fell shy of the optimistic prerace projections. Talk of repeating the event fizzled before the end of the year.

My own first experience with ultrarunning came in 1981 when I signed on as part of a relay team in a 24-hour charity run. I couldn't believe that anyone could be capable of running the entire time, but that's exactly what a Scotsman named Al Howie did while I watched from the side of the track. He was out there on his own, moving like clockwork, eating, drinking beer, and smiling as he plodded methodically and accumulated the laps. The wiry little man covered more than 120 miles by the time the event came to an end. In my mind, the inconceivable moved from the outer limits of possibility to irrefutable fact.

Now, waiting to start the Trans America Footrace, there were four transcontinental veterans among the entrants. One fidgeted with the other competitors in the sand, while another adjusted his tie for the umpteenth time. The mist was still thick, but the sun slowly brightened the tone of the sky. At 6:27 A.M., the PR man gave the race director the signal; there was finally enough light to get the mandatory shots of the start.

One last announcement and the race was under way. No profound words or celebrities; no flock of doves or earsplitting blast. Just Jesse Riley, bellowing for the first time in his life: "On your marks. Ready! Let's go!" With a roar of excitement, the athletes started out from the beach and exulted in the scattered applause.

The runners passed beneath the red, white, and blue banner with the freshly inscribed words: "*Runner's World* Trans America Footrace." They wound their way around the corner, spreading out rapidly, like a long, twisting serpent in a splendid Oriental parade. The race had come a long way, but the real work had only begun. Amid the chaos, New York City seemed light years away.

2

Harsh Realities

I first met Jesse Riley in Washington state, but the convoluted path
that led me there, and ultimately to my involvement in the Trans America Footrace,
actually began the year before I saw Howie perform his 24-hour run.

In 1980, a young man named Terry Fox left his home in British Columbia's Fraser
Valley for an impossible quest. He traveled to Canada's East Coast, determined to run
until he reached the parliament buildings in his home province of British Columbia.

Fox had been much like me—young, energetic, involved in a variety of sports—
until he lost a leg to cancer. Once he became aware of the devastating results of treatment,
he dreamt of seeing the disease that affects one out of five wiped out once and for all.
Fitted with a prosthesis, he decided to take his vision to the people of his proud nation,
in an extraordinary way: by running into their hearts and their homes.

I remember seeing him on the news, striding along with an awkward, off-balance
gait, gritting his teeth against the raging wind. He waved at passersby and spoke to
assemblies wherever he went. I also remember the tears that came upon hearing that after
144 days of averaging 26 miles a day, Fox had fallen ill again and was forced to abandon
his run.

Like hundreds of other young Canadians, I started running more, half believing that
I could prepare myself to take up the torch. By the time cancer took the life from Terry
Fox's ravaged body in 1981, I had seen Howie perform his miracles on the track. I ran
my first marathon later that year, with the young cancer victim's Marathon of Hope a

constant reminder when the going got tough. Terry Fox's effort continues to raise money and motivates thousands to this very day.

Running is like a drug, they say, and I know that from then on, during the times I was forced to do without it, I became cranky, like an ill-tempered bear. By 1988, I had competed in races at a variety of distances but was constantly on the lookout for something different, more extreme, a little bit new. The Lewis and Clark Preview Run was an ideal window into the world of ultrarunning, and after my brother and I won the team division of the 120-mile race, I knew I had found my sport. I met Jesse Riley at the real race the following spring.

Shortly after 5 P.M. on April 9, 1989, the eight- day, 505-mile journey from the Idaho border to the Washington coast ended as the last of the competitors in the Lewis and Clark Trail Run staggered across the finish line.

"What's next?" I asked, scrutinizing Riley closely for the first time. I regretted the question almost immediately.

He was an absolute mess. Both of his knees were terribly swollen. Bloody toes stuck through a gaping hole in his right shoe. His glazed eyes peered at the road through thick goggles, barely able to focus. He clawed at the week-old growth on his chin, wrinkled his peeling nose, and ran a raw tongue across his sun-chapped lips.

I had seen the early leaders in the solo division fizzle, succumbing to pain, injury, and loss of spirit, until only Riley and one other remained. I had seen the psychological roller-coaster ride that dogged every painful step. Yet the most amazing aspect of the entire event was not the reaffirmation of an ancient belief that sheer determination can overcome almost any discomfort—it was the answer Riley gave to my vacuous question. His words lured me across sixteen time zones to an ultramarathon race in Siberia and started the friendship that landed me in the parking lot looking out at Huntington Beach.

Michael Kenney's idea was to stage a transcontinental race of the runners, by the runners, and for the runners. He was fed up with business, but he felt he knew what would be needed to survive the ordeal of the road. That and not money, said the quiet nonpromoter, was what counted the most. Riley seemed to agree: "If one person enters, then we're going, full steam ahead."

Ignoring detractors, the pair decided that the race should start as a low-key, well-organized event, with plenty of room to grow. Putting what little savings they had on the line, they mapped out a route, hired a consultant to assist with production of the race, and formed the Ultramarathon Runners Association Inc. (UMRA) to legitimize the event.

Like the Pyle and ALS races, their Trans Am '92 was to be run in a stage format, with daily start and stop points planned well in advance. For $200 anyone could enter, up until 24 hours before the sixty-four-day race was scheduled to start. Stage times would be kept and cumulative totals used to determine the standings. If a competitor couldn't complete a day's stage within a predetermined cutoff time, he or she would be allowed to continue as a "journey runner," getting credit for accumulated mileage but no longer eligible for competitive awards. Prize money was a long way down on the list of essentials; just supplying food and water would be difficult enough.

Riley's life revolved pretty much around his running schedule: After each competition, he returned home only as long as it took to save enough money to get him through to the next scheduled event. During a layover at my house between races, he mentioned the plan for the transcontinental event.

I knew Riley was dedicated to the sport of ultrarunning, but the organizational nightmares behind such a massive undertaking had frustrated much more professional men. From what he didn't tell me, I realized that both Riley and Kenney had far more preparation to do than they were willing to admit. I admired their determination, but on learning that their paid consultant was doing little to justify his monthly fee, I was more apprehensive than ever before. If the event was really going to work, they needed help, and they needed it fast.

I volunteered to lend them a hand, wondering if it was a move I would live to regret. Before I knew it, I was involved with data bases and mailings, sponsorship packages, and liaising with the press. My reasoning seemed sound enough at the time: The more solid the race became, the better for all parties concerned. Since my own fantasy revolved around participating in the event, I figured if I was going to be out there running, I wanted all the help I could get.

The fall months were an absolute blur. Kenney finished mapping the course, set the daily stopover points, and traveled to Southern California to scout the first part of the route. Riley visited his mother in South Carolina, his uncle in Arkansas, and friends in Key West, borrowing money to cover the start-up costs of the race. Then he loaded up a pack, got a Greyhound pass, and went west to start a tour of the course. I spent endless hours at the library, on the telephone, and in front of the computer trying to track down viable sources of funds. As an elected official on the board of the UMRA, I became a bridge between the concept and the practical needs of the transcontinental race.

Now, on the California coast, I wondered if any of it would actually work. I recalled Wallace Stegner's essay, "Living Dry:"

> The West is a region of extraordinary variety within its abiding unity and of an iron immutability beneath its surface of change. The most splendid part of the American habitat, it is also the most fragile. It has been misinterpreted and mistreated because, coming to it from earlier frontiers where conditions were not unlike those of northern Europe, Anglo-Americans found it different, daunting, exhilarating, dangerous, and unpredictable, and entered it carrying habits that were often inappropriate and expectations that were surely excessive. The dreams they brought to it were recognizable American dreams—a new chance, a little gray home in the West, adventure, danger, bonanza, total freedom from constraint and law and obligation, the Big Rock Candy Mountain, the New Jerusalem. Those dreams had often paid off in parts of America settled earlier, and they paid off for some in the West. For the majority, no. The West has had a way of warping well-carpentered habits, and raising the grain on exposed dreams.

As publicist and sponsor liaison for the race, it was my responsibility to be sure the finish area was set up, that banners were properly placed for maximum exposure whenever a photo opportunity occurred, and that the media were given whatever information they might need for their reports about the epic event.

Riley's main job as race director was to cycle slightly ahead of the lead group, marking turns on the pavement with arrows drawn in flour and offering the leaders water or electrolyte replacement drink from the bottles he carried in saddlebags on the side of his bike.

Race manager Kenney planned to place aid stations along the course every 2½ miles, complete with insulated coolers of water and Gatorade, energy bars, and miscellaneous snacks. After the big Ryder truck was loaded, he was to drive the route and stop at pre-determined points to set out his supplies.

The first 17 miles of the race followed the Santa Ana River from Huntington Beach to Anaheim, mostly on a bicycle path that was accessible only at crossroads. All of the runners had been given detailed instructions before the start and carried photocopied pages, known as turn sheets, explaining the day's route.

Kenney had said that he would be ahead of the leaders long before they emerged from the bicycle path, but when I got to the 22-mile mark in my rental van, he was nowhere to be seen. The front runners had already passed, and Riley was frantically pedaling after them, his bottles totally dry. I filled them, gave him several extras, and replenished other athletes until Kenney finally arrived.

"Gutdayzke is lost," he said in a panic, referring to the driver of the support van that was trailing the slowest runners in the group. "He was supposed to pick up the first five aid stations and bring them to me after the last runners had gone through."

I suggested he set out supplies ahead of the front runners before heading back to look for the missing driver and van.

"I need G-Man's coolers, or I won't have enough to get me through to the end."

Rather than drive ahead, Kenney elected to backtrack to search for the van. By the time I caught up with Riley, he was laboring up the narrow, winding climb over Carbon Canyon Road. The front runners had 20 miles still to go, under the hot California sun.

James "Echo" Edmonson had taken the lead on the 6-mile ascent of Carbon Canyon, and by the time he reached the summit he had decided to go for the win.

"Feeling good," said the forty-nine-year-old as he looked over the San Bernardino Valley and began the steep descent into Pamona, "and goin' to keep on keepin' on, right through to the end."

Edmonson's headband and clothes were speckled white—the result of sweat turned to salt—but the handsome African American ran comfortably in spite of the heat. His intense eyes were blazing; his muscles glistened with sweat. He looked almost invincible as he blasted down the hill.

A widower with four children, Edmonson yearned to follow in the footsteps of Ted Corbitt. "There's nobody like Corbitt left," he told me on the phone before the race began. "No one representing our race the way he used to do."

Edmonson was an 800-meter specialist in high school and attended San Jose University on a track scholarship, but before reaching his full potential in running, he relocated to New York City to pursue jazz dancing as a potential career. While attending a party, he was stabbed in the back. The wound punctured a lung. After a long period of convalescence, he returned to Los Angeles and running but never regained his previous speed.

Instead of running faster, Edmonson started going farther, stepping up from 10-kilometer races to marathons, and eventually beyond. In 1989, he finished second in his age group in the Los Angeles Marathon, and several months later he won the Southern California 50-Mile Championship. The following year he posted the fourth best North American performances for both 24 hours and 100 miles.

"I remember when we moved from Texas to California," he said when asked why he had entered the Trans America, "we drove along old Route 66. Looking out the back window, watching the country go by, left a big impression on me as a kid. Ever since then, I've had a thing about running across the country. Seeing an HBO movie about Terry Fox really pushed me over the edge. It showed me what determined people can do. Winning this race would be like so many dreams coming true."

The Chaffey High School in Ontario, California, had been the first scheduled finish and stopover point, but when Kenney contacted the principal the night before the race began to confirm the arrangements made months earlier, he learned that the facility was unavailable for use. In a mad dash to secure an alternative, the race manager called ahead to the VFW hall in Rancho Cucamonga, where a spaghetti dinner was planned. Post commander Phil Didio agreed to let the runners eat, clear the tables, and bed down on the concrete floor. Although staying at a scenic campus on the tree-lined boulevard that runs through rural Ontario would have been preferable to the Veterans Hall, the real concern was the additional 5 miles the new finish added to the stage. It wasn't a good sign, on the very first day.

By the time I got to Rancho Cucamonga, met the people in charge of the hall, and prepared to set up the finish, I knew all about the trouble that was taking place on the road. The medical team had stopped me in a panic, looking for someone to help them care for the runners that lagged far back from the lead.

"These guys are dying out there," yelled Dr. Mark McKeigue, "and they're strung out for miles. There's no water, no Gatorade, nothing for them to eat. We're picking up whatever supplies we can find along the way, but I haven't seen the big truck or any coolers since this morning. What in the hell is going on?"

Only three of the entrants had the benefit of a personal crew. The rest relied on Kenney's aid stations, Riley and two other young Floridians on bicycles, and a pair of roving vans. One van driver was lost, Kenney had fallen behind schedule looking for him, and the cyclists had run out of supplies and become weary themselves.

It was probably comical for bystanders that happened upon the long, drawn-out parade, but for the participants, it was a struggle that seemed impossible—an interminable campaign with a page of instructions, no supplies, and never an end. If participants weren't running together, they were totally alone, trying to read the sweat-stained piece of paper that told them where they should turn. By the time the more conservative athletes reached the corners, most of Riley's markings had been obliterated, erased by gusts of wind or the steady flow of cars.

I was torn between obligation to my official duties and the needs of the athletes out on the road. As I would 126 more times in the upcoming weeks, I set up the two wooden ladders and secured the banner between them. I strapped my stopwatch to the clipboard that held the timing sheet—and tried to make sense of the things that remained to be done. I decided to go and help on the course as soon as the first runner arrived.

It turned out to be Helmut Schieke, completing the 50 miles in 7 hours and 25 minutes.

"What happened to Echo?" I asked, surprised that the gentle little German had charged past Edmonson in the final miles. Schieke was even more surprised than I.

"No Echo? I have not passed him. He must have gone a wrong way . . ."

Edmonson had been well ahead of Schieke when he came upon what should have been his last turn of the day. Riley was nowhere in sight, and the sharp right that took the runners off the major road they had been following for 3½ miles was unmarked—just another intersection to an athlete running on empty after more than 7 hours on the road. Less than 100 meters down the side street lay the finish line and a jug of cool lemonade, but Edmonson continued straight for 2 more miles before realizing his mistake.

Kenney was only 5 miles out from the finish when I caught up with him, and he now had all of the aid stations in place. He assured me that everything was under control, so

I rushed back to the finish, expecting to find the slew of reporters that hadn't made it to the prerace press conference or the early-morning start. Edmonson and several other finishers were there. A lone newspaperman looked on while Echo kicked the dust in a rage.

"This is total B.S., because that turn was supposed to be marked. I should have won, but what happens? Instead I run a bunch of extra miles, without any help, and for what— to come in sixth? No way I'm putting up with that."

The reporter was writing frantically, taking in the scene, already shaping his condemnation of the race and envisioning the way it would work on the page. I listened to the other runners' comments before making a feeble attempt to deflect the damage done by the irate Edmonson's rapidly shortening fuse.

"Obviously there was some sort of miscommunication," I explained, the voice of diplomacy, "but that's why you have turn sheets, to guide you on the course . . ."

He wouldn't hear any of it, and turned his frustration on me. The others calmed him down by saying they agreed that following the paper directions while running was a difficult chore, and reaching a consensus that Riley, as race director, should really shoulder the blame. His job was to be there, ahead of the runners, marking the course. Howie, who crossed the line 14 minutes after Schieke, spoke strongly in favor of compromise.

"Why not give Helmut the race leader's number one," he said, "and let Echo 'ave the same time as though they came across both at once. We 'ad a bloody awful day wi'out help in the heat, but we know for the next time we 'ave to be careful on turns."

I tended to agree but knew that the decision was up to Riley and Kenney. They were the race organizers; they were there to make rulings on such predicaments and to ensure that they didn't happen again. As much as I had become involved with the details in recent weeks, I wanted nothing to do with the administration of the race.

With few solid contacts and a minuscule budget, Riley's scouting trip over the route in the fall of '91 had been of debatable use. Kenney's attempts to secure road permits were held up because the race had no liability insurance, and the few entries that trickled into his post-office box in Eugene were from relative unknowns with little chance of meeting the competitive schedule. Like many people who have spent any amount of time involved in sports and pursuit of adventure, I realized that a good idea does not a sponsorship make. High-profile athletes, media interest, and the credentials of the organizers were crucial parts of the mix. Trans Am '92 had none of the required elements, and I had been brick-walled by dozens of corporations thought to be ideal supporters of the transcontinental race.

In early December, the tide suddenly turned. Besides an onslaught of qualified entrants, Kenney had been contacted by Amby Burfoot, the executive editor of *Runner's World* magazine, who felt that his company should be backing the race. In the months that followed, I negotiated a sponsorship agreement with the magazine's marketing manager and enlisted as official media liaison for the newly named event. I blamed a lack of finances for my own retreat from the ranks of people scheduled to run. The fact was, I was scared to death. I had little faith in my running abilities and didn't believe I could survive past the first week of the race.

Schieke crossed the finish line just before 2 in the afternoon, but more cautious runners trickled in until 8 o'clock at night. Of the twenty-eight entrants, three started as journey runners, knowing they could not possibly complete each stage of the race. Four of the remaining twenty-five were forced out of the competitive division on the very first day.

A few of the runners left immediately upon finishing, heading for motels or to spend the night with family or friends. For the vast majority, however, wounds had to be nursed in the Veterans Hall, on the cold cement floor. Blisters, sunburn, and nausea were the most common complaints, as the athletes washed down with cold lemonade the spaghetti dinner prepared by the ladies auxiliary. One of the runners was disoriented, some had headaches, and almost all showed symptoms of exhaustion or dehydration brought on by the heat.

I tried to compile the results and make my scheduled calls to reporters between snatches of conversation and the odd bite of food. Several runners were still struggling toward the VFW hall as we held an award presentation to recognize Schieke as the winner of the stage. Riley took Howie's advice and entered Edmonson on the results sheet as tied for first, with an identical time.

Compact, blond, and bearded, Schieke was an exceptional ultrarunner, yet he had not even been scheduled to start. The fifty-two-year-old German mailed his entry after the deadline and, like many others, was sent notification that the race was already full. He turned up in Huntington Beach anyway, claiming that a mail strike must have kept the rejection letter from arriving at his house. Kenney and Riley listened to his story, evaluated his credentials, and decided they could do worse than letting him run.

Schieke, like Howie and Skagerberg, brought a wealth of ultramarathon running experience to the race. In 1971, he ran across the United States in 59 days, 10 hours, and 20 minutes, with his wife and four-year-old son along as support. Since then he had completed more than sixty marathons, forty 100K races, and ten 24-hour events—with some impressive results. He averaged 6,000 miles of running per year and held numerous age-group records. Three weeks before the Trans Am was due to begin, he won the European 24-Hour Championship in Apeldoorn, Holland, running 153 miles. In mid-June he left his wife and son at home in Westphalia and traveled to America for the second time.

"Never will I haf this chance again," he said. "Especially not to make a part in the greatest race in the worlt."

I switched on my laptop computer, hooked up the printer, and struggled to write a positive summation of the day's results. George Hirsch, the publisher of *Runner's World*, was in New Orleans for the Olympic Trials with Burfoot, and as I plugged the portable fax into a dusty phone jack, I envisioned them waiting at their hotel for my glowing report.

Although the cutoff had passed, journey runners and aid stations were still scattered between Rancho Cucamonga and Huntington Beach. Incoming calls told the story from out on the road. Everyone assumed that the back-of-the-pack runners were well taken care of, but we learned that the trailing van had broken down more than 25 miles away. Realizing that there was only a single vehicle covering the remainder of the course, the medical team jumped into action. Meanwhile, Riley lounged in an isolated corner of the room, scribbling notes and joking with his cyclist friends.

Amid blisters, birthday cake, and bitter complaints, Erv Nicholls appeared at the VFW hall. He was compact and full of energy, pensive and organized, quick with a smile. Nicholls is a runner who owns a print shop in the mountain town of Big Bear Lake, California. When he heard the Trans America was being planned, he immediately offered to help. Kenney linked up with Nicholls during his first scouting trip on the course, and the hospitality he had received gave him nothing but hope.

"Erv is a great guy," he said, "and seems willing to do whatever he can." During the visit to the mountains, Kenney met a friend of Nicholls's, a man who expressed skepticism about the feasibility of the transcontinental event. By the time Kenney left the clean air of the mountain resort, he and Nicholls had warmed the friend to the idea. John Emig was a newspaper editor, former race director, and ham radio operator extraordinaire. He too offered to help.

After introductions, Nicholls laid out a series of maps and outlined his plan for the following day. He and Emig had taken their tasks as coordinators of stage two seriously. They had recruited a network of volunteers and were ready to cover the course between Rancho Cucamonga and Victorville, California, from beginning to end. Their crews not only had ice chests, Gatorade, soda, fruit, sandwiches, cookies, first-aid supplies, and a radio communication network—they also had a sensible plan of attack.

All of the runners still on the course except two were picked up safely on the first sweep by the medical van. Carol Carter was not far from the finish and wanted to cross the line under her own steam, even if she was late. She had been the last person chosen from the waiting list of entrants and was the only female in the full competitive race. One of the doctors opted to run beside her in the darkness, while the student who was with them drove ahead, leading the way. The slowest entrant, an unorthodox walker named Leon Ransom, was nowhere to be found.

At 10:50 P.M. the telephone rang. It was Ransom, calling from a booth in a gas station. He was still 20 miles out. When no one else volunteered, the medical student went to pick him up, another cross he would bear. Struggling to keep awake, I finished and faxed my report, then followed Patrick Taylor to the hotel where he and Jane Serues had rooms. Both were *Runner's World* people; Taylor headed up the public relations department, and Serues was the person who had agreed to sponsor the race.

Too tired for a shower, I focused on the television while Taylor clicked through the channels, looking for the news. He found two segments based on the footage he had delivered to the networks that afternoon. We exchanged high fives and whoops of delight. All the work has not been for nothing, I told myself as I disappeared into a black hole that was nothing like sleep.

The way back was difficult, but when I finally emerged at 3:30 the next morning, a fuzzy, elated feeling hit me. I saw things with a clarity I had never felt before.

Standing under the cold shower, I realized that problems were an inevitable part of what we had taken on. We were all in the thing together and had to pool our resources to come out on top. All the planning in the world, I told myself, could not have prepared anyone for all of the first day's snafus. As Kenney had pointed out before, situations were bound to crop up every step of the way. Flexibility on everyone's part would be the key to enduring the roller-coaster ride that was bound to last all the way to New York. For every summit there is an equal abyss.

Kenney's direction sheets on day two were impeccable. Mileages were written next to descriptions of landmarks so that runners could gauge progress as they went; the many turns were explained in detail with reference points; and access spots were given for crew vehicles that couldn't make it on the steep, rutted secondary roads. Kenney pointed the way from Cucamonga to Victorville, and Nicholls's group of volunteers made sure thirsty bodies had the fuel to get them through the long, hot miles.

The race began with very little fanfare under the banner where it had ended the previous night. After cleaning up at the VFW hall and stopping for breakfast, I checked in with the ham operators who were monitoring the race. According to their tally sheets, three of the journey runners had fallen behind the 3½ mile-per-hour cutoff schedule and were struggling. Those at the front were running easily, they said, at a pace almost two times as fast. Barely three hours into the race, the leaders were almost 10 miles ahead of the slow movers at the back of the pack.

I caught up to the lagging journey runners and offered them supplies, then shot a series of photos with the distant brown hills as a backdrop. The drought was still on in Southern California; there was a severe shortage of green. Leaving the slowest runners to their work, I followed the dry, winding road to a busy intersection. The branch to the left seemed the natural choice, and after searching for markings, I saw faint tracks of flour pointing the way. I looked right to check for traffic and caught a glimpse of a rhythmic, flashing pattern far down the steaming road.

"I'm just following him," replied John McPhee when I pulled alongside and told him he was running off track. He pointed to another figure that was moving slowly, like a mirage, half a mile farther down the road. I returned them to the corner where they had gone astray. They both pulled out their turn sheets of directions and studied them, seemingly for the very first time.

"It looks 99 percent certain that we can use I-15 between the Cajon Pass and Hesperia," Riley had said about the route the runners would follow during the second stage. "That'll save us about 7 miles, lots of bitterly tough hills, and a whole bunch of ups and downs on rough dirt roads."

A week before the start, however, final word had come in: Running on the freeway would not be allowed. An alternate plan would have to suffice. Luckily, Kenney had scouted a slew of possibilities during several trips to the area and knew the options well. The route of choice approximated that taken by Pyle's runners sixty-four years earlier, and was identical to the one used in the Skagerberg-Campbell race in 1985.

Following Kenney's directions, I drove up I-15, exited, and backtracked on the narrow dirt road to where the runners were supposed to emerge. After parking among the dusty brambles, I set out my coolers and Power Bars, then scrambled up a hill overlooking the road. The earth underfoot was like prehistoric clay: cracked and rutted and in need of a drink. Crushed by the heat, I set up my cameras and waited for activity from below. Howie and Schieke appeared in the distance, moving slowly together, making steady, painful progress to the summit of the hill. I took photos of them with tongues hanging out from an unquenchable thirst. Ten minutes after the parched leaders passed through, Tom Rogozinski arrived with a smile on his face.

"You gotta love it," said the twenty-four-year-old as he filled his bottle from my cooler and stretched his hamstrings in the shade. "This is incredible, and I feel pretty good."

Three weeks before the race had begun, I had received a message from Kenney saying that Malcolm Campbell was injured and unable to run. It was a shame he and Skagerberg wouldn't have a rematch of their race during the Trans America, but there was an up side. Rogozinski was next on the list. I contacted the young teacher and told him the news.

"I've been training for a six-day race instead of the Trans America," he told me on the phone, "and I'm not sure I'm really prepared."

But his schedule of racing back-to-back marathons on most weekends for the previous two months seemed to have done justice to the young runner's talents. Here he was in the hills of California, a long way from his Pittsburgh home, running strong and feeling on top of the world.

Schieke and Howie arrived at the Victorville Recreation Center together, raising their arms in the air as they ran across the line in a tie for first in the stage.

Prerace favorite Al Howie of Scotland trails Germany's Helmut Schieke on the climb over California's Cajon Pass on the second stage of the sixty-four-day event. Two of the most experienced ultra-marathoners in the group, the pair jockeyed for position, enjoyed each other's company, and traded advice for the first week of the race.

"We took it easy today," burred Howie, hidden behind a hat, dark glasses, and the black shield that protected his nose from the sun. "The real desert is comin' and there's plenty of time to think about a race."

They had completed the 47 miles in 7 hours and 20 minutes, despite the grueling 4,000-foot climb.

The looks of the tiny pair were a study in contrast, somehow belying their athletic skill. Schieke was in full running gear—outfitted with hat, singlet, shorts, socks, and shoes by Adidas—but he looked more like a pixie than a runner who could churn out endless miles on the road or the track. If Schieke didn't fit the standard vision of an athlete, Howie appeared all the more unlikely. The day before, he had worn shorts, headgear, a button-down shirt, and colorful tie. This time he was bundled up in sweatpants and long sleeves, with a bandanna over his shoulders as if he expected it to soon be cold.

"Skin cancer is too easy ta catch," he explained, "and I've done my time in the sun."

Rogozinski finished 34 minutes after the leaders, with Edmonson right behind him, only 1 minute back. With two days down, the top four runners were within an hour of each other in total cumulative time. Schieke held the lead by 13 minutes over Howie, but Edmonson and Rogozinski sat well within range. A pattern seemed to be taking shape, but some of the entrants who were running more conservatively questioned the wisdom of those at the front.

Jane Serues and Patrick Taylor arrived from helping on the course with a good indication of what lay ahead for the rest of the race. Nicholls and his supporters had been essential in the heat, but the next day was a Monday and they would all be back at their jobs. The broken-down van would be several days in the repair shop, and the cyclists simply could not keep up with the demands of the road. It looked like Kenney and I would have the only vehicles to care for the unsupported athletes as they ran into the desolate Mojave Desert.

Jane realized the situation was dangerous, but she had seen a man named Bobby Wise at work throughout the day, and he had volunteered to help for the duration of the race. She made a deal with Kenney: He could keep her van, use it for general support, and pay for the rental after it was dropped off in New York. She suggested that Wise would be an ideal driver.

The arrangement made complete sense, but I wasn't sure it would work because of a deal Riley had made in order to get Wise to help crew for the other runners. Bobby was expecting to work and run on alternate days. When Jane packed her gear into Taylor's car and prepared to leave, I was overcome with emotion and had to fight back the tears.

A local television reporter arrived and was amazed by the jovial demeanor of the faster runners as they picked their gear from the curb where Kenney had laid it and selected a spot on the rec center's floor. He spoke with Schieke and Rogozinski on camera after they had showered, questioning their sanity for taking part in such an event. Meanwhile, Howie tended to the finish line, cheering the other athletes as they rounded the baseball field and made their way to the line.

Though Riley's contact in the San Bernardino sheriff's department couldn't swing the permission to let the runners take the main route over the Cajon Pass, he did help out in a very tangible way. Pat Klootwyk organized a dinner at the recreation center, and the spaghetti, salad, and garlic bread were a welcome source of carbohydrates for the second night in a row.

By the time the reporter finished his interviews, most of the competitive runners were in. He had hoped to get footage of a finisher, but there was only one person left on the course. Just as he was preparing to leave, there was a shout from outside.

"Here comes Dial," yelled Howie, his accent twisting the pronunciation of the name of the burliest athlete in the group. The reporter quickly unpacked his video gear while I looked down the road. Sure enough, Dale Beam was making his way down the home stretch, just shy of the cutoff time. I attached the long lens to my camera, prepared for a shot—and saw that something was wrong. Beam was wavering along the sidewalk, his thick beard filthy and caked with a dirty, crusty mess.

The group of runners at the finish had grown. They were cheering Beam in.

"Can I have a few words with him?" the reporter asked while taking a wide shot of the scene.

I suggested that the runner would be tired after nearly 13 hours on the road.

"Maybe we'll let him clean up first," I said, turning the reporter back toward the kitchen. "Perhaps you can catch him once he's had a chance for some rest. Have you spoken to the people from the sheriff's department yet? It's their sort of spirit that's going to get these athletes across the country."

He went inside, oblivious to the state the last runner was in.

I'll never forget the dazed look on the big man's face—or the massive stain that had seeped through his lycra shorts and dripped slowly down his leg. When I was certain the reporter was out of earshot, I yelled for the medical team at the top of my lungs.

3

Desert Oasis

And I said to the man who stood at the gate of the year:
"Give me a light that I may head safely into the unknown."
And he replied: "Go out into the darkness and put your hand
into the hand of God. That shall be to you better than light
and safer than a known way."
—M. Louise Haskins

C. C. Pyle knew nothing about distance running, but his vision for the
1928 transcontinental race had been incredibly complex. Not only did he have to plan and control the event, he also had to house and feed the competitors, as well as the support entourage, to ensure that at least some finished the race.

The ability to generate publicity seemed to be the dapper little promoter's true calling, and he felt that if he could offer exposure to towns, companies, and products through his epic event, they should pay for the association. He expected to garner tremendous revenues by charging local authorities fees for the privilege of having the race pass through a town, but when his scouting agents sent back news from the course, it was depressingly bleak. The first part of the route led through the Mojave Desert, where facilities were inadequate, if they existed at all. There were very few towns with decent accommodations, and those that lay along the route refused to shell out Pyle's extravagant fees.

The solution was to hire a work gang, a convoy of trucks, and all the equipment necessary to create a mobile town. Once the kinks were ironed out, the system was amazingly efficient: Each participant was given a locker, a cot, and a space in a tent. As soon as the race got under way for the day, the workers moved gear from the morning's start to the afternoon's finish. The whole process was eased by a team of advance men who made all the necessary arrangements just ahead of the group.

A mobile kitchen was contracted, and a cook was constantly on hand to ensure a steady flow of food for the athletes. Maxwell House supplied a van in the shape of a coffeepot and positioned it on the road each day. It offered hot coffee and peanut butter sandwiches to the runners throughout the race. A doctor and chiropodist were part of the crew, as were a whole complement of specialists, including shoe repairmen, timekeepers, referees, and patrol judges.

Route 66 started in Chicago, then headed southwest through Missouri, into a corner of Kansas, and through Oklahoma, Texas, and New Mexico before crossing Arizona and California. In Pyle's day, it was little more than a tightly woven patchwork of old wagon trails and Indian paths between hundreds of towns, but it crossed deserts, mountains, valleys, rivers, and streams on the way from Lake Michigan to the shores of the Pacific coast.

Leading from the dust bowl states of the Midwest to the land of opportunity, Route 66 was called by author John Steinbeck a road of flight; the "Okies" who traversed it by the thousands saw it more as a gateway to their dreams. They hoped it would lead to a new life in a better place; instead they found bitterness and strife. Armed gangs often greeted the migrating hordes and forced them through to the next state.

The out-of-place transplants eventually arrived in California with their dreams still alive, but the best they could do was build tent villages and shanty towns—and perform seasonal labor, if jobs could be had. Children died from malnutrition, sickness, and dysentery, while the adults did what little they could. The situation was all but unknown to the rest of America until *The Grapes of Wrath* was published in 1939. Steinbeck's controversial depiction of an Okie family's plight set the country into an uproar, but little was actually done. A faraway author of destruction indirectly helped resolve the problem: World War II rejuvenated the American economy and united the nation in a common cause.

The California stretch of Route 66 probably looks much the same today as it did when Pyle's convoy followed it into the Mojave: desolate, barren, cracked pavement and steaming sand. Day three of the Trans America was identical to the fourth stage of Pyle's 1928 race—and was the first of six consecutive days in the deep desert. The course followed Route 66 all the way into Barstow, the last town of any consequence for several hundred miles.

Although he had athletic ability, Dale Beam lacked self-confidence while growing up in Milwaukee and never really pursued sports on a competitive front. It wasn't until he finished military service and graduated from the University of Wisconsin that he learned of Frank Shorter's accomplishments in marathoning and became inspired to run. Beam completed his first marathon in 1972 after only ten weeks of training and had run dozens of races at various distances in the twenty years since.

"To me, the Trans America Footrace is a wonderful mystery," Beam had said before the race began. "I don't think anyone knows what will happen out there, or what we will all become."

Beam was used to extended travel, but the concept of ultradistance running was something entirely new to him. Most of his month-long trips throughout the United States had been on the seat of a bicycle or with a backpack in the woods. The daily grind of running megamileage would be like entering virgin territory, he had said, but he felt his years of manual labor and constant movement were perfect preparation for such a grueling event. He didn't know what to expect, yet had been ready to give it a try.

Beam's arrival in Victorville had me worried. He had lost control of his bowels and vomited through the last miles of the stage. He looked bad on the surface, but the worst of his problems were revealed when he took off his shoes: Thick blisters the size of baseballs covered the bottoms of both feet. While the others enjoyed the spaghetti dinner, the Grizzly Adams look-alike tried to shower. He screamed from the pain.

The medics from Illinois were gone, but we had a new team consisting of a pair of students from the College of Osteopathic Medicine of the Pacific. Eric Filbiger and Bill Moore tended to Beam throughout the evening, wrapped his feet, and settled him in for the night. When he got up off the floor in the morning, he could barely balance on his heels. He knew it would be crazy to continue, but he had sacrificed too much to simply abandon the race.

"I had visions of making the stage," Beam said later, "as I tried to find a way of moving through the first 10 miles."

He kept ahead of the slowest of the journey runners for a short time, but it wasn't long before he was struggling just to put one foot in front of the other. His pace dropped to 1 mile an hour.

"It was then I gained a sense of what it would be like to die in the desert."

And yet Beam refused a ride from the support van when he learned that a food shack lay just up the road. His feet and body were on fire, but summoning up his last bit of courage, he stumbled on to his goal. Sitting on a cushioned seat in air-conditioned comfort, he ordered hot dogs and an ice-cold Coke. He was delirious and believed he had reached heaven after the hell of the road. He took a ride the next time it was offered, knowing he was out of the competitive event.

Aid stations every 2½ miles were hardly adequate supply for running through the desolate Mojave Desert. As temperatures reached 110 degrees, sweat evaporated before it could cool the athletes, energy bars turned to mush, and water and electrolyte replacement fluids left on the side of the road became superheated.

The support picture looked bad, and to complicate matters, the insulated coolers Kenney laid out for Gatorade and water had been disappearing at an incredible rate. There had been forty when we left Huntington Beach; we were now down to eleven, and by the end of the day, a pitiful four.

Heat in the desert is a relative thing. An unusual spell of cool weather kept the temperature down to a mere 90 degrees on day three, but the competition at the head of the field remained surprisingly hot. As was his custom, Edmonson charged to the front early and led for a stretch, but he was soon joined by Howie. The Scotsman was a study in consistency, taking over the lead at 34 miles when his rival dropped off the pace. Howie entered Barstow, turned right off the main street, and strode up the final hill to the finish on the lawn of the recreation center, completely alone.

Howie ran the 39-mile stage in 5 hours and 23 minutes, and even though he was bundled up in his sun-protection gear, he had barely broken a sweat. Schieke had been 13 minutes and 34 seconds ahead going into the stage, but as Howie waited beside the banner, he was aware he was gaining with every second that passed.

In 1974, while working in a foundry in Toronto, Howie had quit the smoking habit he had started in his native Scotland at age nine. He took up running to combat a growing aggressiveness and to take off the edge.

Before he had ever heard of ultramarathon running, he ran 90 miles nonstop on a bet. Howie eventually moved to Vancouver Island and twice ran its length to raise money for charity. In 1980, a mere two months after making his marathon debut, he entered and won his first 50-mile race. Then, in 1981, he set a North American record for 24 hours, running 149.2 miles in the Canadian Championship, and downing a case of beer along the way.

Four years later, on a publicity run from Victoria to Montreal, Howie became sick and was diagnosed as having a malignant brain tumor. He was given four months to live. Refusing chemotherapy, he stopped drinking and put himself on a strict macrobiotic diet. He focused his energy on pursuing a positive, healthy lifestyle, and the tumor all but disappeared. His running became easier, his times got better, and he found himself a standout performer in multiday races all over the world.

In the summer of 1991, Howie began his most ambitious project to date. He set out from St. John's, Newfoundland, for Victoria, British Columbia, amid raging winds and a downpour of rain. Aided by his wife, her niece, and Jesse Riley, he covered the 4,533 miles in 72 days, 10 hours, and 23 minutes. He obliterated the previous record for the crossing, averaging more than 63 miles a day. He raised more than half a million dollars for a children's charity along the way.

"The accomplishment has few if any equals in the annals of distance running," wrote editor David Blaikie in *Ultrarunning Canada* of Howie's incredible run. "He got stronger as he ran, not weaker. His pace quickened rather than slowed. He needed less sleep the farther he went."

Hardly one to bask in past accomplishments, Howie took little rest upon completing his journey: Three weeks after reaching Victoria, he was back racing on a loop course in New York. He beat his own record in a 1,300-mile race, clocking the third-fastest 1,000-mile run of all time as a split.

Now, a tiny figure appeared at the bottom of the hill. It wasn't Schieke or Edmonson, but Rogozinski, running as well as ever through the heat of the day. Schieke finished several minutes later, and the tallying began. The final calculations placed Howie in the overall lead, with Schieke in second place. After 135 miles, the German was 38 seconds behind.

Bob Ross, the director of the recreation center, let me take over his office to communicate the news of the race. I did a radio interview, spoke with several newspapers, and faxed the preliminary results back to *Runner's World* in Emmaus, Pennsylvania. The early finishers lounged under the trees by the finish line, waiting for their gear to arrive. Kenney and the big truck were at the bottom of the hill, directing the runners onto the sidewalk on the right side of the street. In spite of all the work the consultant had supposedly put into getting permits, nothing was arranged. The Barstow sheriff insisted that the athletes stay off the road.

By midafternoon, the runners were getting hungry, but an organized dinner was not scheduled until 6. This problem would become an ongoing concern, but in Barstow, a local runner who had read about the race got together with Ross, drove to the nearby Pizza Hut with a pair of my press kits, and told management any donations would do. They returned with a stack of pizzas, and then visited McDonald's, with equal success. Take advantage while you can and load up, I thought to myself. A whole lot of nothing is all that's available after this.

Kenney hadn't known what to do when he was flooded with entries, but he and Riley decided to set a twenty-five-person limit, taking competitors first come, first served. Riley still wanted to let extra people take part as noncompetitive runners, provided they would act as volunteers for at least half of the race. The plan was vetoed for a variety of reasons, but after the pair looked at the numbers and realized how few of the entrants were providing their own support crews, the idea resurfaced. Rather than encourage *Runner's World* to appeal to its readership and contacts across the country, Riley tried to entice volunteers from the ultrarunning community with the promise they could run part of the race.

Bobby Wise was the only one who went for the bait. After his third day of crisscrossing the course with supplies for the other runners, he felt it was time to collect.

"Take me back to where we started this morning," the volunteer told Riley in Barstow after finding him asleep on the lawn. "I'll cover the distance to the finish by walking through the night. I'll drive the van tomorrow, no problem on that."

The dispute between the two obstinate ultramarathoners was more Monty Pythonish than the British comedy troupe's famous argument skit.

By the time they were done, Riley had lost both his temper and his ever-present smile.

"Bobby, you're a pain in the ass," he yelled, "so get the hell out of my life! Take your gear off the truck and leave! As far as I'm concerned, you've got nothing more to do with the race!"

I tried to mediate but had already come to realize it was fruitless to reason with Riley when he had made up his mind. Wise quietly found his bag and hitched back to Victorville with the medical staff.

It was almost 11 when Ross, the recreation center director, locked me out of his office and said his farewells for the night. I surveyed the dining hall where we were staying. It looked like a MASH unit, with bandages, debris, and bodies scattered all over the floor. Spotting my sleeping bag, I dragged it and my duffel of gear outside to the lawn. I could hear the hot rods down on Main Street. The security lights shone brightly in my eyes where I settled, but I remembered that Ross had warned against sleeping too far away. The town was not small enough to be entirely safe.

For those of us on the grass, the morning started earlier than usual: The automatic sprinklers were programmed for 3 A.M. Luckily we had access to kitchen facilities, so I plugged in the borrowed coffeepot that had been set up the previous night. Howie fired up a batch of oatmeal while the other runners slowly prepared themselves for another day on the road. I packed up my portable office and noticed Beam filling up a new set of plastic water jugs, hobbling gingerly and in obvious pain.

Shortly after dismissing Wise as a troublemaker, Riley had asked Beam if he would take over the support van Wise had been handling. Like several of the runners who had dropped from the competitive division early, Beam wanted desperately to remain a part of what he saw as a historic event. And yet he stood apart: While the other injured runners chose to run bits and pieces of the course and get shuttled to the finish when they had had enough, Beam's attitude was different. From the moment he realized he was out of the competitive race, the wild man from Wisconsin forgot about his own problems. His main concern became the athletes who were still pursuing their dreams.

"I'll do what I can," Beam said, and was handed the keys.

Riley woke up the late-rising runners and his cycling friends and packed up his gear. Kenney barked for the runners to bring their bags to the truck, just as he did every morning when it was getting toward time for the start. The local who had obtained the pizzas and burgers the afternoon before showed up as promised and helped Kenney organize the load in the truck. The runners gathered under the banner and on the start command ran off into the dark.

It was shortly after 5 A.M., and Wise's whereabouts were completely unknown. I thought back to the Lewis and Clark Trail Run. Wise had been there, walking, as he always did, with a bent-over stoop. In the middle of the race across Washington state, he was almost a day behind schedule but kept going at his own precise pace. At some point he was picked up by the local law-enforcement authorities, who wondered what he was doing, staggering around in long underwear, alone, on the open road. Wise was tired, low on blood sugar, and barely able to speak. Before he knew it, he was in a mental hospital under observation, but he was released several days later and went on to complete the distance. The race had been over for nearly a week when he finally reached the finish at Cape Disappointment.

I decided that if race management had cut Wise loose, it wasn't my problem to worry, but I was troubled just the same. Examining the situation with a weariness that would dog me for the rest of the trip, I convinced myself that he was resourceful and self-sufficient and that the athletes in the race needed my help far more than he. Ahead lay 52 miles of scorching desert.

German Stefan Schlett had put it succinctly just before starting the stage: "The party, my friends, has only just begun."

Edmonson approached the day in his usual manner. By the 20-mile mark, he was more than 10 minutes ahead of Howie. The Scotsman ran easily alongside Schieke, sharing strategies and experiences from his previous events.

"We tried to tell Echo not to run like a madman, but he took off like a shot," said Howie when he stopped for Gatorade on the desolate road. "He canna' last, runnin' like that on a day like today." The temperature was in the high 90s already, and it was well before noon.

Kenney had been very excited when relating the potential of day four. The section of Route 66 we followed was true desert, eerily beautiful in a harsh sort of way. Crumpled hills rose off in the distance, looking like purplish brown velvet pillows through the haze, surrounded by blazing blue sky. I-40 was visible, but the pair of trains that went by on the tracks paralleling our route was double the number of cars on our road. The stage was

The mystical Bagdad Cafe, a.k.a. Sidewinder, was like an oasis during a long desert stage. Runners received lemonade, oranges, ice, and encouragement from the residents of Newberry Springs before continuing their trek into the blistering heat.

long and desolate, but 22 miles from Barstow there lay an oasis whose inhabitants were waiting for the runners to arrive.

The film *Bagdad Cafe* had never enjoyed huge audiences, but it became a hit with the art house crowd because of its whimsical, dreamlike tack on life back of the beyond. When Dick Devlin first visited the Mojave Desert for a barbecue, something appealed to him, just as it had to the German tourist in the film. Four days later, Devlin bought a house in Barstow. He fixed it up and traveled there from Los Angeles whenever he could.

With every trip came an exploratory journey a little farther out into the Mojave. When Devlin saw a ranch in Newberry Springs, he knew he had found the location that would convince him to move.

"I figured I would farm sand," he chuckled. "I actually wanted to go thoroughbred, but I hated the thought of having to inoculate." He decided to search for a real reason to settle down in so different a place. Several years after *Bagdad Cafe* was completed, the coffee shop where it had been filmed went up for sale. Devlin snapped it up to justify his life in the desert and has been having a ball ever since.

As the race passed Devlin's renovated landmark, the Newberry Springs welcoming committee did the owner proud. The fire department cranked up their sirens each time a runner went by. Senior citizens cheered; young children waved balloons; truck drivers pulled over to see what the commotion was about. Like a scene from the movie, time seemed to stand still.

Buckets of ice, sponges, lemonade, and oranges were carefully arranged in a line. The thirty spectators were interested in the runners and spoke with them in earnest, applauding their quest. A *Penthouse* model was there in skimpy shorts and cowboy boots, sipping a beer. Bob Lundy, president of the California chapter of the Route 66 Association, held up a banner as the athletes ran through the brief oasis in time.

"Fresh fruit in the mittle of the desert," said Schlett, "is like the finest champagne. Today will be goot."

The thirty-year-old had come to the Trans America with a wealth of ultradistance experience and, more important, a fun-loving attitude ideally suited to the nature of the race.

"I do this to haf a lot of fun," he said in his clipped accent, "and to meet a lot of excellent runners and old friends. For the finish? I just want to survive."

A runner since age fourteen, the native of Kleinostheim bills himself as the complete adventurer, the craziest endurance athlete in all of Germany. A paratrooper during his five years in the military, Schlett became a salesman for a time: "Just long enough to realize it is better to test my limits than the little bit of patience that some people haf."

"I like to do what some think is impossible," he said when pressed about the long list of mountaineering, bicycling, running, and multisport events he has completed. "I love the high that comes when you are competing at such an unbelievable level in such challenging sports."

Schlett quotes Nietzsche while admitting he knows little about the philosopher other than the fact that he is a countryman, of German descent: "What does not destroy me makes me stronger. I like this thought, because I think this is true."

After more than 460 parachute jumps, 26 major mountaineering expeditions, more than 50 ultrarunning events, and several Double Ironman competitions, Schlett has yet to be destroyed. He came close when he broke his leg on a solo mountaineering expedition in Europe, but within a year of recovering, he was back on his previous track. Perhaps the most alluring thing about the lean, goateed blond is his prankish sense of humor.

"Ultramarathons are like nuclear war," he would say in one form or another at the starting line, every day of the race. "There are no winners, only survivors. The word of the day is for us survivors: bull-sheet."

The man who had started the only newspaper in Newberry Springs, Jim Ellison, together with his wife, Sue, was responsible for the overwhelming support the runners received in front of Devlin's Bagdad Cafe.

"Normally people around here don't get involved with a whole lot of anything," explained Ellison when he took me inside Devlin's establishment and pulled out the June edition of the *Silver Valley Sentinel*. It was a special issue, dedicated exclusively to the Trans America race. "The response has actually been quite a surprise."

While we spoke about the paper and life in the desert, one of the runners entered the air-conditioned room and ordered a meal. It was Serge Debladis. The forty-four-year-old Frenchman had been suffering from tendinitis in his ankles since day one, but his appetite was very much intact. He sat at the counter and pointed to a picture on the wall.

"Amboorger et Koe-ka-Koe-la," he said, as well as he could.

Riley and Devlin joined the Ellisons and me in our discussion about some of the problems we had already encountered. Talk soon turned to what lay ahead.

"You realize there's absolutely nothing in Kelso, don't you," said Devlin, "and that there are no decent supply points between Barstow and there?"

For the next two nights we would have shelter. There were no prearranged meals, but at least there was a small restaurant at each stop where the runners could scare up some food. The big concern was the Kelso stopover on day six, which neither Riley nor Kenney had taken the trouble to plan. We would be camping out beside a deserted railway station, but there were no facilities. The only sights were abandoned trailers and desert, whichever direction you looked.

As the last of the runners passed through the Newberry Springs aid station, the medical students pulled up in their jeep.

Sleeping conditions usually were far from ideal, ranging from cement floors in armory buildings to tents set up on the side of the road. On this occasion, runners and crew members relaxed under the crumbling facade of an old train station in Kelso, California. An earthquake centered 5 miles away shook the building two days later.

"Ed Kelley is out of the race," Bill said while unloading his kit. I watched with my mouth open as he and Eric helped maneuver the red-faced runner from the back of the truck.

In the early stages, the thirty-four-year-old from Los Angeles consistently finished in the top five and looked incredibly tough. While studying sports management in college, Kelley had run from Sacramento, California, to Washington, D.C., averaging 42 miles a day. He believed he was a strong contender for the Trans America, but it looked like he had given it everything he had—and it wasn't enough.

Bill went to work massaging Kelley's back, a continuation of the stretching Eric had already performed on the athlete for more than an hour on the side of the road.

"I'm cramped up so bad that I can't even walk without pains shooting right through my legs," said Kelley through his grimaces.

The students spent another 90 minutes with Kelley, who drank fluids steadily while trying to relax. He sat up suddenly, concerned about the time. When he said he felt better, the medics took him back to where they had picked him up.

Half an hour later, Kelley ran past the Bagdad Cafe, waving. He moved at his regular pace, chasing the clock. He made it to the finish in fourteenth place, 2½ hours ahead of the cutoff and still in the race.

Ludlow, California, according to Ellison, had been a railroad town in the 1930s, with a population close to 1,200 at its peak. The town was shrinking all the time and was little more than a truck stop and motel when the Trans America arrived.

Howie and Schieke finished together in 8 hours and 2 minutes, and then wandered across to the gas station store. The Scot bought beer and chips for whoever chose to indulge, while the German stocked up on pretzels and nonalcoholic malt. Riley and Kenney had booked the entire ten-room Ludlow Motel, and although several of the entourage went without beds, the semiprivate rooms proved a luxury after the hard floors of previous nights.

Edmonson finished 38 minutes behind the leaders, with Rogozinski and David Warady hot on his tail. Howie held a 38-second lead over Schieke in the overall standings. Rogozinski sat in third, 1½ hours down on Howie's total time; Edmonson held on to fourth; and Warady was fifth, nearly 3 hours back. Kelley's mid-stage break had cost him time, but he still held sixth place of the nineteen who remained in the competitive race.

The 28-mile stage from Ludlow to Amboy, California, was a short one, and since there was no media expected, I opted to get some exercise after seeing the group off from the start. I had been inactive since the race began, and it took some time to find a rhythm, but once I got going, I savored the effort in spite of the heat. I caught up to Carol Carter and several other journey runners, chatted briefly, and continued on my way. Up ahead I saw one of the competitive entrants, running easily, enjoying the day.

"I kind of pity the guys in the lead," Marty Sprengelmeyer said when I pulled alongside. "They're actually in a serious race up there—and missing out on this . . ." He gazed into the nothingness and took a deep breath of the stifling air.

The road stretched out into the distance, a dry patchwork of cracks. Every so often the white line moved—tiny lizards scattering as our footsteps approached. The Santa Fe rail line ran off to the left, while strange craters rose from the desperate ground on the right. Somewhere out there lay the remnants of the army training center where Patton had prepared his troops for battle against Rommel, the notorious Nazi Desert Fox. Down below the surface of the scorching moonscape ran the Mojave River, meandering through the worst of the barren inferno as an underground stream.

Sprengelmeyer and I spoke as we ran, our sweat evaporating the moment it came out of our pores.

"This is what I came to this race for," he said, "not a competition where everything is lost in an absolute blur."

An eleven-year veteran of ultramarathons, the forty-five-year-old computer programmer from Iowa loves new challenges. He once competed in Australia's famous Sydney to Melbourne race. He won the Sri Chinmoy 1,300-mile race in 1987, coming the closest to the distance before the 18-day time limit was up. And the year before the Trans America, he had finished second to Howie in the 1,300 mile event and completed the race. Sprengelmeyer had read about people crossing America on foot and for more than a decade dreamt of someday doing it himself.

While we ran, I asked him what was going through his mind. "I've been thinking what it must have been like out here before there were any roads," he replied. "I've become an Indian warrior, galloping on a beautiful horse, hunting game. Or better still—chasing a squaw." We laughed and were quiet again. I shall forever envision the thoughtful, softspoken, black-bearded athlete on horseback, chasing young Indian girls through the desert. Somehow it fits.

We soon caught up to Rogozinski, who had backed off the pace and was taking a walk to put some spring back in his stride. We expressed surprise that he was not up near the front. "I had leg speed in the early stages," he explained, "so I figured I might as well use it. Yesterday I really had to work to stay in touch, and to me, at this point, that's crazy. Besides, I don't want to miss anything. I'm out here to really see this country, so that's what I'll do."

We spoke about Pyle's so-called "Bunion Derbies" and tried to imagine more than a hundred runners plodding along in flannels and hard leather boots. Attire aside, what Pyle's athletes saw around them couldn't have been very much different from the dry expanse that surrounded us now.

By the time Edmonson led the runners across the finish line at 11:20 A.M., the thermometer registered 100 degrees. The sun was beating down with all of its might, but Gutdayzke had returned with the broken van. Between his and Dale's effort to get everybody ice, the day on the road was bearable for most. The complications didn't really start until we arrived in town.

Town, in Amboy's case, consisted of a post office, several houses, a garage-cafe, and a nonfunctional school. The whole shooting match was owned by a seventy-eight-year-old named Buster, and it was up for sale. Amboy had been a popular tourist stop when Route 66 was well traveled, but when I-40 opened in 1973, traffic and business dropped off by 90 percent. The original asking price was reportedly $350,000, but inflation had driven it up to $2 million by the time the Trans America ran into town.

We couldn't spend a plugged nickel, because the cafe closed its doors when the owners caught sight of the first of our group.

"We've got a film crew coming tonight," the waitress told the famished athletes. "We've got to get cleaned up, so we're shutting at 2."

The woman who let us into the school where we were staying knew of a tiny Mexican restaurant 12 miles down the road. The runners shared takeout beer and burritos. Those without injuries helped the less fortunate tend to their wounds. From the time the group had left Ludlow in the morning until the slowest of the journey runners had enough, Beam drove back and forth on the course, making certain no one was left without support. He did everything but give his feet the rest they so desperately needed to heal.

The next day, stage six, the Trans America course veered north from Route 66 and headed into high desert, leaving the path of the original transcontinental race for good. Pyle's runners had continued on the Main Street of America through Arizona and New Mexico, but Kenney's route went straight through the desert to Nevada, traversed the Silver State, and entered Colorado. There we would encounter the Continental Divide.

Once the stage was under way, crews drove back to Ludlow to fill gas tanks and stock up on supplies. The runners passed under I-40 and began a 4,000-foot climb into the Bristol Mountains toward Kelso.

As a result of a mass mailing of press releases, an ABC crew from Los Angeles now joined us to gather footage for the national news. Steam rose from the roads as they dogged the runners, taking shots of every aspect of the race. They captured Howie and Schieke running together; Beam pouring ice and soda; and Edmonson making his move at 20 miles, taking over the lead. The full day of attention from the outside world gave us a new focus, something other than the stifling heat.

David Warady won his first stage of the race, and Richard Westbrook came in third, just behind Kelley, who had recovered his form. Warady and Westbrook had full-time handlers, and both looked remarkably fresh.

When Howie arrived, he took off his shoes, revealing feet that were blistered almost as badly as Beam's. The blisters had burst; the dead outer flesh was obviously creating painful friction between itself and the raw layers below.

"I 'ad a bit of a blister the first day," he said, "but I've no idea why. I've never 'ad foot trouble before."

When the student doctors arrived, they were not certain just what they should do. Moleskin would be ineffective. They had no supply of second skin, the sterile gel that is often used on burns when deep tissue is exposed. With the Scotsman's consent, Bill

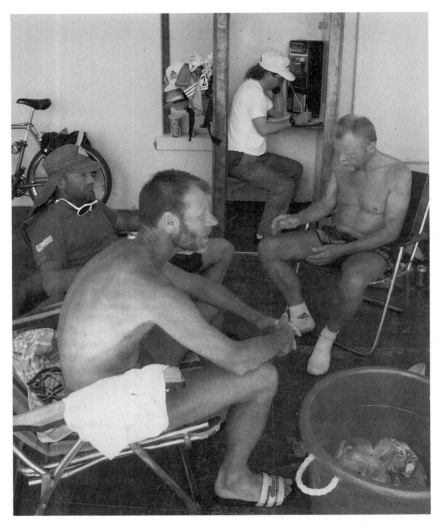

Most of the western stages were in isolated areas, with little in the way of activity when the day's running came to an end. Race manager Michael Kenney, on the phone, checks on the arrangements for the days ahead. Relaxing in the foreground, from the left, are Emile Laharrague (France), Helmut Linzbichler (Austria), and Helmut Schieke (Germany).

cut the outer skin from the bottoms of his heels, cleaned the exposed areas, and bandaged them up. I couldn't bear to watch, but the television crew was there, as were several people with cameras, capturing the process forever on film.

The medics were even busier than usual after this hot, climbing 40-mile stage. Fifty-five-year-old John Wallis passed out on the concrete platform of Kelso Station shortly after finishing his run. Wallis was as experienced as anyone in the race, but heat and dehydration had taken their toll. When he came to, Eric gave him a thorough examination and told him to take in as much fluid as possible for the rest of the night.

Skagerberg was feverish and worn out, despite having had help for several days from his girlfriend's son. Milan Milanovic, the Swiss runner, had painful tendinitis in his ankle, which had swelled beyond belief. Everyone scrambled for buckets and what remained of the ice.

Kelso had first been developed as a water stop for the steam engine trains in 1905, and when the Union Pacific took over the line in 1924, it built a Spanish-style depot to provide food and lodging for its railroad workers. The Bureau of Land Management is trying to raise funds to restore it, says area manager Bob Collins, but when we arrived it looked rather like it was crumbling. Like the group, it was falling into rapid decay.

Into the destruction came Dick Devlin, an apparition sent from above.

"I told you this was a six-pack day!" he yelled from his truck. "Get these guys to the relish tray! They've gotta be starved!"

Devlin's pickup was stocked with plates of cheese, crackers, and cold cuts, but the other essentials, like ice and cold beer, were the first things to go.

There was an old water pump out by the train tracks, and one by one the runners stripped off to wash sweat and dirt from their withering frames. Most were already thinner than they had been when the race began, but Devlin and his nephew Jim had come prepared to start reversing the trend. The Ellisons arrived in their camper and unloaded more food and beverages than we had seen in a week. A picnic table was soon stacked with potato salad, pasta, pickles, baked beans, rolls, fresh vegetables, and fruit. Bob Lundy came next. He secured his Route 66 banner in the background and took photographs of the hungry runners attacking the spread.

Over by the truck, Jim had the barbecue fired up high. The side dishes were all I could handle, but the runners' mouths watered just listening to the main course sizzle on the grill. Bodine's buffalo ranch was just down the road from the Bagdad Cafe, and Devlin had swung a deal to give the runners a treat. They attacked the buffalo burgers like starved refugees. It was a feast they would not soon forget.

"It's high in protein, low in cholesterol, and has hardly any fat," said Devlin as though he were a snake-oil salesman pitching his product at a Wild West fair. "It's the aphrodisiac of the nineties."

After dinner, I climbed a knoll of sand behind the depot to photograph the sunset. The runners had already scattered out to sleep. The depot offered some shelter beneath its overhang, but many had spread out under the stars. Devlin and his nephew set up a tent, and the Ellisons retired to the comfort of the camper on the back of their truck.

Far off in the distance I saw the lights of a vehicle coming our way. Five minutes later, a Blazer drew near, crossed the tracks, and turned in to where the other vehicles were parked. The doors opened, and a pair of women emerged. A young boy followed, pointing toward where I sat perched on the hill. I waved, confused, wondering who they were and what they were doing out in the desert at that time of night. They ran up within earshot, but all I could see were silhouettes against the background of light.

4

Sting of the Scorpion

The world breaks everyone and afterward, many are strong at the broken place.
—Ernest Hemingway

The start beside the old depot on day seven was eerie, all silence and
desolation and purple desert light. After preparing an enormous batch of pancakes on a
kerosene stove, the troupe from the Bagdad Cafe cheered the runners as they went on
their way. The athletes' moods were upbeat despite the desperate conditions, the result
of good hospitality and the arrival of help.

After crossing another 48 miles of empty desert, the runners would leave California.
The stopover was right there on the border, at one of the two casinos that made up Stateline,
Nevada. Everyone was looking forward to hot showers, air-conditioned rooms, and
twenty-four-hour buffets.

Surrounded by cinder cones, towering sand dunes, and barren brown hills, the Kelso-
Cima Road sliced through a forsaken landscape, slowly gaining altitude, before turning
a corner to an unlikely sight. It was as though the Trans America group had been
transported to a planet from a Heinlein novel, an uninhabitable territory with warped
vegetation that looked more humanoid than plant. In actual fact, we had entered the high
desert, the only place in the nation harsh and isolated enough for use in developing
supersonic jets. Tom Wolfe described the spectacle in *The Right Stuff*:

> It looked like some fossil landscape that had long since been left behind by
> the rest of terrestrial evolution. It was full of huge dry lake beds. . . .Other
> than sagebrush the only vegetation was Joshua trees, twisted freaks of the
> plant world that looked like a cross between cactus and Japanese bonsai.
> They had a dark petrified green color and horribly crippled branches. At
> dusk the Joshua trees stood out in silhouette on the fossil wasteland like some
> arthritic nightmare. In the summer the temperature went up to 110 as a matter
> of course, and the dry lake beds were covered in a sand, and there would be
> windstorms and sandstorms right out of a Foreign Legion movie.

After passing through the world's largest Joshua tree forest, the route reached a crossroad at Cima, the site of several mailboxes, a telephone booth, and a tiny, under-stocked store. I supplied the runners with food and drink before stopping to make a series of calls. Several athletes went into the store searching for ice cream, but without luck. They settled for cold sodas instead.

The tangled trees provided novel thoughts for a time, but once past Cima, the scorching desert heat began extracting its price. As the runners began a long downhill with nothing but rangeland in the distance, their muscles began to tighten, weary and worn from continuous work. By the time they reached a potholed dirt road, many of the athletes had slowed to a regular walk. Even the previous leaders' pace dropped off: Schieke because of a troubling hamstring strain; Howie to keep his friend and rival company, and because of his feet. For the second day in a row, two of the three runners with full-time handlers emerged at the front.

Thirty-five-year-old David Warady had planned his race strategy for almost a year, but his athletic background went back much farther than that. He grew up with swimming, basketball, and football, and began running in earnest while attending the University of California at Berkeley. He never ran on college teams, but when he moved from Sacramento to Huntington Beach, he joined a running club and put himself under the tutelage of a coach.

"He was surprised at my ability to train hard, work, and then come back and train hard, day after day," Warady recalls of the first months with his new mentor. "He told me if there was ever a stage race, my conditioning was ideal."

Warady became a steady marathon performer before moving up to ultradistance races in 1987. He won the Southern California 50-Mile Championship in his first year, clocking a respectable 5 hours and 58 minutes. By the time he learned of the Trans America, he had brought his marathon time down to 2:34 and was convinced that he could handle the grueling regimen of two months on the run. He and his coach mapped out a plan of attack, considering every possible situation that could crop up in the race.

"You really can't train specifically for this type of event," he said before the start, "because only years of high mileage can develop strong enough tendons and ligaments to handle the stress."

Leading into the race, Warady continued his regular training, putting in anywhere from 110 to 150 miles a week. He ran his first six-day race in December 1991 as a test, learning early that his biggest problem was controlling his pace. While the traditional six-day strategy calls for constant movement and accumulation of mileage on very little sleep, Warady's plan was to simulate the conditions of the Trans America: to run 50 miles a day with good rest periods in between. Even with thirteen years of training behind him, Warady suffered from severe tendinitis; by day five, he could manage only 29 miles.

"That was the race to make mistakes in. That's why I went there: to try out and learn."

Besides his experimentation on the track, Warady researched Pyle's races, as well as individual transcontinental crossings that had taken place over the years. He determined that in order to stay healthy he would need regular food, fluid, and quality rest. Knowing that even those basic needs would be impossible to come by in the context of the race Kenney and Riley had planned, he worked a deal with his wife. They saved their money so that he would be able to stay in hotels, eat decent meals, and rent a van for supplies. She quit her job to act as his one-woman crew.

The day into Kelso had been good for Warady; in fact, with his wife, Kelley, stopping whenever he needed supplies, the run through the whole of the desert had gone like a

Only two of the finishers had full-time handlers; the other athletes relied on aid stations and the help of overworked communal crews. Kelley Babiak tended to her husband, David Warady, every mile of the race. She gave him ice, sodas, cookies, sandwiches, and TLC—whatever he wanted, whenever he wanted it most.

dream. With a van full of ice, soda, cold electrolyte replacement drinks, sandwiches, fruit, and a variety of snack foods at his disposal, he suffered none of the problems that came with relying on superheated aid stations and sporadic communal support.

Warady's wife was there to support his effort and his effort alone. More than once while running alongside another competitor, Warady pulled up at his van to get himself a drink. Despite the 100-degree temperatures, when rivals asked for ice or liquids, he bluntly refused.

"Kelley is here to help me," he said. "If she assists someone else, it wouldn't be fair."

Georgia's Richard Westbrook also had the luxury of a handler: A college student named Shelley Tyler shadowed the forty-six-year-old, stopping every mile or two to refuel him and check on his needs.

While running for Westbrook's cross-country team at Riverdale High, Tyler learned that her coach was getting into ultramarathons. She decided to try one herself, a 50 miler, at age seventeen. She did incredibly well, and has idolized Westbrook for his tenacity in races of all distances ever since experiencing the world of ultras herself.

When her former coach and friend said he was contemplating the Trans America, Tyler debated what she was going to do for the summer—and then offered to help. The pair rented a car and loaded it up with tent, sleeping bags, and coolers full of supplies. The ex-student became the teacher's crew for the race.

Helmut Linzbichler, the Austrian entrant, had more support than anyone else, but he was far back in the standings in the competitive race. Even with a masseuse, driver, roving cyclist, and medical assistant, Linzbichler was entered only to finish. The members of his support team were helpful to anyone who happened upon them, but they shadowed their athlete closely. He was the one paying their bills.

"We have beaucoup volunteers," Riley had said during the last scout of the course, "and on top of our full-time helpers, there will be tons of support."

Two of the full-time crew members were the cyclists, and another was Bobby Wise, the man whom Riley had so hastily dismissed. The last was the fellow we knew as Gutdayzke. The promised flood of assistance was a meager trickle at best.

With the ham radio operators and Dick Devlin's Bagdad Cafe crew behind us, things looked desperate, but the Blazer that appeared from the darkness in Kelso carried much-needed replacements who were eager to help. Even so, the reality was that the organizers were providing less than the bare minimum; they were several dozen steps away from meeting even the most lax requirements for a competitive race.

Riley's cyclist friends had already proven to be practically useless: They tendered neither moral nor physical support. They knew little about running, had expectations of a frolicking vacation across the country, and were terribly unfit. After helping with registration and water on day one, they had taken to sleeping in and riding slowly amid the runners, making little more than a token effort to help.

Gutdayzke was a tremendous assistance, but his focus had changed significantly from the original intent. Before the race began, Kenney had offered to have a van belonging to one of the competitors transported to each day's finish, on the condition it be made available for roving support. Entrant Ed Williams agreed wholeheartedly: He wanted his vehicle on-site so he could use it whenever he needed supplies. Williams drove from Missouri to California, picking up Gutdayzke in St. Louis on his way to the start of the race. The runner and the volunteer became good friends, and by the time they reached Huntington Beach, Williams had changed the rules for use of his van. Gutdayzke shifted from a general support role to personal handler for sixty-three-year-old Williams, the oldest participant in the race.

Gutdayzke was a tattooed Vietnam-era ultradistance competitor who wore earrings and peace signs and old, flowing, hippie-style shirts. He had a vague and mysterious air, but underneath it all displayed a heart of absolute gold. He provided welcome relief to the runners who ran within range of Williams, at the back of the pack.

Beam and I drove back and forth between the rest of the uncrewed runners, but we simply couldn't supply all of them often enough. Sporadic as support was, there were times when the front runners were so intent on racing that they refused to lose precious seconds by stopping for aid. "Those guys are either the most incredible athletes on the planet," Beam reflected, "or else they're too stupid to be believed."

Pyle's runners had encountered similar support problems in 1928, but at least the crews that were there helped everyone out. Englishman Peter Gavuzzi, one of the top contenders, recounted the situation when he spoke of the race: "Sometimes you couldn't get a drink between water holes in the desert," and when you got to those you had to bargain with the Indians before you took even a sip."

During the second transcontinental race, which went from New York to Los Angeles the following year, Pyle required all entrants to bring their own trainers and handlers. Even with $25,000 at stake, good sportsmanship and common sense prevailed when it came to a rival in need. Gavuzzi remembered fighting it out with Johnny Salo of New Jersey all through the race.

"Often I'd be up in front, with Salo's car watching me. And my car'd be back with him, seeing how he was doing—and giving him drinks."

Warady knew that his planning gave him an advantage, but he held fast to his philosophy. "I wanted no surprises, so I prepared as well as I could." Even in the deathly hot desert, he figured, it was every man for himself.

The Mojave was tough on everybody, but the strung-out entourage kept moving forward, relentlessly, a thin trail of marchers at a continuous pace. Past Cima, we turned at a cattle gate onto a narrow dirt road. It petered out after 3 miles, until there was nothing at all.

"Beginning of dry lake bed," read Kenney's instructions. "Leave graded roadway and follow markings across lakebed surface. Aim at hotel . . ."

When the casinos of Stateline, Nevada, finally appeared in the distance, the runners thought they were either nearing the finish or having hallucinations of an amusement park mirage. Ahead lay neon lights and a giant ferris wheel--strange signs of civilization arising out of the dust. The temperature was 120 degrees.

Warady took the stage in 7:53, and Westbrook came in second, 21 minutes behind. After clocking them in, I cycled back across the lakebed to take photographs and came upon Howie on the final stretch to the hotel.

"Helmut wanted to walk the last 5 miles," he said while taking a drink from my bottle, "but I 'ad to push on. I've got to get off of these feet."

Schieke was only 15 minutes back. The little German seemed to be limping, but he smiled when he saw me.

"Ah, this is truly America," he said, waving first back at the emptiness and then ahead to the building that rose like a rocket out of the sand. I recalled reading an interview with author Ian Frazier, who had said that a traveler today has a completely different sense of time from that of a traveler a hundred years ago. For 6 more hours, the Trans America runners struggled across the barren desert, while travelers on the interstate drove by at seventy less than a mile away, oblivious to the incredible race.

Warady's run moved him an hour ahead of Edmonson in overall time, bringing him into third and within 2 hours of the lead. Howie held on to the number one position, 32 minutes ahead of Schieke. Rogozinski stayed in fifth, 2 hours back of Edmonson, despite his resolution to take a more conservative approach. Williams was the slowest for the day, completing the 48 miles in just over 13 hours. After one state, seven days, and more than 300 miles, nineteen runners remained in the competitive race.

The group that entered the Primadonna Casino that day reminded me of the old American Express commercial where the unshaven man emerges from the jungle, dressed in filthy safari gear, all covered in sweat. We may not have had endless lines of credit or dressed in tuxedos for dinner, but we were able to bask in the luxury of real beds inside air-conditioned rooms.

The contrast between the Primadonna and where we had just been was like comparing the Roman Empire in the days of Caligula with a visit to the far side of Mars. Lights, mirrors, and glitter balls sparkled in every corner of the flashy building. The constant ringing of slot machines was unfamiliar to ears accustomed to parched conversation and the silence of the desolate road.

There were people everywhere. They were either pale and bloated from days of overindulgence at the gaming tables or else lobster pink, burnt by the sun. Almost all carried large plastic cups in their hand, jingling coins as they crossed the lobby, returned from the change counter, or lounged near the phones. Children chased each other up a spiral staircase that led from the slot machines to the mezzanine level. They were dripping wet, having just come in from the pool.

After showering, the runners ravaged the casino buffet like vultures, making trip after trip until they could no longer move. Most went to bed early, holding off on their vices until the following day.

"Each Saturday, starting with Stage Number Eight," wrote Kenney in the prerace information packets, "competitive runners will be required to run a time trial. This should make each Saturday a unique and exciting 'Trans-Am '92 style' focus for the week."

The first Saturday time trial did anything but generate the interest it was meant to entice; it created irritation instead. The original format called for the race leader to head out alone at 5 A.M., with the rest of the competitive runners leaving according to their deficits in overall time. The standings after the first week of running meant that Howie would start at 5:00, Schieke at 5:32, and the others at 6:00 since they were more than an hour out of the overall lead. Kenney's theory was that the first finisher of the time trial would almost always be the overall leader of the race.

Howie felt he was being placed at a disadvantage if he headed out alone, however, and although annoyed at the suggestion that the initial plan was less than ideal, Riley decided to modify the start without thinking it through. The main pack left the quiet parking lot behind the Primadonna Casino together, with Howie following, 5 minutes back. Schieke began his run 32 minutes after Howie. He shrugged, knowing he would be the one who was alone, at the back, for the first part of the day.

The disorderly start was one thing, but the highway wreaked a different sort of havoc on the support crews. The runners ran facing traffic, on the left side of the road. For the handlers to gain access, they had to drive ahead to the next exit, get off the interstate, and double back, watching for speeding traffic when they pulled off the road. Once the athletes were supplied, the vehicles had to drive to another exit ramp, veer off, loop around again, and continue beyond. The process was nerve-racking, and it became more time-consuming and difficult as the pack spread out through the course of day.

With the Blazer and new volunteers came a whole extra support vehicle and the opportunity to orchestrate an actual plan. We split the course into thirds and developed a system that seemed to actually work. I stayed with the front runners, the new arrivals roamed the middle, and Beam took care of the rear. We circled back and forth, overlapping occasionally, and kept most of the athletes fairly well supplied. Kenney's aid stations were always there, but the runners preferred a friendly face and a van that offered variety to the warm jugs of fluids on the side of the road.

I ran for a short while with Howie along a particularly bad strip of road. The shoulder was pitted, as though an aerating machine had raced along it, digging divots in the blacktop like it would on a lawn.

"Do you think this'll hurt the feet?" Howie asked while floating along at an impressive clip.

"I don't know, Al," I answered, while wondering how it possibly could not. "I guess the question is, how do you feel?"

He was running well and was already past most of the people he had started behind. Somewhere up ahead was Edmonson, running powerfully, as he always did in the early part of the day. It was only 36 miles from Stateline to Las Vegas, and it seemed possible that Edmonson would hold his lead through to the end.

Arrival at Vacation Village in Las Vegas was a pleasant surprise for the Trans America group. Lying on the extreme west side of the strip, it was rather more basic than the gaudy madhouses that light up the heart of the town. The level of smoke was bearable in the early afternoon, and best of all, Kenney had done some schmoozing during his scouting trips and had wangled free rooms for the second day in a row.

Edmonson broke the tape in front of a television crew in 5 hours and 27 minutes and gave a positive interview about his goals for New York. Warady and Westbrook arrived 10 minutes later, running under the banner side by side. A reporter and photographer from the *Las Vegas Dispatch* turned up just in time to catch Ed Kelley crossing the line, and then several minutes later scrambled to get shots of the leader of the race. Howie was coming toward the finish, running with Rogozinski and another tiny athlete, a newcomer who had become familiar to us all since he appeared on the scene.

The trio veered off the main road, their hands joined and held high in the air. The neophyte's smile was all teeth; the photographer snapped away at the heartwarming scene. The group converged at the water jugs that sat in the back of Kenney's big, yellow truck, and the reporter asked about the kid.

"This is Louise's son," replied Rogozinski. "We call him the Brandonator."

Though none of us had met them before, and we knew them only by their pseudonyms Thelma and Louise, the new volunteers took their crewing tasks to heart. Lori Walker and Thelma Porter had both worked as handlers during 100-mile races in California, and Lori's eight-year-old son, Brandon, loved to be in the thick of things, helping however he could. The trio had driven all the way from San Diego to Kelso, taking a week of summer vacation just to assist the Trans America group.

"No one seems to understand why we'd leave our husbands and families for a week on the road with a bunch of runners we didn't even know," wrote Porter in a letter to *Ultrarunning*. "Well, I'll tell you why. Even on the hottest, most miserable of days through the desert, these men and women were as friendly, upbeat, and thoughtful as humanly possible. It was incredibly inspirational, seeing what those people could do."

Thelma and Louise may have been on vacation, but they were essential to the success of the transcontinental event. The race organizers had severe budgetary constraints and were unable to meet the full needs of the athletes in the race. For the $200 entry fee, they had promised to house the runners for sixty-four nights and to feed and water them out on the course.

Kenney balked at buying new jugs for fluids after those provided by the sponsors were stolen. When several of the second batch disappeared, he began to use flimsy plastic water jugs, setting them directly on the side of the road. The Gatorade and water became undrinkable almost as soon as the bottles were placed on the scorching desert ground. With Power Bars as the sole means of sustenance early on, the athletes ate their share until they could stomach no more. The chocolate and malt nut packets of energy may have been excellent sources of easily digested calories, but melted and gooey from the sun, day in and day out, they quickly lost their appeal.

Riley refused outright when asked to stock Beam's support van with ice, soda, and some alternate food. Several athletes donated money so that the runner-turned-volunteer could supply them with cold fluid and snack foods on the course without going broke. Thelma and Louise and I were funding our vehicles' supplies from our own pockets, but occasional contributions by the athletes helped to balance the accounts.

Louise pointed out that there was too much for too few to do because the runners were spread so far apart, but by the time we reached Las Vegas, the system was working as well as it could. Thelma and Louise were getting to know the group in the middle of the pack and came to realize how appreciated a cup of iced Kool-Aid and a sandwich could be.

An article about ultramarathoning had appeared in the Las Vegas paper the previous week, and the Trans America received a short mention at the end of the piece. Several curiosity seekers turned out to cheer the athletes as they finished, but with a 4-hour spread among the nineteen competitive runners, the race was not exactly an exciting spectator sport. The race director of the Las Vegas Marathon stopped by to give everyone T-shirts and see if there was anything he could do to help out the group. He talked hotel management into letting us use an air-conditioned conference room as a lounge area while our rooms were being cleaned.

Dave Pearle, a friend of Jane Serues's who lived in California, showed up in Vegas and stopped by Vacation Village. He had been a tremendous help in the days leading up to the start, stockpiling the product shipments from sponsors, making posters of the entrants, providing food for the prerace press conference, and helping to load Kenney's enormous truck. He said he had driven out to Vegas from the coast in order to get his parents out for the weekend, but I knew he was there at Serues's request.

After looking at the worn-down athletes, he offered me a heartfelt piece of advice: "You look worse than they do. You'd better start getting some rest. And try to relax. At this rate, you're not going to get anywhere near to New York."

Besides good wishes, Pearle brought padlocks and chains for Kenney to secure the aid stations to posts or trees at the side of the road. He had been dismayed at hearing the coolers had been stolen but relayed the message from Jane that a new shipment would meet us the following week. Pearle also carried with him a huge chocolate cake, courtesy of *Runner's World*—a congratulatory offering to the athletes for making it through the grueling first week and successfully crossing California. Most everyone was too hot and weary to pay it much attention, so we decided to take it upstairs and divvy it up later, while watching Edmonson make his network debut.

The medical team set up in the conference room and went immediately to work. Bill and Eric were joined by Ed Hoffman, an osteopathic doctor from the area. While the students tended to the minor problems, Hoffman was bombarded by a series of significant complaints.

Tendinitis, shin splints, aching knees, severe sunburn, painful rashes, diarrhea, and inflamed ankles were just some of the ailments Hoffman dealt with throughout the course of the day. He was appalled by the general condition of the athletes, especially when he learned of the inadequate support and total lack of hygiene. Riley shrugged off the concerns as though the physician should have known better—these things, the race director believed, were part of the game.

When the rooms were ready, keys were distributed, and the athletes went to shower and rest up before an evening of entertainment or going their various ways. The medics moved their tables to the hallway outside the rooms, keeping on with their work on the athletes who were left. Many were hurting, but it was Howie's feet that worried everyone the most.

The little Scotsman had been delaying the inevitable visit, but Hoffman finally came into his room. When Howie undid his shoes and bandages, the physician couldn't believe what he saw. The rough road had done more damage to the raw heels, and blood seeped from the exposed layers of tissue the way sweat does in a sauna, dripping from pores.

Hoffman spent close to an hour trying to determine how best to deal with the wounds. Most of the other runners swung by on their way to the hotel buffet and asked how the patient was doing. Hang in there, Al, they said optimistically, hiding the truth they already knew. This is like the many problems encountered so far, they said, and can only get better with time.

"There is no way you should be running on those feet," Hoffman finally said.

"There's far too much damage. I'm going to have to pull you from the race. Tell me you won't run anymore so I can cleanse the wounds properly and give them a chance to repair."

A minor debate took place, but Howie lost steam on hearing that long-term damage could result if he didn't relent.

"Go ahead," whispered the athlete, "and do whatcha 'av ta. Fix 'em up so they'll start up ta heal."

Howie twisted the sheets into knots and gnashed his teeth as Hoffman applied peroxide to burn dirt and infection out of the flesh. Howie remembers crawling to the bathroom that night; he was unable to stand. He also recalls Warady's wife looking into the room at some point, trying unsuccessfully to put on an expression of concern.

"She was spying for David," he told me the next day. "I could see she was glad I was out of the race."

5

Follow Your Bliss?

Even if strength fail,
boldness at least will deserve praise:
in great endeavors even to have had the will is enough.
—Propertius

Everyone involved with the race thought that it was ripe for cover-
age—that the press would be on it like fans to Michael Jordan after the Bulls' second
championship win. According to *Runner's World*'s Patrick Taylor, however, when it
comes to public relations, theory and practice rarely converge.

When the staff of *Runner's World* first evaluated the proposal to sponsor the Trans
America, they had seen the potential for publicity as one of the event's major appeals.
Though the magazine could not offer up-front financial support, extensive editorial
coverage before and after the race was promised, as well as a wide array of services aimed
at promoting the event. Besides taking me aboard, Taylor hired a journalism graduate
to work as an intern specifically assigned to the race. Maria Farnon was the main contact
at headquarters; I was the on-site man, out in the field.

Weeks before the race began, Taylor and Farnon sifted through a data base of
thousands of media contacts to try to determine who might be interested in covering the
cross-country event. Hundreds of press kits were printed and sent, becoming the basis
for a constant stream of follow-up calls. By the time I left for California, the publicity
effort was off and running. Farnon staffed the media hotline back in Pennsylvania, kept
on top of the mailings, and began organizing my schedule for updates and telephone calls.

"You make damn sure Michael and Jesse get their act together by tomorrow," Taylor
yelled at me the day before the race actually began. "If they screw this thing up, we'll
pull our support so fast they won't know what hit them. We'll see to it they never work
on another race in this country, not ever again."

Taylor had dealt with dozens of high-profile events and knew that the press
conference generally set the tone for the rest of the race. The race organizers had been
disorganized and slovenly, and they hadn't even bothered to show up on time for the kick-
off event.

The time and location had been finalized two weeks before; anyone vaguely connected with the race had been duly informed. Several of the athletes had come straight from the Los Angeles Airport in order to attend the meeting and make themselves available for the press. Kenney and Riley, on the other hand, had been in Huntington Beach for more than a week, yet they showed up at the press conference more than half an hour late.

I grappled to find an up side: At least the media turnout was poor. President Bush's visit to Los Angeles must have captured the lifestyle reporters, I thought. The U.S. Olympic Track and Field Trials started that evening in New Orleans and had likely hooked all the media involved with sports. Despite our barrage of information, the Trans America remained fairly unknown.

"We could be a sensational draw," Taylor had said, "or we could be an absolute flop." The initial indication was toward the latter, but given the circumstances, I saw that as a blessing in disguise. If the race was to get off to a bumpy start, I figured it was good that it would happen away from the camera's vulturelike eye.

The Las Vegas start was set for 5 A.M. sharp, but at five minutes to, only half of the runners were ready to go.

"Today there is no leeway," said Riley in an irritable voice as he stood under the banner and looked at his watch. "At 5:00 we're starting. I don't care if nobody is here; I'm going and we're starting the clock."

Curses could be heard across the dark parking lot as tardy athletes dragged their gear to the truck. On day nine, at least, Riley was as good as his word.

I drove out ahead of the leaders as they passed the flashing neon that lit the world-famous strip. Caesar's and Bally's Grand made for interesting backdrops, but I was particularly keen on getting photographs at the Flamingo. The Route 66 man, Bob Lundy, had put me in touch with the person in charge of the Flamingo's marquee. He had promised to flash a 50-foot-high message to the Trans America athletes between 5 and 6 A.M.

The strip was unusually crowded, alive with people heading out of the casinos and into the streets. The runners are celebrities in this town, I thought to myself. We had made both television networks on the prime-time and late-night news and were in the paper this morning. But all these people? I wondered. Are they really standing around just to see us?

I came upon the Flamingo, but it was a disappointment. The neons were totally dead; nothing flashed on the glorious sign.

Once the runners reached the far side of town, I went back to Vacation Village to help load the trucks and collect the rest of my gear. I helped Howie down the stairs and into my van.

"Do you think I should 'ang around," he had asked the night before, "or would I be best to pack up and go? I don't want to be in the way—but maybe I can do somethin' to help."

I didn't quite know what to say. Like Beam, Howie had every right in the world to head home to try to recover; in fact, as a proven elite athlete with far more to lose if he didn't heal properly, I figured the Scotsman had more motivation to make himself right and get back on his feet.

To be out of the race was devastating, but Howie found some consolation in the fact that he had been pulled. After examining the potential reasons for the blisters, he determined that friction from new insoles had been the actual cause. Six weeks before the Trans America, a physician friend at a race in New York had recommended that Howie replace the inserts that came with his shoes.

It was interesting to see such a remarkable athlete grapple with his own vulnerability. Howie was trying to find the best way to cope with personal heartbreak while looking beyond himself for a validating reason to stay with the group. I suggested that he do what was best for Al Howie—return to Cowichan Bay in order to heal. At the same time, I knew his presence would have a positive effect on the athletes left in the race, and somewhat selfishly, I hoped he would choose to stay. Howie said he would check flight costs and bus schedules. If he did, it was a halfhearted effort.

"Where to?" I asked when he closed the door to my van.

"Let's do what you 'ave to do, get some brekky, and then get out and help the boys on the course."

Once through Las Vegas, the runners reentered the desert—and were relegated back to the shoulder of I-15. The 55-mile stage to Moapa, Nevada, was the longest yet, and the temperature soared to 120 degrees by early afternoon. With Howie out, Schieke started the day with the yellow leader's number, but it was Edmonson who ran as though he was in command of the race. Throwing caution to the wind, he charged from the start. He held on again, winning his second stage in a row in spite of the heat.

The support crews were joined by Erv Nicholls for the day. He had been so impressed with the athletes on day two that he couldn't resist the opportunity to help them again before they were too far out of his range. It was a long, hard stage for everyone, with the only resupply point at the Valley of Fire State Park. I stocked up on soda and ice for the runners at a store run by Indians from the nearby reservation, while Howie had a hamburger and loaded the cooler with beer.

The stage ended in a dusty parking lot in front of the Moapa Moose Lodge. A strong wind was blowing, but it was hot, offering nothing that even resembled a feeling of relief.

The Moose people were expecting us and had ice-cold lemonade prepared when the first runners arrived. The locals had, in fact, been buzzing with anticipation for a good several days. The first real payoff for all the prerace media work was upon us, and it seemed we were the biggest happening for the desert town since they installed the slot machine in the bar.

CBS This Morning had a crew waiting in nearby Glendale; they planned to be at the Lodge at 3 the next morning to videotape the athletes preparing to embark for Mesquite, Nevada, on stage ten. As the runners assembled under the banner, the Trans America would be broadcast live over national airwaves.

The thought of a big media splash helped bolster the spirits of the worn athletes until a call came through: Everything we had been preparing for was suddenly off. The crowded streets in Las Vegas that morning had had nothing whatsoever to do with the runners or the race. There had been an earthquake, just as the athletes were getting ready to start. Our CBS crew was being sent back to the Mojave to film the damage, which had occurred as far away as Newberry Springs. Roads and water towers had been ripped up and cracked. There were no casualties, but I couldn't help wondering how our friends and the depot at Kelso had weathered the shock. The epicenter was only 5 miles away from where we had slept.

I called headquarters, left a message, then returned to the room where the athletes sat waiting for their meal. I hated to relate the news, but I had already handed out new race shirts for the runners to wear in front of the cameras. I told everyone to try to keep the tees shiny until the following week.

"This was my worst day," said Sprengelmeyer that night as he spoke into the phone. "I developed shin splints going into Vegas, and now I'm so tired I'm dragging my feet. If Donna was here right now, I'd be in the car and heading for home."

Serge Debladis was even worse off than Sprengelmeyer: He had severe tendinitis, shin splints, and circulation problems caused by terrible varicose veins. He was almost as vocal as Edmonson in his harangues about organizational issues, but his yelling was entirely in French.

During our first telephone conversation, I had struggled valiantly to dredge up my high-school language lessons while Debladis waited patiently on the line at his home outside of Toulouse. We barely communicated, but I did get his flight details and figure out that he hoped to be met at the airport and housed before the start of the race. I slowly learned about his background by hacking my way through our subsequent talks.

Debladis had run his first marathon in 1978 while visiting an aunt in New York. Seven years later, he discovered ultramarathons and the lure of the beyond. His first major event was the Spartathlon, a grueling 250K race that follows ancient country roads between Athens and Sparta in Greece. For three years in a row, Debladis completed the Spartathlon challenge, and then moved to 24-hour races, competing on a track. The forty-four-year-old librarian had raised money for a variety of children's charities during his previous runs. He planned to create awareness for the handicapped when he returned to his wife and son at the conclusion of the Trans America race.

His transcontinental dreams, like my own, had started when he read *Flanagan's Run*. Debladis saw the Trans America the same way Kenney did: It was an incredible opportunity, the start of something tremendously big.

"The Tour de France," he said often, "is tremendous, magnificent. The [Trans America] runners are like the cyclists, and me, I will be a hero when I arrive in New York."

The Trans America should be embraced by the whole nation, he believed, the athletes treated as if they were Gods of the Feet. The gates to every city should be opened wide, its wine made ready to flow as the runners came through. First-class treatment is what the Tour de France riders get; the Trans America runners should have the same, from the moment they left Los Angeles until they set foot in New York. The race was less than 3,000 miles long, but Debladis's vision was a million light years away.

Helmut Linzbichler, the Austrian, suffered along with the others, hobbling into the Moose Lodge last, at 8:30 P.M. Nine days into the race, he sat in thirteenth place, 24 hours back of the leader in cumulative time. On day ten, he could barely stand. He got up for the cooked breakfast but didn't bother to line up for the start. The spirit that had made him an accomplished mountaineer abandoned him, and he gave up the race.

Linzbichler had turned up at my hotel in California at nearly midnight on the day I arrived. The Trans America was due to start three days later, and he wanted my help in finding a vehicle to transport his four-person crew. His problem was related to a complication that had arisen while sponsorship negotiations were still under way. For a time it looked as though a car rental company would provide the race with several vehicles, and since Riley knew he didn't have enough volunteers to drive them all, he informed the Austrian that his group was welcome to use one of the donated vans. But the sponsorship deal died a week before the start of the race.

Linzbichler wound up renting a maroon Dodge van and loaded it with enough equipment to survive a year on the moon. Among himself, a driver, a medical advisor, a masseuse, and a personal handler, the van was packed to the absolute brim. They had several thousand packets of vitamins, six microcassette recorders, four cameras, two bicycles, a portable computer, a massage table, and who knows what all hidden in their stacks of personal gear. He may not have been the most accomplished ultramarathoner in the group, but Linzbichler appeared to be the best prepared. He had to finish the race, he told me the night we met—he had a contract to write a book about the experience of running through American lives. Here he was in the desert, with severe tendinitis, dismayed at having to drop from the competitive division.

The new $16 million high school in Mesquite, Nevada, was our stopping point for stage ten. After climbing out of Moapa, the course followed I-15 through a desolate stretch of dry desert plateau, then veered off and took secondary roads along the meandering Virgin River as far as Mesquite.

The 37-mile stage belonged to Rogozinski from beginning to end. The young teacher clocked in at 5 hours and 28 minutes.

"Good sights and good music," he said as he pulled off his headphones at the finish. "Combined with a good run, they make for a beautiful day." Bruce Springsteen provided the music, and Rogozinski's brother was responsible for to-the-point introductions and motivational words.

Westbrook finished 12 minutes later, followed by Warady, more than 1 hour back. As Schieke, England's Peter Hodson, and Kelley completed the stage, I noticed that Edmonson had not yet arrived. The atmosphere was almost peaceful without the Angry Dude here, I reflected. Edmonson was a good runner when he stayed on course, but he was even better at stirring up shit.

Edmonson, it turned out, had been struggling with a sore knee. He finished thirteen places after Rogozinski, dropping 4½ hours and one place in the standings over the course of the day. Edmonson was followed only by Skagerberg and New Jersey's Paul Soyka, who made the 10½-hour cutoff with a mere 25 minutes to spare. Like many of the others, Skagerberg had already battled shin splints and blisters. Now he was at war with a severe pain in his foot.

We were comfortable and well fed at the school, but Edmonson threw a fit just the same. He seemed to have made a vow to blow up at least once every day of the race.

"Where in hell is my sleeping bag?" he yelled after retrieving his duffel from Kenney's truck. "This is the second time someone has stolen it. I'm sick of this discrimination. Why is it everything happens to me?"

No ice, hot fluids, poor food, not enough support, and the leeching journey runners all entered into Edmonson's tirade. Although Edmonson's gripes were often petty, I saw them as symptomatic of the constant state of weariness that plagued almost every member of the Trans America group. We were all tired and irritable only ten days into the nine-week event.

The journey runner division had been problematic even during race planning, but both Riley and Kenney had backed it as a valid part of the race. They wanted the Trans America to be nonelitist, they said, open to all who chose to experience the event. On paper their ideal sounded noble, but its impracticality became evident early on, and its problems were amplified tenfold when the stages were long.

Dissension resulted from the fact that the journey runners were getting all the benefits of the full event without any of the hardship. When they fell behind schedule, they were picked up and dropped in the midst of the competitive field. If they became tired during a stage, they convinced kind-hearted Beam to give them a ride to the end. If they were

Those who couldn't meet the 3½-mile-per-hour cutoff schedules were eliminated from the competitive race, but many stayed on as "journey runners." Relaxing on the roadside are Carol Carter, John McPhee, and John Kim.

too sore, or tired, they took days off. They held to no schedule, running as little or as much as they pleased. They relaxed at the finish, with food, refreshments, and time on their hands.

Besides diverting the efforts of the crews from the competitive runners, the situation had a devastating psychological effect. John Wallis, although the most positive of the competitors, explained the problem one day while stopped for a drink.

"It's so discouraging to see someone up ahead, to set your focus on catching them, and finally when you do, to realize it's Bruno. And you're passing him for the third time in the day."

This was twentieth-century America, but the athletes seemed to be dividing into very distinct castes.

Before the race began, there had been a tremendous amount of debate about the runners' chances of completing it. In an "estimate the outcome" poll taken by *Ultrarunning* magazine, most respondents believed there would be few finishers, if any. Howie was the first of the truly hardened runners to drop from the field, and the pessimistic predictions seemed a depressing possibility as Skagerberg, Sprengelmeyer, and several others with a serious shot at going the distance began to struggle.

The race started without Edmonson on day eleven.

"It's not my knee that's bothering me," he said. "I've just had my limit of this disorganized shit."

Rogozinski started off well, but a stabbing pain in his knee suddenly slowed him to a walk.

"What's up, Rogo?" Howie asked as we pulled alongside.

"Beats the shit outta me. I felt great at the start of the day, and now I can't even run."

Annoyed and worried, the twenty-four-year-old downed a cup of Coke, filled his bottle with Gatorade, and began the slow trudge through the final 8 miles.

Westbrook won his first stage of the race, covering the 46 miles into St. George, Utah, in 8 hours and 7 minutes. He finished more than ½ hour ahead of Warady. Next came Hodson, followed by Schieke and Kelley together in a tie for fourth.

Besides helping crew for the athletes, Howie had taken on the task of timing the finishers and calculating the overall times at the end of the day. The Scotsman now did his math on the lawn in front of the National Guard armory as Rogozinski struggled across the line in a disappointing sixth place, 1½ hours behind the stage winner.

"David's pulled ahead a' Helmut into first," said Howie just after Rogozinski arrived, "and he won't know it till tomorrow. He's probably asleep by now, 'is feet up in the motel."

Skagerberg had a much better day, finishing eighth, but Soyka suffered as never before. He finished the stage, but it was his last in the competitive race. He withdrew the next morning complaining of shin pains, believing he had muscular infections in his swelling legs. This latest in the series of casualties brought the Trans America down to fifteen athletes in the competitive field.

No one was particularly happy with the prospect of another cement floor, but the armory's showers were warm and the building was relatively cool. When everyone had arrived, we took time to revive the daily award ceremony, giving Westbrook an old Utah license plate for taking the stage. Warady was absent, as usual. Howie surmised that he was having his fourth meal of the day.

Unlike Warady, Westbrook had chosen from the beginning to be one of the group. Although he had a full-time handler in Tyler, both were eating and sleeping under the same conditions as everyone else. Most of the entrants stayed up at night to enjoy one another's company, and each was delighted whenever I asked him or her to spend a few minutes giving an interview over the phone. Warady, on the other hand, remained apart, getting involved with the goings-on in camp only when they were impossible to avoid. More than once I had been unable to hook him up in interviews with East Coast reporters because the new race leader felt it would cut into his sleep.

St. George, like Mesquite, had been settled by followers of the Mormon prophet Brigham Young, but nearby petroglyphs suggested that Anasazi Indians had been in the area nearly a thousand years before. The lava beds, cinder cones, sand dunes, towering bluffs, and spectacular canyonlands that surround the town may not have meant much to the early pioneers as they struggled to eke out an existence, but with roads came tourism and, in recent years, a population boom. For the Trans America group, that meant options for getting a meal.

After the awards, fifteen of us went for a special dinner to honor the contributions of Thelma and Louise.

"If it weren't for these two and Dale Beam," said John Surdyk once we were settled, "I know for a fact I wouldn't be here today." The Chicago native went on to relate how many times he had been brought back from the brink of disaster by the sight of a van appearing from the vast nothingness of the desert, angels coming forth out of a distant mirage.

"A cup of ice, a bad joke, and that good ol' TLC," he continued in his best Ditka voice, "that's the stuff that made me what I am today."

Surdyk was one of the true characters of the bunch, a man with a sense of humor that just wouldn't quit. On the road he was a study in determination, one of the underdogs

There were times when the roads went on forever and the day's finish line never seemed to get any closer. John Surdyk never expected to make it past Las Vegas, but with patience, perseverance, and plenty of help from others, he kept moving forward. Every night he dumped his duffel bag on the stopover floor and slept amid a disorganized pile of gear, but by the 5 A.M. start, he was always repacked and ready to roll.

who had entered the race for the absolute challenge yet knew he was in far over his head.

"I didn't think I'd make it to Las Vegas," he told me, "so each day I'm here is gravy, far more than I thought."

At first glance one would be inclined to say the sturdy thirty-seven-year-old looked more like a clean-shaven lumberjack than an ultrarunner, but one of my early lessons in the Trans America had been not to associate image with ability.

As self-deprecating as they come, Surdyk says he realized long ago that he was exceptionally slow. He ran his first marathon in 1977, and two years later entered a 50-mile race. It was nearly a decade before the many-degreed medical technician tried multiday running. His first experience was a dismal attempt in a stage race that spanned the length of New York state. Knowing nothing about pacing, he injured his knee on the second stage of the 400-mile event. He learned a lot and says that with each subsequent six-day effort he discovers a little bit more.

"As you get into multidays, you find that the guy who wins has endurance and brains, not necessarily speed. I've definitely got more endurance and brains than speed, so maybe this is for me."

A great outdoorsman who believes that enjoyment should come first, Surdyk has never let training take over his life. Prior to the Trans America, he hit the road for an average of 12 miles a day and kept on with recreational hiking and canoeing as he normally would.

Thelma and Louise accompanied the athletes through the next stage to Cedar City, Utah, the latter walking with a suffering Surdyk for the final miles, constantly urging him on. The following day, as the band of runners started their 55-mile stage to Beaver, Utah, the ladies and their eight-year-old escort left for home. They had won many hearts with their kindness, generosity, and humor, and though their departure was difficult on the weary athletes, some took Wallis's advice and looked on the positive side.

"The fact that they have gone to such trouble on our behalf," he reflected, "shows that this race is worth something to those who take the time to try to understand." The mysterious ladies from San Diego left behind a feeling that affected us until the end of the trip.

A sudden rash of media interest offset some of the negative emotions that resulted from the volunteers' departure, but it did little to alleviate the strain of three long days above 6,000 feet. Traveling on frontage roads, some paved, many dirt, and all virtually deserted, the athletes were transported to the pioneer days of the Wild West.

Free-range cattle looked on as the Trans America runners followed sweeping alpine valleys and passed by the remains of mining towns that had boomed during the silver rush of the late 1800s. Visions of Butch Cassidy were conjured up by a historic marker pointing towards Panguitch, the town where the infamous outlaw had met his mother for the very last time. One of his better-known hideouts lay among the limestone spires in Red Canyon, just a short horse ride away.

The course now veered from the northward direction of I-15 and turned east, leaving the towns of Cedar City, Summit, and Beaver behind. Passing through the canyon that had provided access to the Sevier River basin for thousands of years, one could almost see the Indians as they had lived centuries before.

On the morning of day thirteen, the group climbed over the 7,000-foot Clear Creek Cove Fort divide. The temperature was down to 48 degrees. I ran for a while with Rogozinski, who had walked the whole of stage eleven and then had recovered enough to finish first on the following day.

"This is unbelievable out here," he said as we moved slowly toward the summit, watching enormous beetles scurry out of our path. "In spite of all the crap, there isn't any place I'd rather be."

Warady blitzed the 52-mile climbing stage in 9 hours and 46 minutes, increasing his lead on Schieke to nearly 5 hours in cumulative time. Westbrook was second into Monroe, Utah. He seemed to have his eye on Schieke's position in the overall standings. The little German was still nursing his tender hamstring; the coach from Georgia was running well and only 30 minutes back.

Utah's Sevier School District wasn't exactly thrilled about hosting a group of runners while summer maintenance programs were in full swing, but they did allow the entourage to camp outside the high schools in Monroe and Salina. They even arranged for a janitor to provide access to showers and toilets for two hours during the hot afternoons.

In Monroe, a storekeeper named A. J. Polson came to the school to greet the group, offering directions to a natural hot springs that bubbled from cliffs on the far side of town. "It's a beautiful spot," he said, "and only the locals know where it is. It'd be good for weary muscles, I'll bet that much for sure."

Polson was a second-generation local who had traveled extensively in many parts of the world. "I came back for good, 'cause there's nowhere like this on the face of the earth. I was born here, raised here, and I'll probably die here. Yessiree, this is my kind of town."

Another friendly interlude occurred when a *Runner's World* reader tracked down the group on the road.

"I come down to visit grandpop every now and then," he said, "and when I read about the race, I knew I had to see you guys. Is this for real? What are these ultrarunners really about?"

He introduced himself only as David. He and his girlfriend shuttled runners to dinner that night and reappeared to applaud the athletes the following day.

The race was two weeks old and it was Saturday, the Fourth of July. The second time trial was only 29 miles, and it started with little complication, reverting to the format Kenney had originally planned. Warady left at 5 A.M. accompanied by Riley on the bicycle and his wife in the van. Since no one was within an hour of the leader, the rest of the pack started at 6. For most of the athletes, the short stage offered a well-needed rest.

Warady finished well ahead of the others, but it wasn't until the next runners appeared that he was certain of having run well enough to claim the win for the stage. His time of 4 hours and 41 minutes bettered Rogozinski and Westbrook's tie by 1½ minutes. Schieke managed to run fifth for the day but was bumped from second place overall by Westbrook. It didn't escape anyone's attention that the crewed athletes had moved into the top two spots, but to most it appeared that Rogozinski was every bit as strong.

Later, Kevin Ashby, the publisher-reporter of the local newspaper, showed up at the school. After giving him some of the race background, I directed him to where Howie, Kelley, and Skagerberg were relaxing in the shade. As he had done with a television

Marty Sprengelmeyer earned the moniker Easygoing for his demeanor and stride. Well known in his hometown of Davenport, Iowa, he spoke to his newspaper daily during the early part of the race.

reporter several days earlier, Howie downplayed his own previous achievements and deferred to the athletes left in the competitive race.

"This isn't about me," he said, "it's about all these incredible runners who people think are a little bit weird. They're every bit as superhuman as the cyclists in the Tour de France."

The others answered Ashby's questions keenly and before long were deeply involved in a philosophical discussion of ultrarunning and its relationship to the greater issue of everyday life.

A pair of packages had arrived at our mail-drop point in town. One was from my wife: a loving card and a tin of homemade cookies that she insisted I keep for myself. "Don't let anyone else see them," she wrote in the letter that accompanied the goodies. "You need them—and those guys are probably like a pack of hungry wolves."

The other parcel was a care package sent by Sprengelmeyer's friends in Iowa. "It's from the MacDonald's Morning Running Club," he told me as he ripped off the brown paper. Inside he found two new pairs of Nike Air Max shoes, letters, cookies, and several tubes of silicone for repairs. Just as mine had, his mood brightened visibly. I knew he felt better when he offered to call his newspaper. "I'd rather not say anything," he had told me earlier in the week when I learned he had stopped phoning in his daily reports, "than tell him how bad things have actually become."

Those words had hit me like a brick on the side of the head and forced me to recognize what I had already known. Blaming Edmonson for exacerbating already bad situations had been a form of denial: The real root of the problem lay not with an overstressed athlete but in the thought processes of the pair who had created the race.

Kenney was indisposed in Salina because of a stomach virus, so Riley had to forgo his customary afternoon nap to deal with my questions about what lay ahead. It had come to that a week ago: The athletes were so fed up with race management's vague and evasive attitudes that they brought their problems directly to me.

Edmonson, the Angry Dude, had caught a bus for home the day he dropped from the race. He had been gone for the better part of a week when the problems came to a head.

6

Mutiny on the Highway

There must be a beginning of any great matter,
but the continuing unto the end until it be thoroughly
finished yields the true glory.
—Sir Frances Drake

Shortly after meeting Riley at the 1989 Lewis and Clark Trail Run, our paths had crossed again. His mention of a running trip to the Soviet Union had snared me straightaway, with very little bait. When the small group of athletes of which Riley and I were a part arrived in Moscow that summer, the attitudes of the organizers were hard to decipher at first. They claimed the event we were involved in was an international ultramarathon, a stage race that would cover 1,000 miles, and yet after a welcome reception we were shuttled off to Siberia on a sightseeing trip.

"We have not the permission to go toward North Korea," said our Ukrainian liaison when a meeting was called. "Instead we will run along the Baikal Amur Mainline Railway, from here to Lake Baikal."

As soon as the supposed race began, most of us saw through the facade: The event itself was merely a front for the personal business dealings of the American entrepreneur who had enticed us along. It was disappointing to a group of athletes hoping to make their mark on a major international event, but we did what was necessary to make the trip a success. Five weeks of cultural immersion hosted by Soviet citizens, far away from the authoritarian tourist mechanism, made up for the farcical race.

The Trans America was far different from the situation in Siberia, for Riley and Kenney had no ulterior motive. They really believed in the event, but they had become paralyzed by the pressure of actually pulling it off. Their decisions were so random and unpredictable that one never knew quite what to expect.

Kenney had promised to provide me with a complete set of turn sheets for each of the sixty-four stages at least two weeks prior to the start of the event, but the night before the race began, he was still working on his notes for the very next day. Once we got under way, his main task was attempting to keep ahead of the game: preparing routing directions for the following stage. Between loading and unloading his truck, laying out aid stations, and transcribing the course notes from his scouting tapes, the race manager's days were relatively full. He had no time to roam the course as originally planned, but neither was he worried by the lack of mobile support.

"We didn't promise them anything but the basics," he said. "If they want more than that, they should have been more like David and Richard and come with a crew."

As for Riley, marking the course seemed to be his sole area of responsibility. Kenney had taken on multiple duties and worked himself to a frazzle while his partner's days proved to be far more relaxed. Riley had told me he would have his driver's license long before the race began, yet by the time we left California it was obvious he had never taken a test.

I wondered whether Riley would have considered driving the van that Jane left for support on the course. The cynical side of me said no—that he had probably foreseen just some such possibility and consciously decided he did not want to drive, no matter how serious the need. Without a license, there was no way he could be expected to jump into the breach. I was thankful, even though I hated to think in such a way, that Beam had become injured when Wise's departure left the vehicle without a volunteer who could drive.

When Riley wasn't stranded on the side of the road waiting for the Austrians to come along and help him fix a flat bicycle tire, he took it easy and rode with his friends. More often than not, the race director rode alongside Warady or Westbrook. They were two of the few who still spoke to him and Kenney with civility, mainly because they had no need to rely on race management for support. Where others criticized, the crewed pair offered nothing but praise.

"To have this opportunity is a miracle," said Warady so often he sounded like a record stuck in a groove. "We should thank Jesse and Michael from the bottom of our hearts."

Nearly everyone agreed that the dedication it had taken to put together the route, arrange the daily stopovers, and get the mammoth event off the ground was inspiring. It was almost too much to believe. The problem was that we were now far beyond the planning stage, but the organizers didn't seem to be able to make the jump from concepts in the mind to the realities of life on the road. Complaints had been coming from all the runners since day one, yet race management had no system for dealing with them. Nor did they seem to have any desire to do so.

Initially, Riley was very defensive when anyone offered comment. Then he went through a short phase of dealing with suggestions in the same way he had handled Jane's input before the race began: He had a response ready immediately and made an emphatic pronouncement, based on his original plan. Before the end of the first week, however, he had become ornery and uncommunicative. If an issue arose, he simply avoided the problem, hoping it would go away.

If Riley was an unyielding dreamer who had his head in the clouds, Kenney was the silent workhorse who hated a clash.

"The way I look at it," said Ed Kelley, "is right now, the race, this is the test. The planning, the scouting, the setting up—that was all homework. This is what counts: the Final Exam. It's hard to believe they could flunk out so badly after working so hard, but as far as I can see, the boys are sleeping in class."

In Salina, Riley suggested that his cycling friends cook a meal for the group, yet with ample restaurants in town, no one was too keen on pasta spirals and Ragu sauce in front of the school for $5 a head. Paradoxically, stages sixteen and seventeen would both end at rest stops on the side of the road, but the race director was loath to follow anyone else's suggestions about planning for meals.

From Salina, we would travel into wilderness as desolate as the Mojave for two consecutive days. There was nothing en route by way of facilities: no coffee shops, gas stations, or means of resupply.

"Why don't we just get wieners and beans," said Howie, "or something that's simple and quick to prepare? I can make oatmeal in the morning; served with raisins, that's grand energy food, and easy to make."

"That's stupid, Al," replied Riley with obvious ill humor. "Who wants to eat that shit? Besides, I don't know how to work the stove."

Kenney had purchased thirty tents for the nights out, as well as a propane stove, but he proved as belligerent as Riley when it came to planning for food.

"Everybody knows we're heading into the desert," he said in Salina, "and as far as I'm concerned, if they don't bring anything with them, that's their problem."

Only the arrival of fresh volunteers enabled the group to make it through the isolated stages in the canyonlands without several more casualties.

Don Choi is legendary in the world of ultramarathon running for his incredible performances and his tireless efforts on behalf of the sport. On Independence Day 1980, as a thirty-one-year-old, Choi kicked off the first six-day race in the modern era at a California track. After many years of organizing ultras in the Bay Area, the six-day event was his last as a race director.

"No more worry about organization or postrace responsibilities," he said at the time. "Now I can just run and run and run."

Ever since he has done exactly that. During his inaugural six-day race, he posted 401 miles, and less than two months later, at a cinder track in New Jersey, increased his mark to 426. By 1983, he had upped the record to 460, and the following year he became the first American this century to go over 500 miles.

Choi is a postman in San Francisco; it is said he delivers more mail in a day than several of his coworkers could hope to put out in a week. A true believer in the power of challenge, he has helped many of the solo transcontinental athletes at various points in their runs. When he learned of the conditions facing the Trans America group, he drove to Utah to help with the cause. He knew Skagerberg and several others from various races over the years.

I met Choi for the first time on a dry stretch of gravel as he scrambled to see what he could get a weary runner from the overstocked trunk of his car. I had heard about him for years and wasn't at all prepared for his quiet, semidisorganized, almost uncoordinated style. His hair was cut in a page-boy, and he smiled when he spoke.

"Marvin has told me about you," he said with an outstretched hand. "I'm glad for the sake of these guys that you're here, helping out with the race."

I was instantly embarrassed, unable to accept praise from such an unselfish man. I was trying to balance the dreams of the race organizers with the needs of the sponsors and the harsh conditions facing the runners but felt totally inadequate in my conflicting role. All I really knew was that the road resembled a battle zone—and the patchwork I was attempting seemed to make an incredible mess. No one was happy with the meatball surgical job. I floated in a strange no-man's-land, doing too little in any one area to make a difference in the overall scheme.

Besides Choi, the other saviors on day sixteen were from my hometown in Canada: a former roommate and a friend. Sharyne Herbert had spoken about coming for a visit and I encouraged her, knowing that I would be insanely busy and we really needed the help. When she and Lorraine Harrison arrived, the pair picked up where Thelma and Louise left off, filling coolers and then setting out for the course. By the end of their first afternoon, they were known as Laverne and Shirley.

At least there was running water at the stopover Kenney dubbed "The Rest Area at Milepost 84." Warady took the 33-mile stage from Salina in 5 hours and 57 minutes, his third in a row. The route passed huge sandstone cliffs and deep gorges, winding its way to almost 8,000 feet. Rogozinski finished 38 seconds behind the leader, chasing through the spectacular scenery for the whole of the day. Westbrook came in third, while Schieke tied with Milan Milanovic for spot number four.

Thanks to Choi, Sprengelmeyer ran comfortably into seventh place, but even with the help of the new crew people, Skagerberg was last again, strung out to the end. As soon as the veteran was finished, he piled into Choi's car with Sprengelmeyer and Wallis and was whisked into town.

"These guys need some ice, good food, and a decent night's sleep," said their effervescent helper. "I'll take them to Green River and have them back by five tomorrow, all ready to go." Warady was the only other one who went for a hotel. He had departed several hours before.

Things at that first rest stop actually went relatively well. After setting up their tents, many of the runners took rides with Beam, me, or Laverne and Shirley for the 30 miles back for meals and supplies. We took orders for those who stayed behind. Riley and Kenney paid their $5 and ate another stove-top meal with their cyclist friends.

In spite of Riley's initial resistance, he and Kenney had finally purchased some basic supplies. They felt that canned fruit was fine for breakfast, and the rice and vegetables the cyclists planned to eat would be plenty for one of the two evening meals. They hadn't taken a vote or asked for feedback, but the turnout at the rest-area dinner spoke for itself: Obviously no one agreed.

Howie awoke early and prepared the stove to cook oatmeal as he had the morning before. Rustling among the boxes that lay in the back of the filthy Ryder truck, he located powdered milk and rolled oats but couldn't find matches. When he asked Riley if there were any extras, the race director went completely out of control.

"I told you yesterday not to lose them!" he yelled at the tiny Scotsman with uncalled-for venom in his voice. Howie recoiled in absolute shock.

When the porridge was finally cooked, none of the athletes wanted any: They weren't about to pay $2 to the race director. Howie knew that the money from the day before had more than paid for the supplies, so he dished out generous portions without charging a cent. Riley came for a bowlful, tasted it, and lit into Howie again.

"How can you be so stupid! You didn't clean out the pot properly and the oatmeal is burnt! Everybody complained about that yesterday! I can't believe you did it again!"

Howie bit his lip, but by the time we reached the second rest stop, he decided he had to either punch Riley to release his tension—or head the hell home.

"That condescending little shit," he said during one of his more vocal moments, "is a bespectacled bloody dishwasher with an ego the size of a barn. Do you remember what he wrote about my run across Canada? We started as friends, he said, but ended as brothers. What a bloody little hypocrite!"

With day seventeen came Rogozinski's turn to crank up the pace. He cruised through the 30-mile stage in 4 hours and 12 minutes, racing away from the pack over several difficult climbs. Westbrook came next, in 4:58, followed by Kelley, then Warady, and the rest of the pack. Skagerberg fared a little better than the day before, but he told me his foot was beginning to worry him. Choi had taken him to a doctor, but he refused to get X-rays. "He'll probably only tell me what I don't want to hear."

Wallis had zinc oxide plastered all over his hands as protection from the deadly effects of the sun. He had become so badly burnt in the Mojave that his hands looked like boxing gloves. If the thick blisters burst, said the doctor, there was no telling how long the damage would take to repair.

Riley arrived at the milepost 114 rest area with Rogozinski, found a shady spot, and was immediately asleep.

"I'm not the race director," I told the athletes when they gathered a little later under the trees. "You need to talk about the problems among yourselves and somehow get Jesse and Michael to deal with your gripes."

Everyone had reached the breaking point with the organizers' lax attitudes. It was time to take action before the race crumbled and dissolved into dust.

"So far," said Linzbichler, "this race has gone ahead because of the determination of the runners. I have made serious commitments. If it's going to end here because of lousy management, I need to know so I can get my way out."

After covering 730 of the toughest miles of the course, no one else even wanted to consider the possibility of packing it in, but they knew something had to change or they would never survive. Complaints ranged from poor course markings to the bugs that regularly bathed in the aid station jugs; from poor overnight facilities to the need for more food on the course.

Perhaps the most serious of the problems was the inconsistency of the medical help. Blisters and bunions were getting infected, and more severe injuries were resulting from changing running styles to compensate for the myriad nagging little pains. Riley had promised that a network of physicians would visit every other day, but since the group had left Las Vegas, not even a student had showed. Choi had driven Wallis and Skagerberg 70 miles to get someone to look at their wounds.

Compounding matters was Kenney's disregard for cleanliness. He had become lazy, refilling the same water jugs for his aid stations day after day. He rarely washed the large coolers he used as a source, yet the Ryder had held thirty new insulated coolers since Cedar City. Those unpacked by Laverne, Shirley, and Choi were the only three to be cleaned and put into use.

Beam was being worn to the bone, the runners said. He alone did more than Kenney, Riley, and the cyclists combined. With the Rockies looming large and narrow, winding roads at altitude not too far ahead, everyone was concerned that there would be nowhere near enough coverage on the increasingly difficult course.

Another major bone of contention was a lack of information about what lay ahead each day of the race.

"We should know at the end of the stage," said Carter, "exactly what is planned for dinner, or if there is even anything planned."

"That and what's happening tomorrow," said Kelley. "We need an accurate distance, the road conditions, altitude gain or loss. That should all be posted at least a day in advance."

"It's not usually one thing that will get you," an ultrarunning friend had told me when I first became involved with the sport. "It's an accumulation of small problems that keeps building, until you simply can't deal with anything more."

The group talked of a strike to force change before they reached the mountains and found themselves under serious strain. I didn't have any solid answers and started feeling like a revolutionary plotting a coup. For some reason, I felt guilty, and yet I knew they were right. Something had to be done—and soon.

I suggested that the runners come up with some positive proposals and present them in a way that made Kenney and Riley feel empowered, as though the ideas had actually come from within. Criticism and suggestions had been taken as personal affronts, so perhaps by stroking the pair they would feel less threatened and take the situation in hand. Howie couldn't imagine its working, especially after the porridge incident, but Rogozinski said he would try to talk sense with the organizers the following night. It seemed like a long shot, but as far as I could make out, it was the only way we could salvage what was left of the race.

After our discussion, the runners were driven ahead to the town of Green River in search of a meal. The rest area had a toilet pit, no running water, and one single light.

Rogozinski came with me and let loose as we drove, quite a change from his regular calm: "You know, Jesse ought to be strung up for the ignorant way he treated Al. No one can believe he did that, but as usual he's just sleeping, and being let off the hook."

I later learned that one of the cyclists gave Riley a piece of her mind when he awoke. The race director made a sobbing apology to Howie for the way he had behaved.

When we returned to the lookout, the sun was throwing a purple glow over the multileveled buttes and wooded tablelands that surrounded the mesa on which we were perched.

"Can't you talk to them?" Laverne asked me as we looked out over the stunning spires of Sinbad Valley that lay stretched out below. "You and Jesse are supposed to be compadres—you should be able to work things out."

Looking at it from her perspective, I would have felt the same, but communication had proved impossible since the third day of the race. "It's as though I'm the enemy now, and I don't think I'll ever be able to consider him a friend . . ."

I had run with Warady for a short stretch earlier in the day, and he told me that Riley was merely a concerned entrepreneur who was protective of the project he had so lovingly begun.

"You, Michael, and Jesse have very strong personalities," he said, "and you just have to find a way to work together, with mutual respect."

Perhaps it was juvenile of me, but I knew that I could hardly stand to look at Riley any longer, so thoughtless had his treatment of Howie and others been since the Trans America began. The concept of respecting the race director in his self-important world seemed a ridiculous joke.

To me, Riley now represented a shell-shocked soldier, huddling at the bottom of a bunker instead of facing the reality of what he had to do to help his comrades in arms. That in itself didn't bother me. It happened, and no one can predict how he or she will handle a difficult situation until it actually occurs. The problem I had was with Riley's attitude: He felt that he was doing all he could, that no one had any right to complain. In his mind, there were no valid concerns. Not only did he do nothing, but time and again he refused the outstretched hand that offered to help.

The route from Huntington Beach, California, to New York City had been well mapped out in advance and followed dirt paths, frontage roads, local highways, and interstates. The athletes encountered everything but snow as they traveled through scorching desert, striking canyonland, rugged mountains, and endless plains on their way east. They passed through fourteen states and more than four hundred cities and towns.

Kenney caught wind of the meeting and asked how it had gone. I told him the runners had come up with several suggestions and wanted to talk with him and Riley at the very next town.

"It sounds pretty productive," he replied, "and maybe they'll knock some sense into Jesse. He's really not doing what a race director should."

It was my turn to be stunned. Not once since leaving California had I been able to get through to the pair, so inseparable had they seemed in their opinions on matters related to the race. This was the first acknowledgment that the job they were doing, at least in Kenney's eyes, was not the absolute best. I wondered if Kenney might be somewhat more approachable than Riley.

"What do you see as the best way to deal with Jesse?" I asked.

"Your guess is as good as mine. All I know is I'm doing as much as I can, and if Jesse doesn't handle his responsibilities, that's life. There's nothing I can do."

The stage from the rest area to Green River was 45 miles through an isolated canyon, and terribly exposed. Roadwork made support incredibly difficult, but as we had done when Thelma and Louise were on the course, Beam, Laverne and Shirley, and I split the field into thirds. Choi focused his attention on Skagerberg, Sprengelmeyer, and Wallis, as well as anyone else who ran among them in the latter part of the pack. The day dawned blissfully cool, and thanks to a long downhill and drizzle, all of the times through the fascinating landscape of sandstone mountains were exceptionally quick.

The town of Green River, Utah, sits alongside its namesake, which originates in Wyoming's Wind River Range more than 600 miles to the north. In May 1869, Maj. John Wesley Powell had set out down the Green from the Wyoming Territory, with an outfitted expedition and heavy oak boats. He followed the sediment-filled river to where it meets the mighty Colorado and then turned with it, through the raging Cataract Canyon and southwest to the spectacles of the Grand Canyon that lay beyond.

The Green is the largest tributary of the Colorado River; their confluence lies through Canyonlands National Park, 60 miles south of the town. Although it once boomed because of nearby uranium mines, Green River seemed like little more than a service point when the Trans America entourage descended from the wilderness to the west. We were all too caught up in the process of surviving to visit the River History Museum or the multimedia presentation about the nearby Colorado Plateau.

Stage eighteen finished at the O. K. Anderson City Park, beside an old missile casing, in the center of town. The actual stopover arrangements had been made at a local campground, some 2 miles away.

"We can shuttle the runners," Kenney had said when he told me of the plan, "or they can walk from the finish, with no problem at all."

Showers and beds were priorities for the athletes, however, especially after three legs of hard running with neither amenity waiting at the end of the day. The first thing I did after securing the finish line and dropping Howie off to handle the timing was to check the local motels for prices and the availability of rooms.

Negotiations down the street were not terribly fruitful, but the motel across from the park had plenty of rooms. As the runners trickled in, they paired up, checked in, and came back to search for baggage in Kenney's overloaded truck. Rogozinski blitzed the course in 6 hours and 44 minutes, taking the stage win convincingly for the second day in a row. He moved ahead of Westbrook in the standings to second place but remained behind Warady by more than 5½ hours in overall time. Kelley came in second in the stage and was followed by Warady, although both were assessed penalties for cutting across highway exit ramps instead of running them through.

It was not the first time that allegations of cheating had cropped up, but when the two were asked about the accusations, they readily admitted they had made a mistake.

Rumors of one sort or another made their way through the group every night; it was almost as though gossip took the runners' minds from the ills of the road.

I was filled with anxiety after dinner while I tended to my calls. Rogozinski and I had decided to share a room at the motel, and he, Kelley, and Linzbichler borrowed my van to meet with the race organizers at the campground about the athletes' concerns. I called in my daily report to the touch-tone hot line, as I always did, but when playing it back, I noticed my voice was unusually flat.

A pair of telephone conversations with *Runner's World* headquarters left me feeling uncomfortable with my role in the race. I knew I was putting far more time into the support effort than into generating publicity, but as far as I was concerned, the athletes' lives were on the line. Taylor gave me flak for neglecting my job responsibilities, but I responded that somebody had to do whatever was necessary until Riley started taking his duties to heart. When I spoke to Jane, she said she supported my position, but nevertheless I felt totally trapped. Damned if I do, damned if I don't; the win-win we had spoken so much about during the sponsorship negotiations seemed like a childish dream from a faraway past.

My next phone call maddened me more than anything, but it also gave me hope in a typical, contradictory, Trans America way.

Dr. Mark McKeigue, at the Chicago College of Osteopathic Medicine, answered my page within 4 minutes, just as he had promised he would do at any time of the day. "Just mention race, run, or Trans America," he had said as he left for the airport with his team on day two of the race. "They'll find me. Even if I'm in surgery, I'll get to the phone."

When he realized it was me, McKeigue's questions set me straight as to why we hadn't received any medical visits since the departure of Eric and Bill: "Where have you guys been? Why in hell hasn't anyone called?"

Riley had not spoken to the medical director of the Trans America since leaving California; the calls he had promised to make daily had never occurred. It turned out that McKeigue had had doctors waiting to see the runners on three nights of the previous six, but when he didn't hear from Riley, all he could do was apologize to the physicians who had volunteered their time. He stopped prospecting for assistance farther on in the race.

The positive aspect of the conversation was that in spite of the blatant disregard the race director had shown for the professionals who had offered to help, McKeigue was willing to rejoin the effort. The medical visits began again the very next day.

Once the prerace press conference had actually gotten going, Riley spoke about the friendships he had made with certain runners yet was strangely elusive on details of the upcoming event. I was introduced as the publicity person, while Serues and Taylor were *Runner's World* representatives, on site simply to see the athletes on their way. When Dr. McKeigue and his medical team arrived to conduct prerace examinations, Riley skipped introductions altogether.

"These guys want to take some blood before you get started," he said, "so they can see if they can find out what makes you tick." It was an uncomfortable way to start for everyone concerned.

Andrew Lovy was a psychiatrist, osteopathic doctor, and sports medicine expert who was well respected in the multiday running community for his steady flow of humor, determination, and verve. A participant in many 24-hour, six-day, and seven-day running events over the previous decade, he and Riley had met several times at events in New

York. Lovy impressed the walker from Key West with his understanding of the ultramarathon experience and solid medical sense. When *Runner's World* became involved with the Trans America and Serues asked what sort of medical support Riley had planned, the race director thought of Lovy. They hadn't spoken about it yet, but Riley believed the short, stocky, ultrarunning doctor was almost ideal.

Lovy was the chairman of psychiatry at the Chicago College of Osteopathic Medicine and an extremely busy man. With only three months of lead time, there was little he could do to actually help with the race. He did have enough interest, though, to pass the idea on to a friend—McKeigue. The director of sports medicine had no more time than Lovy, but as a marathon runner and medical director of one of the Chicago area's most prestigious road races, McKeigue was intrigued by the physiological implications

No one was immune to injury: All experienced multiple problems on their way to New York. Mark McKeigue, D.O., right, pulled together the network of medics that were on hand through the race. A marathon runner himself, the chairman of sports medicine at the Chicago College of Osteopathic Medicine was fascinated to learn the implications of ultradistance running over such a prolonged period of time. He draws blood from Michael Hansmann, an Austrian cyclist who was a crew member for a countryman

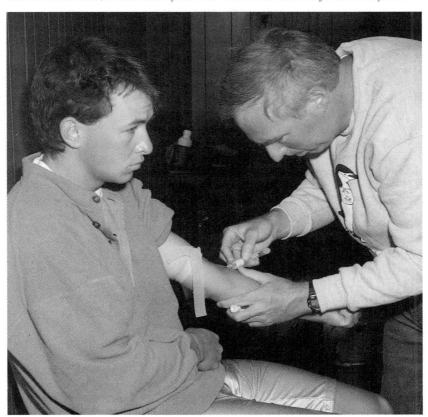

of the sixty-four-day event. He had vast experience in treating running-related injuries and, like Lovy, believed that osteopathic manipulation could be of particular benefit in such a continuous race.

McKeigue contacted Riley and told him he would be of limited help, able to consult on little more than a few stages when the group reached the Midwest.

"That's more medical coverage than we have now," Riley replied at the time, "and way better than nothing at all."

With the help of Lovy and a student, McKeigue made hundreds of calls to colleagues from one end of the country to the other, asking for assistance covering the course. Miraculously, by the time the Trans America began, the trio had stitched together a network of contacts that covered 80 percent of the route.

McKeigue, Lovy, and CCOM osteopathic fellow Jordan Ross flew to California at their own expense for the start of the race. If they were disconcerted at the lack of organization at the press conference, they could hardly believe the state of affairs they encountered when the Trans America actually got under way. I felt more strongly about them than any other members of the ever-expanding list of people who came to the rescue when we needed them most: I couldn't imagine what would have happened if they hadn't been there to help.

Rogozinski returned late that night with the van, but I was still trying to fax the results back to headquarters in Pennsylvania and was very much awake. Howie and Kelley came in and passed around beer.

"Jesse is so far out of it," Rogozinski laughed, "that it's hard to believe. He said to hell with the sponsors and the medical team. 'Who needs them?' he said. 'I'll do it myself'."

Kelley explained that the meeting had ended with the athletes insisting that sponsors and medical care were crucial to the runners—and, ultimately, to the success of the race. Kenney said little but seemed to agree. After much heated discussion, Riley reluctantly relented, stating in the same breath that I would never tell *Runner's World* how laborious things had actually become. For me to let Jane in on the reality of what we faced, he said, would be like cutting my own throat. Surely I wasn't foolish enough to do myself out of a job.

The knowledge that Riley's attitudes were deeply rooted and that his capitulation at the meeting was mere lip service sent me spinning. I barely slept that night, feeling sick to the stomach. It was as though I had eaten until bloated, and then taken a violent ride at the fair.

7

On the Edge of the Road

Bring on the night, ring out the hour.
The days wear on but I endure.
—Guillaume Apollinaire

The course from Green River to the next stopover was reminiscent of old Route 66: quiet, desolate, and on its way to being reclaimed by the desert from which it was carved. It was beautiful in a stark sort of way. Halfway through the stage lay Thompson Springs, Utah, where the temperature had been hovering around 108. The town was typical of those we had seen earlier, consisting of little more than an Amtrak station, an abandoned warehouse, and a tiny cafe.

I stopped at the local phone booth to call Jane. Our discussion the night before had touched on various possible solutions to the leadership problem we so obviously faced, but I was convinced none would get cooperation from Riley. I also knew I hadn't the knowledge, desire, or ability to head up the race. Serues herself was in no position to come to the field for more than a few days, and her relationship with Riley was even more antagonistic than mine. She spoke of sending temporary help, a person with organizational experience to bring some order to the chaotic event.

Race services manager Bart Yasso seemed like the ideal choice, for he had some ultramarathon experience and knew the type of people he would encounter in the Trans America race. He loved the transcontinental idea and had already started using his contacts in the running community to gain support in towns farther east. The problem was that he was overwhelmed not only at work but also in final preparation for an adventure of his own. While the Trans America wound its way through the Ohio valley, Yasso would be out West on his bicycle. His goal was to ride across the country in a little under three weeks. Still, Jane said, he would come to assist the Trans America for a few days, as soon as he could.

I left Thompson Springs with a smile on my face, afloat from the news. I felt incredibly relieved, actually hopeful for the first time in days.

Rogozinski and Kelley were up ahead, laughing hysterically as they ran easily along a lonely stretch of road.

"Wait till the Europeans hit that last aid station," chuckled Kelley as he filled his bottles from my cooler. "They're going to freak out, even worse than us."

The pair had fallen victim to a prank started by Westbrook and his handler, Tyler, who were moving along comfortably nearly 2 miles ahead.

A dead rattlesnake lay on the side of the road, not far from where Kenney had placed Gatorade coolers for one of the regular stops. Westbrook and Tyler noticed the reptile and moved it nearer to the jugs. When Rogozinski and Kelley arrived, they were apprehensive but quickly realized the snake was deceased and could cause them no harm. They moved it yet again, coiling it around the base of the container—and achieved comic results.

"We came upon the Gatorade," said Milan Milanovic later that day, "and a big snake was there, ready to bite. I was so very thirsty. It took me ten minutes to find something to move it, but finally in the desert, I came out with a stick. I poked the beast very carefully, and it moved! I jumped back, but some time later, it never did make a movement again. I pushed it away, and I laughed. I'm not sure if it drank Gatorade or didn't, but finally I knew it was no longer in life."

Westbrook, like many of the athletes in the race, had wanted to run across America for a number of years. A baseball and football player in high school, he ran cross-country

There were plenty of hardships en route—and plenty of laughs. Fifty-five-year-old John Wallis hams it up atop a pile of the athletes' gear outside an abandoned garage in Cisco, Utah. The stopover was one of several that were little more than a handful of trailers and a post office. The area was used in a scene for the movie Thelma and Louise.

for a year in college and then helped coach during his master's studies in Clarksville, Tennessee. Road races led to marathons and eventually to ultras. In the ten years since his first ultramarathon, the father of four has competed in most of the long races in the nation's Southeast. He has run across his home state twice, covered Vermont from north to south, and done the same in Massachussets—just for the challenge and fun.

"This race is a big experiment," he said before the Trans America, "and my goal is simply to complete it, to see how things evolve. The kids say it's pretty crazy, but they're excited and pitching in to help." Once the race started, they followed their father's progress in the *Clayton News/Daily* from their home in Georgia and plotted his course on a giant map they had pinned on the wall.

Westbrook won the 48-mile stage from Green River to Cisco, Utah, crossing the finish line beside a porcelain toilet bowl in 8 hours and 5 minutes. He was 26 minutes ahead of Warady, and almost 40 ahead of Rogozinski and Kelley, but the overall standings were unaffected by the results of the day.

The ladders and banner were set up according to Kenney's directions, alongside an abandoned gas station on the south side of the road. Across the street sat a pair of empty railcars on rusted sidings, converted to living quarters for the maintenance people during their rare visits to town. The building that had once been a gas station was little more than timbers and insulation, a decaying wasteland on a broken concrete slab. Paint peeled from the panoramic murals that adorned the crumbling walls inside and out. A weathered pump stood beside the toilet; a rotting couch lay slightly off to the side. In the distance, there were several trailers and a minuscule post office. A postmaster paid a visit three days a week, from 10 A.M. until noon.

The runners arrived throughout the afternoon and appeared refreshed by the cloud cover and the extra help they received through the day. Choi had gone back to San Francisco, but another body arrived in his place. Stan Baker was a retired back-of-the-pack ultrarunner from Kansas who planned to stay with the Trans America until the course got close to his home. Laverne and Shirley still had two days left, and if we were lucky, Yasso or another *Runner's World* representative would arrive by the following week.

After setting up their tents, the runners nibbled on cookies and sandwiches brought by the ladies and washed them down with the ever-popular beer. There was no water in sight, and dinner was still a couple of hours away.

Howie organized the beer purchase. Like Beam and me, he had learned the hard way to collect money before distributing the goods. He had passed the advice on to the new arrivals at the rest stops, and they quickly became proficient at taking head counts and collection in the mornings, before hitting the road. Food on the course had improved noticeably, and the meal Laverne and Shirley lovingly prepared was gourmet compared to the begrudging pasta and Ragu made by the cyclists several nights before.

I tracked down Riley and asked him to take a walk with me, away from the group. We headed east in silence until the road curved. Crossing the railroad tracks, we stopped, turned, and looked back at the camp.

"It's amazing we can come all this way, after all this work together," I said, stumbling over the words, "and find ourselves unable to talk."

Riley looked at me through his thick goggles. His lips were chapped and bloody. He looked much as he had the very first time we spoke.

"I know. But there's just such incredible tension, and I've felt like I'm the only one who is really committed to this race. Everybody talked about bailing out, and the runners do nothing but bring their problems to me—and bitch just because they're tired and stressed. I know that's just the way it goes, but I've done so much work, and no one appreciates it from my point of view. There's only so much I can possibly do."

I listened while he talked, surprised when he finally admitted that he had shut down under the pressure. He slumped and suddenly appeared vulnerable, as if unloading a terrible burden that weighed on his soul. I put my arm around him to offer comfort, and he reached out and embraced me. We actually hugged.

We talked about the importance of cooperation, not only between race management and the athletes, but also with sponsors and medical staff. We spoke of working together

Relations between the athletes and race organizers were tense because of poor conditions and planning, but volunteers seemed to arrive just when they were needed the most. Lorraine Harrison and Sharyne Herbert, who spent a week with the group, prepare a meal at the Cisco stopover, while John McPhee and Billye Butler look on.

for the betterment of the race, and he said that he would try to be more attentive to the needs of the athletes. The sky was a magnificent orange, and the distant hills glowed purple as the sun dropped lower in the sky. I wasn't sure whether I really felt any better as we trotted back to where the food was waiting, but I knew I was suddenly starved.

The chili, rice, and salad went down well in the open air, especially with tortilla chips and hot-as-hell salsa piled high on the side. The entire group ate their fill, washing it down with the last of the beer.

Water was a particular problem in Cisco, and since I had to drive back to Crescent Junction to make my calls anyway, I told Beam to relax and give himself a break. Oliver Volk, a German volunteer with the Austrian crew, helped me load up all the available containers, and we drove back toward the sun as it disappeared behind the darkening hills.

I asked Volk how he had come to be in the United States with the Austrian group. "Stefan Schlett and I are good friends," he replied. "We do some crazy adventure once in every year. I come here to help Stefan, to see the country of America, and to have some good type of fun."

Volk was a fourth-year medical student in Bavaria and had been learning more about blisters and bandaging than he ever could have hoped.

"This is like a crash course on the front lines," he said, "but it is good to be useful. I keep very busy at night, and learn as I go."

Earlier that afternoon, a physician and an assistant who were friends of McKeigue's contact in Grand Junction, Colorado, had arrived on the scene. They set up shop beside the crumbling gas station and, together with Volk, were kept busy for close to four hours.

Debladis, the Frenchman, had been struggling since the beginning, and on the stage into Cisco he came in his usual last place. Were it not for the patient pacing and prodding of Emile Laharrague, Debladis would have been out of the race before leaving the Mojave Desert. As it was, he moved painfully forward, hovering dangerously close to the cutoff schedule nearly every day.

Laharrague had entered the Trans America as soon as he realized it was a legitimate race. He had been preparing for just such an event for more than a decade, since moving from France to the United States. A former Green Beret and paratrooper, he was a solo adventurer of the Rambo mold. He had hardened his mind and body in the jungles of Central America and Southeast Asia and had put his abilities to the test in many multiday races over the years.

In a sport of soft-spoken athletes, his unparalleled intensity had led to controversy at ultradistance races in the past. Despite strong performances in several six-day events and an impressive victory in the poorly managed Race Across Texas in 1986, the sturdy little Frenchman was better known for his fiery temperament than for his athletic accomplishments. Before the Trans America, Laharrague had researched Pyle's events and spoken to many runners who had done solo transcontinental crossings before. He adopted an uncharacteristic strategy of prudence. Those who knew him from previous races were convinced he would burn out inside of a week.

"Slowly, slowly," Laharrague said during the difficult desert crossing. "I must go slowly, like a monk in the woods."

He was not only sticking by his belief that the runners who started out quickly would fail to complete the race, but he was also forced to take it easy in extreme heat because of the malaria he had contracted during his travels in the wild. Laharrague's tactical plan kept him running just ahead of the cutoff pace; he was playing it safe. When Debladis became injured, Laharrague stayed close and encouraged him, diverting attention from

A disparate group of athletes from seven countries entered the Trans America. Stefan Schlett, left, was a gregarious German adventurer who loved to take part in ultra-distance races for the challenge and fun. Frenchman Emile Laharrague, on the other hand, was intensely focused: "This type of race," he said, "is run in the mind."

the injuries that were a constant concern.

Fruita, Colorado, our next stop, lay 45 miles from the ghost town of Cisco, Utah. From the moment we entered city limits, it was a welcoming place, especially in comparison with the wilderness behind us. It hadn't always been so, I was told later: Not until 1881 had a treaty with the Ute Indians opened the area to settlers from the East.

Mabel Kiefer's essay in the fall 1930 Special Cowpuncher's edition of the *Fruita Times* told of the past:

> In the early 1880s, soon after the Indians had been moved on, a few intrepid white pioneers halted on the hills to the eastward, and looked out over the valley, bounded by mountains on the north, mountains on the south, and losing itself in the dim distance where the blue base of the Book Cliffs apparently shut in from the world beyond. . . . Desert to the right of them, desert to the left of them, desert in front of them, and yet—what a land of promise.
>
> With the prophetic vision of the hardy adventurers they saw the waters of the river diverted from its channel and spread over fertile fields, they saw farms and orchards and cattle on a thousand hills, and taking courage from their visions, they came and conquered, braving hardships and deprivations and danger. Such was the spirit of the pioneers. . .

The pioneers had planted many fruit trees, and before long, the town was the home of World's Fair–winning produce. Fruita, it seemed, was perfectly named.

The man in charge of our stopover was bank manager Carey Horton. "This is going to be great to have people actually meet you guys," he said excitedly while he showed me a flyer advertising the Trans America Evening in the Park. "We've sold about thirty tickets in advance."

A decorating crew was already stringing banners around the circular green that sat across the street from Horton's office; tables and chairs were unloaded from a truck as we talked.

"Is there anything else we can do before the barbecue gets started tonight?" he asked.

I took the opening, knowing that crew access was bad on the road and that the athletes were strung out by the length of the stage.

"Do you have any extra bodies around who could help the runners out on the course?"

In a matter of minutes, a burly biker came strutting to where I was making calls, at the back of the bank.

"How's it going, Tony?" Horton asked before introducing his friend.

Tony Olmstead was a member of the Fruita chapter of the Goldwing Road Riders and a Vietnam vet. He promised to gather several friends, load up with supplies, and escort the slower runners to the school at the far end of town.

"It was one of those 'oh-shit, here-we-go' type of feelings I had," said John Surdyk later when describing the sight of the motorcyclists pulling up on the road. "I thought these guys were the bikers from hell, just out after some kicks. By the end of the day I was thanking God they were there."

Olmstead and his group were like Nicholls's ham operators and the Bagdad Cafe crew: generous in the extreme, and appreciative of the opportunity to become involved with the historic event. They nursed Surdyk and Debladis through the heat of the day.

For the Frenchman, the crossing into Colorado was one of his worst days of the race. He spoke many times of quitting and going home. The pain, he said to Laharrague early in the stage, was becoming too much to bear. Somehow, even though they couldn't communicate, Olmstead knew just what the desperate runner needed. The biker spent 4 hours with the Frenchman, guiding him slowly along. Debladis finished last again, in 12 hours and 11 minutes. He had only 37 minutes to spare.

At the front of the pack, it was Howie who finished first. His feet had healed miraculously well, and he made the transition from my van to the road with relative ease.

"If I start today," he had said in the morning, "I can use the rest of the race as a trainin' run. Since I stopped in Nevada and will get some runnin' in Utah, I'll not have actually missed out on any of the states."

The Scot ran with Rogozinski for a time and then took off from the head of the pack. The surprise was the person who followed him: Linzbichler had already returned to the road as a journey runner but had yet to extend himself or run particularly hard. Howie crossed the finish line first, followed by the Austrian, and then Rogozinski, the stage winner in the competitive race.

The party in the park was the first solid community turnout since the Newberry Springs aid station, and it felt good to see the efforts of the athletes appreciated by everyday people, young and old. A band played as volunteers from the Chamber of Commerce dished out barbecued chicken, corn on the cob, and generous bowls of delicious hearth-baked beans. Local citizens paid for their meals to raise funds for an antidrug campaign, but Horton insisted that the Trans America group eat free of charge. We could hardly refuse.

Laverne and Shirley made special arrangements with the supermarket manager to pick up fresh bagels and muffins early the next morning, then went to a hotel to attempt a decent night's sleep. McKeigue's medical contact stopped by the high school with his wife and another couple, all decked out for a night on the town. Larry Copeland, D.O., introduced himself, made the rounds, and said he'd be back after his concert to get down to work.

Copeland returned at 10:30 as I packed up my van for the night. I half awoke later when I heard footsteps on the concrete path near the shadows where I lay. The physician was heading home. My watch read 1:15.

I got up early, plugged in the borrowed percolator, and waited for the Canadian ladies to arrive with the food. At 4:05, there was still no sign of them. I didn't know whether they had gone to the store by a back route, or if they were still in their room with the money for the baked goods, asleep in their beds. I drove to the hotel in a panic, saw the Waradys' van, and noticed the lights in the room behind. Beyond Laverne and Shirley's Mazda RX7, there was no sign of life.

I raced to the supermarket, paid for the order, and made it back to the school to find the runners mulling around the coffeepot, awaiting their food. Riley had agreed to pay up front and collect a reasonable amount from those who ate, perhaps $1 a head. When I laid down the boxes of steaming bagels and muffins, the athletes pounced like vultures. Riley stomped off in a rage instead of taking collection as planned.

"To hell with it," he said when I asked what the problem was. "Give them their bagels! This is the very last time!"

"But everyone said they would pay for the food if you don't rip them off and charge an arm and a leg."

"I'm not going to try to get money out of them! You do it if you want! I really don't care!"

Laverne and Shirley made it in time for the start and reluctantly said their farewells to the athletes as they set out into the dark. While working themselves to the bone, they had found new strength, and both went home knowing they were capable of running farther themselves than they ever would have believed. They were weary but deeply inspired by the performances they had seen.

I helped Beam load his truck and watched as Leon Ransom, a journey runner, performed his self-appointed chore of cleaning the gym where the runners had stayed.

"All done, Mr. Barry," he said when I came in for a shower. "Can I go now, with Dale, so he can drop me ahead?"

I could never quite figure Ransom out, but I did know he was determined to spend every second he could moving forward along the road. He rarely said a word when I pulled up to him and offered supplies. No matter how much I insisted that he could have whatever he needed, he never took more than the smallest sip of Coke. When he did speak, he generally argued sarcastically that the supplies were for the "real runners." Everyone would probably be far happier, he said, if he gave up and headed for home.

Fifty-five-year-old Ransom was an ex-military man known in the ultrarunning community for his shuffling march at multiday races. Over the course of a thirty-year running career, he had completed 310 marathons and more than 200 ultradistance events.

Ransom's goal in the Trans America was fairly simple: He wanted to be left alone, to do his thing for as long as he was allowed. His appearance made an amusing portrait.

He was deeply tanned, weather-beaten, and sported a crew cut under a permanently affixed, tattered straw hat. His voice was squeaky when it was heard at all, and he rarely looked up from the road as he walked slowly along. He always carried an old army backpack, which seemed to be loaded with gear. Some of the runners cut holes to relieve pressure from their toes; Ransom customized his worn-out shoes by removing the tops almost to the instep. On most days his shuffling pace hovered between 2½ to 3 miles an hour, well below the cutoff. Beam shuttled him ahead at least six times a day.

After leaving Fruita on day twenty-one, I met up with a television reporter from Grand Junction, Colorado and directed him to the course. Backtracking to a complicated section where the runners had to veer onto an overpass and run through an industrial section of town, I came upon one of the cyclists.

"Do you have any flour?" she yelled when she saw the Trans America signs on my familiar brown van. "That idiot Jesse didn't mark any of the turns and two runners are lost."

The other cyclist had gone back to search for Skagerberg and Linzbichler, who had run straight at an unmarked intersection less than a mile from the start. Railroad tracks lay between them and the route, and by the time it was light enough to get their bearings, they were more than an hour behind. Linzbichler was upset, but he was no longer fighting the cutoff schedule to stay in the competitive race. Skagerberg was still in the running, but he was badly hurt. Extra steps were an aggravation he could do without.

Riley doubled back from the lead pack, not because of the course-marking error, but because Warady was running slowly and the race director wanted to be near his friend. When Riley heard of the trouble, he went in search of Skagerberg. He was attempting to commiserate just as I arrived.

"Get the hell away from me, Jesse!" yelled the runner as he hobbled along in obvious pain. "Don't talk to me, don't give me anything, just get out of my life! This is the last race of yours I'm ever going to run in, unless by some misfortune, I end up in hell. One thing I know: That's the only place you'll be directing races, ever again."

Don Choi's presence had been a direct result of Skagerberg's plea for help. The veteran ultramarathoner knew that even Beam's superhuman effort could not deal with all the runners' on-the-course needs, yet even with the support of his friend, he found himself constantly fighting both the cutoff and his frustration with the poorly organized race.

The saving grace in the Skagerberg-Campbell duel of 1985—besides the rare combination of experience, sense, and mettle that each man possessed—had been the support team. For the two runners, there were seven support people available at all times on the course. Even though the route had been planned to the last detail several months before the event began, two advance people kept a day or two ahead of the competitors to notify media, make overnight arrangements, and gather any necessary supplies.

A race referee started the runners in the morning, scouted the roads ahead, and directed the athletes and their crews through any complicated areas to the finish, where he logged in their times. The referee drove a 28-foot motor home with complete facilities for the use of all. Each runner had a van with a two-person support crew and myriad supplies. The athletes put all their energy into forward movement, while the rest of the entourage tended them as well as they could.

Food, fluids, and first aid were available whenever they were needed, at any time of day. Shelter and changes of socks, shoes, and clothing were always at hand. As soon as a day's running was completed, the athletes put their feet up. Calories were restored. Tired legs were packed in ice. Weary backs were massaged. Restaurant meals were frequent, and sleep was good, in comfortable motels. There was no comparison between the joyful experience of 1985 and the reality Skagerberg now faced.

Riley chuckled as he left, unsure of what else he could do. Skagerberg gritted his teeth and continued painfully on.

Across the Colorado River lay Dinosaur Hill, but the runners had no time to appreciate the fact that the first *Brachiosaurus altithorax* had been found there ninety-two years before. They couldn't dwell on the natural beauty of the Colorado National Monument, a parkland that preserves the grandeur of the old American West. Nor could they ponder the geographic wonder known as Grand Mesa, the largest flat-topped mountain in the world, which has been described as an Island in the Sky. With 56 miles ahead of them—but with no Choi, Laverne and Shirley, or motorcyclists to help—the most they could hope for was to reach their next destination before the time limit was up.

Parachute, Colorado, is a tiny place that lies in the shadow of a mountain resort called Battlement Mesa. I checked in with the people who were preparing dinner for the athletes at the local Methodist church. "The area was first developed because of oil shale deposits," Dottie Green, the organizer of the spaghetti dinner, told me, "but now they're building a town. It's the most beautiful place in the world."

Howie completed the stage alongside Kelley in 9 hours and 33 minutes. Rogozinski finished in a tie with Hodson, 52 minutes later, and Laharrague, making his first appearance near the front, came in fourth. Westbrook lost another 23 minutes to Rogozinski, and Warady dropped 70 minutes in cumulative time. Rogozinski seemed to have a solid grip on second and was only slightly more than 3 hours out of the overall lead.

When Howie finished eating, he came to relieve me at the timekeeper's post. I woke Riley when I returned and asked him to take over for Howie, who had done more than enough timing over the previous fourteen days. Feeling dizzy, I searched for a telephone, then struggled to string together coherent words for the daily reports.

Back at the school, Skagerberg and Williams were finishing up after nearly 15 hours on the road. While they were showering, Debladis staggered into the gymnasium where we were spending the night. His shins were wrapped tightly, but the bandages had done little to alleviate his pain. Laharrague helped him get situated and then brought over a plate of food that Dottie Green had wrapped carefully in foil.

I wasn't injured, just sick, and feeling like hell. When the shining white van arrived and the familiar-looking man in the *Runner's World* shirt jumped out, it took all the energy I had left to choke out a simple hello.

8

Rocky Mountain Low

I believe in God. I believe that in men's hardest moments He sometimes
tells them what to do, and that He did it then for Lambert and me.
We could have gone farther. We could perhaps have gone to the top.
But we could not have got down again. To go on would be to die . . .
And we did not go on. We stopped and turned back . . .
—Sherpa Tenzing Norgay

Eric Czechowski had thought the Trans America concept was a recipe for disaster the moment he heard the idea. But since he worked as Jane's assistant in the promotional department at *Runner's World*, like it or not, he bought into the event. We communicated with each other a great deal in the months leading up to the race.

"Just remember, Barry," he said before I left for the start, "no matter what happens, you brought this to us—and actually wanted the job. I hope I'm not the one who has to come and bail you out."

It was Czechowski who turned up in Parachute, Colorado, giving me an I-told-you-so frown.

"Let's talk in the morning," I said feebly after shaking his hand. "I dunna feel so good. A little pain in my stomach. Maybe something I ate . . . "

The hallway in the school was stuffy, but my problem was more serious than that. Shortly after midnight, I scratched my way to the door and sat shaking on the lawn. I heaved for 15 minutes before my stomach was empty. In the morning, I learned that several of the athletes had suffered the same fate during the previous day of running—and more than one had been up in the night.

Czechowski was there to help, but his role was not as hands-on as I had hoped for. His assistance came in a more intangible way. His main goal was to assess the needs of the race and determine if it was feasible for *Runner's World* to assist further without becoming too deeply involved. We spoke over coffee after the start of the race on day twenty-two. Like Pearle in Vegas, he told me I looked like absolute hell.

"Great. My wife is going to kill me for being such an incredible mess."

"Either that or she's going to drag you home. I wouldn't blame her a bit."

It was Saturday, and my wife, Lisa, was scheduled to arrive in the early afternoon. We had spoken several times since I had left home, but during most of our conversations I tried to avoid discussions about the problems of the road. Lisa knew me inside out and could sense when things were not going particularly well. When I didn't have time to call her, she checked the daily race report and judged the state of affairs by the tone of my voice.

I was excited by the thought of seeing her but was petrified at what she would say. I was tired, ill, and unsure of anything. I showered and tried to look presentable before loading the van.

As usual, the Saturday stage was a time trial, and Riley took off with Warady at 5 A.M. They followed the leader's wife out into the dark. The others left an hour later, with Howie setting the pace as he had on the previous days.

The course followed the Colorado River on frontage roads in the direction of Denver, taking the group 44 miles to the finish in Glenwood Springs.

I handed out aid through the towns of Rifle and Silt, then stopped to take photos in Newcastle as the runners arrived. In the distance, I saw Laharrague and Kelley, accompanied by a man in cutoff jeans and T-shirt astride a beat-up bike. The athletes introduced their companion when they stopped for pretzels and Coke.

"Frank Breslin," said the unofficious-looking individual as he stretched out his hand. "Welcome to Newcastle. They're not kidding. I'm the mayor of the town."

I followed the road for another 9 miles, then rounded a bend and crossed a bridge that led toward the end of the stage. Glancing across to the footpath the runners would follow, I noticed steam rising and mobs of people frolicking below. I decided I would have to go for a soak after meeting my wife and finishing my reports for the day.

Continuing through town on Grand Avenue, I noticed historic buildings intermingled with modern shops. Sayre Park with its gazebo lay at the far end, and as I pulled in with my ladders, I saw a face I seemed to recall from the previous night.

Bob Julich had turned up in Parachute, having ridden his bike from his Glenwood Springs home to give the race management team a sense of his plans. Kenney hadn't bothered to introduce us, but I did shake hands and say hello through the pounding fuzz in my head.

Warady arrived at the finish first, but Howie and Rogozinski finished together 30 minutes later. Since the overall leader had started an hour ahead of the others, a simple calculation showed that Rogozinski had gained half an hour, claiming victory for the difficult stage. Kelley and Laharrague also beat Warady's time, but the leader was fourth. He was still ahead of Rogozinski by 2 hours and 47 minutes in cumulative time.

The afternoon was a blur, but I do remember meeting my wife at a crossroad. I filled her in on Czechowski's arrival and my hopes that he would inject some order into the race. We returned to the park, where the runners were relaxing. After compiling the results, we checked in at the Eagles hall, where a dinner was being planned.

"You bet we're expecting runners," said the woman behind the bar as I stepped into the old Odeon Theater. "We're ready for them anytime. What was it they said? Sixty in all?"

Kenney's original estimate of the number of athletes and support people in the entourage was double what we had started with, and by Glenwood Springs we had even less in the group. He hadn't called the people who had promised prearranged meals since his scouting trip, neglecting to update them on numbers or expectations about food. I knew that Julich had invited several athletes home for dinner and that others had eaten their fill of pizza while relaxing at the park. I had planned long ago to have a nice sit-down dinner elsewhere, alone with my wife.

When I told the proprietress there would be fifteen diners at the most, she yelled to the kitchen: "Put the spaghetti on hold!"

She led me around the corner to where five dozen places were set. Salads sat waiting, French dressing dripping from the iceberg lettuce. The leaves seemed to wilt as I looked across the room. I apologized and returned to the park, suggesting to Kenney that he and Riley round up the interested members of the group and head off to eat. I felt sorry that my rebellious stomach wasn't up to barroom spaghetti and struggled to convince myself that the situation wasn't my fault.

Lisa didn't think much of sleeping on a church floor, so we went off in search of a motel. The intimate dinner we had planned became submarine sandwiches between phone calls in the room. After seven attempts, I got the recorded update right. The instant I finished, I dropped off to sleep.

Inside the church where the runners stayed, not one crumb of food was put out for breakfast; no coffee was brewed. When we arrived at 3:45 A.M., Lisa said hello to the runners and tended to the percolator while I searched the back of the big truck for caffeine and other supplies. Rusting tins of canned fruit lay in a box among broken bags of sugar, a thousand loose tongue depressors, and half-filled canisters of Coleman propane. In another box, I found the coffee, powdered milk, and finally, the leftover bagels from two mornings before.

When the coffee was ready, the runners rushed over like addicts in need of a fix. Hodson, the Englishman, ate cold pizza and leftover chocolate cake. Someone else scooped up melted ice cream; others dunked stale bagels. Czechowski arrived at 4:30 and surveyed the chaos. Both he and Lisa were incredulous. To me, it was more or less a typical scene, all part of the preparation for another day on the road.

Peter Hodson's broad cockney accent was hard to decipher, but his attitude was that one could never get enough of something one loved. He enjoyed nothing more than the freedom of running and was always prepared for whatever challenge happened his way. The thirty-six-year-old Englishman cut a comical figure on the roads of America but always made an impression, wherever he was. The other runners knew him as the Alien Warrior, a label he had earned several years earlier for his unusual look.

Hodson had his hair cropped close at all times. When preparing for a day's run, he awoke early for a shave and a wash, and then started on his feet. He always smeared a custom-made glycerin and Vaseline concoction from toe to heel before slipping into a double layer of nylon stockings. Then came his shoes, which after the first week seemed to be amazingly new. I learned he was retrieving Warady's rejects whenever he could. The race leader was sponsored by ASICS and rotated into a new pair every 200 miles.

After his feet were ready, Hodson lubed his naughty bits and pulled on a pair of lycra cycling shorts. His upper body attire depended on the weather, but usually it was layered and consisted of a long-sleeved silky undergarment for sun protection or warmth, with an old yellow running club singlet thrown over the top. Zinc oxide always covered his face, hands, and thighs; a cap with a long kerchief tucked underneath concealed his head and the back of his neck.

When Hodson ran, the kerchief flowed behind him like a cape. His short, shuffling

Britain's Peter Hodson, nicknamed the Alien Warrior, always got a laugh on his way across America as a result of his accent, jokes, and specialized look. Hodson's dry sense of humor brought much-needed levity to the grind of running an average of 45 miles each day.

strides looked slow because one arm dangled awkwardly, but anyone who had run beside him knew the Alien was deceptively fast. He never seemed to push beyond the point of a comfortable cruise, but when he wanted to go fast, not many kept up.

The Alien won the 1990 Sri Chinmoy 700-mile race in 11 days, 13 hours, and 38 minutes, and beat his own time by several hours the following year. He had unusual tactics, sleeping regular hours and then chasing the leaders like a bat out of hell. He seemed to flow without effort, keeping fellow competitors in stitches with his constant prattle and dry British jokes. His shoes were said to ooze a sickly green goo, the result of a thick layer of Vaseline. In those days, the Alien never wore socks or nylons, but he squished his way around the track at an incredible pace.

The lubricating concoction and stockings were unusual, even by Trans America standards, but a decided improvement over the Vaseline ooze that used to seep from his shoes. He never developed any blister problems, but he did leave a greasy trail of footprints at almost every stopover between California and New York.

Everyone involved with the Trans America knew that the Quaker Foods Company had provided Gatorade bottles, coolers, and carbohydrate load and electrolyte replacement mixes for the privilege of being recognized as a supporter of the race. Oddly enough, Kenney had argued when Serues recommended that cups be shipped with the initial order of supplies, but by the time we reached Glenwood Springs, he knew he had been wrong.

Julich had drinking cups left from a race he had once directed. He offered them to the Trans America organizers when they asked what help he could provide but pointed out that his cups said Exceed, not Gatorade—that it might not be wise to use cups bearing the competitor's name.

I knew instantly that we couldn't use the Exceed cups, but Kenney and Riley did not seem to understand. The wall of resistance went up when I tried to explain the conflict, and I couldn't help but wonder about the constant friction. Had I become a negative nitpicker, always looking for the worst from the race management team?

One look from Czechowski confirmed what I already knew: If so much as a single photograph appeared showing Trans America athletes drinking from Exceed cups, all sponsorships would be instantly off. Without the support of sponsors, the race itself was as good as dead. I jumped into the back of the truck where Kenney was loading the athletes' gear, removed the cups, and gave them back to Julich with apologies and thanks.

"It was a high falutin', root'n-toot'n drawing card for the rich and the working man, the famous and the infamous," writes Lena Urquhart in her book *Glenwood Springs: Spa in the Mountains*. "Even before the white man discovered its soothing and restorative powers, Glenwood Springs was one of the oldest known gathering places for the Ute Indians . . .

"Laundry trains from Leadville and Aspen would hit Glenwood on a Saturday morning and unload dozens of miners who spent their day doing laundry and bathing in the plentiful hot water before spending Saturday night in the many saloons and brothels. Thus refreshed and somewhat cleaner, the miners boarded the train on Sunday and headed back to another week of work . . ."

The running had become like work to many of the Trans America athletes, a seven-day-a-week job with no relief in sight. Laundry usually meant scrubbing clothes in the shower. Rare was the day that anyone awoke actually feeling refreshed.

From Glenwood Springs, the route began a series of brutal climbs over the Continental Divide. The first mountain stage had been mapped out by Julich, following a four-wheel-drive-only road over Cottonwood Pass. On Sunday, July 12, the day dawned wonderfully cool. The athletes were supposed to have access to Kenney's aid stations and support from Beam and Baker for the first 15 miles, before veering onto the treacherous dirt path where Julich and his friends had promised to help.

"What the hell happened down there?" yelled Rogozinski, the young teacher, as Lisa and I pulled next to him on our way back from the freeway to the crest of the hill. "We haven't had any aid for the last 17 miles. No turns are marked. Ed and Milan are dying just a little ways back."

Laharrague ran alongside Rogozinski. He gratefully took a pair of cookies from Lisa, stuffed them into his mouth, and washed them down with a glass of Coke. He barely paused between gulps, spitting bits of cookie along with his words. The specifics were almost unintelligible, but the message came across loud and clear.

"Idiots! Idiots! That's what kind of people are in charge of the race!"

Rogozinski told us that Warady and Howie were about 3 miles ahead of him and Laharrague. Knowing that Warady was being tended to by his wife—and fairly confident that she would supply Howie since he was no threat in the competitive race—we drove back in search of those running behind. Milanovic and Kelley were almost out of gas when they came into view. They too were furious and thanked us profusely when we offered them aid. They knew that no one else was within an hour of them, so we turned around and raced toward the finish in the town of Eagle, Colorado, marking the turns from Kenney's direction sheets, all the way to the school.

I barely got the banner up in time for Howie, who crossed the line at the Eagle Middle

School 1½ minutes ahead of Warady. The wiry Scotsman shivered from cold: We were at 8,000 feet, and a steady drizzle had been falling for hours. Lisa gave Howie a spare sweatshirt while he took over the timing board. He said he would monitor the finishers while we went back out on the course.

We doubled back along our previous route, remarking the turns and refueling the runners we had supplied at the top of the hill. We came upon a pair of trembling journey runners, walking slowly in wet layers of clothes. Both refused rides but took small amounts of food and drink before continuing on. Finally, 7½ miles out from the finish, we saw Kenney putting out aid stations. He said the rest of the runners were fine, that the other support people had them under control. We turned around and drove back toward the finish, coming upon the stubborn journey runners we had left only 15 minutes before. We pulled alongside. The pair opened the van door and climbed in, teeth chattering uncontrollably from the penetrating cold. Beam had moved them ahead several times, but after 18 miles of miserable forward motion, they finally decided they were done for the day.

The janitor, Jake Norton, gave me a tour of the school's facilities while Lisa went down the road to secure a spot at a local motel. "They can sleep anywhere in the gymnasium," he said, "and there are plenty of mats up on the stage." Norton's eight-year-old son, Paul, was far from shy and reveled in the athletes' attention for the rest of our stay. He seemed star-struck when I introduced him to Howie and was overwhelmed when Ed Kelley gave him a race T-shirt, autographed by the group.

When Kenney arrived, he parked the truck and disappeared to work on the next day's turn sheets. He had nothing to say to Laharrague and Kelley when they lit into him about the absence of aid stations and markings on the first part of the course. I learned later that Kenney and Julich's group had misjudged the pace of the front runners and arrived too late with the aid.

Riley showed up 1½ hours after the leaders, riding slowly alongside Westbrook and his handler, laughing as though he had not a care in the world. He avoided the other runners, went to the shower, and wasn't seen for the rest of the afternoon.

Lisa returned with sandwich makings and put them out with salsa and chips to tide the runners over until dinner was served. Then she started asking the athletes what they would prefer for breakfast the following day.

"If they're going to run 58 miles at altitude," she said, "they need more than leftover cake to give them the fuel."

Czechowski gained a fairly good sense of the routine, or lack thereof, through comments he had received while out on the course. His day at the back of the pack had gone fairly smoothly, but when he arrived at the school, he received a barrage of complaints. We eventually called a conference of sorts to try to deal with some of the issues and get priorities straight.

Riley was asleep on the stage. When I woke him with the news that we would be meeting in 5 minutes to discuss the day on the road, he rolled over nonplussed and said he'd be there. He still had 4 valuable minutes in which he could nap.

I found Kenney in a back room working from his tapes, and as we walked together to the gathering place, Laharrague flagged us over to where Debladis was sitting.

"Serge has something to tell you," he said in a conspiratorial whisper, "but I think he should not say it in front of the group." The Frenchman looked more gaunt and worn than I had seen him in days, but he summoned enough energy to let fly with an emotional outburst that rivaled Edmonson's worst.

"He says he has been moving well today, in spite of his pain," translated Laharrague. "He has set himself the goal of keeping ahead of Marvin—and other people kept telling him he was doing that by a very long way. Marvin has hardly been able to run the past few days. Serge didn't slow down, but by the finish, Marvin was only 10 minutes behind. Serge thinks that he has been cheating, taking rides on the course."

Kenney said he would keep his eye on things as well as possible but was unmoved by Debladis's complaints.

"It's always something with those two. Food, support, sleeping arrangements, cheating on the course. Tomorrow it'll be something new. Bitch, bitch, bitch. That's all that they do."

Skagerberg had been in serious trouble for a number of days, but the fact was that Beam had turned over the wheel of his van several times in order to keep the veteran company out on the road. Debladis knew better than anyone that having another person with you when you are suffering is the best way to get through a bad spell—and pick up the pace.

Czechowski puffed himself up in true corporate fashion and mediated the meeting in a professional tone. He covered the same ground that had been dealt with at the rest area but used examples from his two days on the course to demonstrate the problems that were a very real part of the race. His approach was very different in a formal sort of way. Kenney's reaction to the lack of markings and aid stations summed up the outcome: "It's happened before, and it will happen again."

The very next day, with head throbbing, legs screaming, and waves of nausea sweeping over him, Rogozinski sputtered words I'll never forget as he neared the 10,603-foot summit of Vail Pass: "I don't care if it gets twice as hard as this, I'm going all the way to New York."

I had been running with Howie and the young teacher for 8 miles of continuous climbing. I struggled to maintain their pace, even though I had started out fresh.

Aid had been good in the early miles leading to the bike path we were on, and thanks to a Vail area running enthusiast named Harald Fricker, it continued along the 9-mile stretch to where vehicular access resumed. Two miles into the bike path, we came upon a man sitting in the middle of the route.

"What can I get you guys?" he yelled when he saw us coming. "I've got chocolate mint cookies, bananas, sandwiches, and Coke."

His name was Orv Peterson, and he was legendary in local athletic circles for his animalistic runs in the hills. He congratulated all of us for our parts in the Trans America undertaking and wished Rogozinski luck while he took in some food.

"The first runner passed by about 10 minutes ago," he said, referring to Warady, "but I'll be here until the last one is through."

We left Peterson with his backpack of goodies and continued our slow attack on the hill. I marveled at the generosity we kept encountering and became inspired by messages that fans had left on the pavement for professional cyclists who trained there. Avanti, they said. Go Lemond. Viva Longo. Yea Sara Neil.

I took photos of Rogozinski, Howie, and Kelley as they ran past a reservoir near the summit, then hopped into the van with Lisa as the runners began a rapid descent. We followed Kenney's directions to various access points, stopping to offer assistance whenever we could get to the course. Disappointed that no television people or photographers showed up through the day, I took more scenic shots than I should have. By the

The climb over the Continental Divide brought successively higher passes over three consecutive days. Edward Kelley—dubbed Hollywood for his hometown and classic look—finds his stride after summiting Colorado's Vail Pass (10,603 feet) on day twenty-four.

time we found our way to the finish at the Summit High School in Frisco, Colorado, Warady was already there. He had finished 1½ minutes before we arrived.

I took the time from Warady's stopwatch and set up the finish line, feeling Riley's smug grin bore through the back of my head. I fumed, knowing I had given him his greatest pleasure of the race. It's happened before, I thought. And it'll happen again.

"I've got to give David credit," said Howie when he arrived alongside Ed Kelley 40 minutes later. "He's a hell of a strong runner, no matter what anyone says."

Since Warady had taken over the lead from Schieke, much had been made of the fact that he had full-time support and spent money every night on restaurant meals and comfortable hotels. The mountains, it was decided, would separate the real runners from those who had been lucky—or had an advantage over the other entrants in the race. The great question was whether Warady could hold up in the hills or would crumble, changing completely the complexion of the race. Most people felt he was far from the fittest athlete but acknowledged that of all the entrants, he had come the most properly prepared. In the mountains of Colorado, however, he showed his true running talent and took command of the race.

Frisco is a pretty little town snuggled among the ski resorts of Breckenridge, Copper Mountain, and Keystone. Its heritage can be traced back to 1875, when a Swedish immigrant built the first log cabin in the area, seeking escape from the gold fever that infected the other towns up the road. Far less touristy than Glenwood Springs, there remains a sense of calm in Frisco. It drew me, like it had the settlers more than one hundred years before.

Miles Porter IV, co-owner and publisher of a local newspaper called the *Ten Mile Times*, showed up at the school to get the full story on the race. He cut his interviews short as the sun fell behind the mountains. "The fish are biting in the lake, " he said, "which means it's time for me to go."

I walked him to his car, and he told me he would get more background material in the morning. When I told him the runners were up at 3:30 and started running at 5, he didn't bat an eye.

"Perfect. After I've done with you, I can go back for more fish." He always kept a pair of rods and tackle in the back of his car.

Bart Yasso, the *Runner's World* man Jane had promised would help reorganize the race, turned up just as Porter left. I was thrilled to see him, knowing he would add another body to support on the course. My hopes of an early night with my wife slipped away as we spoke. Most of the athletes were sleeping by the time I took down the banner and ladders and dragged them inside the school, but two of the journey runners were sitting in a corner, deep in conversation. Beam had mentioned earlier in the day that some of the noncompetitive runners were becoming discouraged. Several spoke about leaving for home.

Fifty-three-year-old John McPhee had discovered running during his early days in the air force, and by the time he retired in 1990, he had run numerous 10K races, nearly two dozen marathons, and sixteen 24-hour events. He felt he could manage the Trans America cutoff schedule, but he was forced from the competitive division on day one of the race.

Mississippi's Billye Butler, on the other hand, says his sole sporting pursuit was softball until he turned fifty, when he started to jog. He found he liked it and has been running ever since. In 1983, Butler ran his first ultramarathon.

"I don't go out to break any records," sixty-three-year-old Butler told me before the Trans America began. "I just get out there to enjoy the experience. I love to run." The grandfather of three completed the first stage 30 minutes before the cutoff; the next day, he managed only 32 of the 47 miles.

When I asked the pair how they were feeling, Butler told me his feet were causing him serious pain. The cycle of good days and bad days was over; each stage had become progressively worse.

"My doc back home thinks maybe he'll have to operate," he said in his southern drawl, "and I think I'd be foolish not to give this up. I hate to leave, but rather than risk not being able to run, I'm going to go home and see what he can do."

I looked at Butler's feet as he spoke, noticing twisted toes and enormous bunions protruding from the first metatarsal of each. He had stopped enjoying the running and the Trans America experience before the end of week one.

McPhee expressed some of the same frustration as Butler, but for him there were deeper concerns than the injuries that had forced him from the competitive race.

"Sure, I'm disappointed that I can't run more than I am," he said, "but I wanted to stay and be a part of the event. I'm thankful to Michael and Jesse for putting on the Trans America, but all anyone does is run them down."

He believed the race organizers were doing the best they could under the circumstances and was sick of the bitching that had become so prevalent.

"My priorities have changed, that's all. I've had about all I can take."

I told the pair that things were looking up, that with input from Czechowski and Yasso, the sponsors were likely to send someone with experience to help coordinate the details of the race. My arguments were futile. Two days later, the discouraged runners both headed for home.

Along with Butler and McPhee, Carol Carter was weighing heavily on my mind. After shuttling her to the school in Eagle the previous day, I had noticed she was having trouble breathing. When the meeting with Czechowski was over, I visited the tiny room she had commandeered for herself. She shivered and sucked on a Ventolin inhaler the whole time we spoke.

She had had trouble with altitude in Utah—and that was only at 6,000 feet. I knew that Vail Pass was 2,000 feet higher than Eagle and that after Frisco, we had another 3,000-foot climb. Concerned, I had called McKeigue, and when he told me that we wouldn't have medical help until Denver, I wondered if I should try to keep Carter from running the highest stages of the race. I knew she was stubborn but didn't think she would object, especially since she had taken time off before. McKeigue agreed that it was wise for her not to run without supervision, but when I put forth the suggestion, I was bombarded by objections—and finally, tears.

"You don't know how much I've had to put up with," Carter cried, "and how I've tried to be strong in the midst of all of the shit. They say I don't run as far as I do, they call me a tourist, they're hardly ever nice. Tomorrow is my birthday, and you want me to sit out of the race?"

I was choked, feeling like a total heel and unable to speak. I recalled my conversations with Carter before the race had begun and how apprehensive she had been. There was a female signed up for the journey division, but Carter was the only woman to enter in the competitive race. Like Rogozinski, she had been pulled from the waiting list just before the Trans America was due to begin.

"I can't believe it," the forty-four-year-old single mother had said at the time. "I'm going to have to do a million things to get my life ready to leave for the summer. And I'm not even in shape."

Formerly an inactive, overweight smoker, the special ed teacher from San Diego had run close to one hundred marathons and ultras in the decade since beginning the sport.

Sensing an opportunity to be a part of something extraordinary in the Trans America, she cast away the complications and started the race. When she was relegated to the journey division, her personal challenge became trying to maintain a positive attitude while engaged in a constant battle for a small piece of respect.

At the roadside meeting with the other runners and me in Utah, Carter had been concerned about the length of the mountain stages—and the lack of medical aid on the course. What will we do, she had asked, if something goes wrong?

She finally accepted my position, although she complained about it to Kenney. He pulled me aside in the morning and took a shot at reaming me out.

"Look, Michael," I said in a horrible tone, "someone has to make a decision around here once in a while, even if it's not what everybody wants to hear. The petty bullshit you guys get uptight about is so stupid, yet you refuse to do what is right for the race. Do you want to be responsible for Carol dying out there while you sit around, scribbling notes in your van?"

I was annoyed. I usually was when conflicts arose with the race organizers, but it surprised me that I let it out in such an unrestrained way.

Czechowski and Yasso got coffee and muffins for the runners before the start of the twenty-fifth stage. The athletes knew the toughest climb of the race lay ahead, but they also knew that by the end of the day, the worst would be past. After arriving in Idaho Springs, Colorado, it was a mere 45 miles to Denver. Getting to the Mile High City, said Skagerberg, would be an incredible boost.

"You know the desert and the mountains are behind you," the transcontinental veteran had told everyone at the start of the race. "And then there are no major obstacles until the hills of the east. If you come out of the Rockies feeling strong, you're almost certain to get to New York."

Laharrague had been biding his time through the early stages, but he knew all about altitude and chose the mountains to show his detractors that he was capable of running a serious race. On the 48-mile stage from Frisco to Idaho Springs, he ran like a man possessed, force-feeding himself to maintain his fluids and strength.

"You don't want to eat or drink in the mountains," he told me when I joined him for several miles on the approach to Loveland Pass. "But you have to, or you get dehydrated and struggle for oxygen. If this happens, you get very sick."

Laharrague remembered visiting La Paz, Bolivia, and the oxygen masks that were waiting for passengers as he boarded the train in the world's highest capital city.

"The young boy," he continued, referring to Rogozinski, "he didn't drink enough fluid yesterday. You saw it yourself, you saw how he ran."

Rogozinski had suffered and lost significant ground to Warady two days in a row. Laharrague, meanwhile, motored on. He was moving up several places with each passing day.

The summit of Loveland Pass sat at 11,992 feet. Laharrague led the strung out field over the top, with Westbrook only 12 minutes behind. Milanovic, the gentle Swiss who had finished fourth in both of the previous mountain stages, came over the summit behind Westbrook. He was smiling, as always, and was pleased when Lisa gave him Coke and pretzels and told him he was running in third.

"This is so beautiful," he said, looking down at the switchbacks from where he had come. Dirty patches of snow met the road in spots, and when one looked off in the distance, the view was of magnificent white-tinged peaks that reached to the sky. "It reminds me a little bit of some places at home."

We drove back to check on the slower runners and handed out the last of Lisa's cookies. After working through the field, we finally came upon a limping Skagerberg, cringing in pain. He told us Dale had walked with him earlier. He was feeling pretty poorly but thought he could keep on schedule until the end of the stage. I joined him for 2 miles of chatter. He seemed to perk up while we talked about his previous transcontinental experience—and what lay ahead.

"Keep at it, Marv!" I yelled when Lisa returned to pick me up. "And remember what you said. This is the turning point of the race. The last difficult day."

9

Roll the Dice

On Monday when the sun is hot,
I wonder to myself a lot:
'Now is it true, or is it not,
That what is which and which is what?'
—A. A. Milne

Lisa and I reached the Clear Creek Recreation Center in Idaho Springs, Colorado, in plenty of time. Laharrague's stage win moved him into eighth overall, but in total time he remained almost 50 hours out of the lead. Warady held his position, finishing behind Westbrook and Milanovic—and just ahead of Rogozinski.

Howie arrived with Czechowski in the van, took over the timing, and sipped on an icy beer. The little Scotsman was fuming from what he had heard in Frisco the previous day.

"It really burns my ass," he spat in disgust, "that I get that sort of attitude after all I've done!" He was speaking about the latest conflict, another mind game that resulted from his return to the road.

Everyone knew Howie was out of the competitive race, but Riley said he was stealing the glory by trying to win every stage. I apparently had fueled the controversy by mentioning in my phone reports that Howie had rejoined the race as a stage runner and on several occasions noting that he had finished in first. It was nothing out of the ordinary; I was always trying to alter the flavor of the messages by referring to different people, places, or special events. I always gave a rundown of the overall standings and the status of the race at the front of the pack.

The problem apparently had begun when Warady called friends in California and was informed that Howie received mention on the tape. In a classic Trans America example of turning a mountain into a molehill, Riley claimed that Howie was limelighting—and tried to make it sound as though all the other runners agreed.

"Everyone is complaining about Al running through the finish line," Riley said, "and they think journey runners shouldn't be listed in the results for the day. It's not fair that he's fresh and they've been running the whole time."

The Scotsman was so badly insulted that he swore not to run another stage in the race.

"If this is the kind of support I get from people," he told me later, "I've bloody well 'ad enough of this sport! I'm seriously thinking about giving up runnin'. I've 'ad it this time. I've 'ad it for good!"

It took dozens of conversations with the other runners for Howie to realize that Riley's "everyone" consisted of only one or two athletes, but despite support from the majority, he stuck to his vow. He had run his last complete stage in the Trans America—and jogged only occasionally when a competitor was hurting and felt company would help.

While I took photographs of finishers in front of the Recreation Center, a burgundy car pulled alongside. As a familiar face emerged, I couldn't believe what I was seeing, and I breathed a deep sigh of relief. If anyone can help get this thing under control, I said to myself, this guy can. He's been out here. He's done it. He's a man who knows what this race is really about.

Bill Shultz was almost as experienced as Don Choi in multiday running; when he turned up at the Trans America, he still held the official Six-Day North American best. Besides having competed in hundreds of marathons and dozens of ultras, he had directed his own 24-hour race for more than a decade. He had run across the country in a solo effort two years earlier.

When I saw Shultz, I started shaking with nervous energy. After exchanging pleasantries, I pulled him aside. "You're just the man we need!" I sputtered in excitement. "You have to help us, Bill. This whole thing is teetering. Believe me, it's falling down bad."

He shook his head and held up his hands as if surrendering to a maniac with a gun.

"I can't get involved. If I stuck around here, there's a good chance someone would die."

Shultz was the forceful type, and it didn't take long to grasp that he meant what he said. If he was in charge, certain heads would have rolled before the end of week one. Shultz told me that he and a friend had actually come to help Skagerberg but were unable to find him out on the course. Word came in as we spoke; 12 miles from the finish, the veteran's foot had become so bad he dropped from the race.

The new arrivals were devastated. They cursed at the directions they had been following all afternoon in an attempt to bisect the course. They half believed that if they had found Skagerberg in time, he would have finished the stage. When they settled down, they told me why they were in Colorado.

"Don Choi is the calmest person you ever want to meet," said Shultz. "He's never negative about anything or anybody, but he sent out the alarm."

Choi was appalled by what he had seen during his brief stint with the Trans America. As soon as he returned to San Francisco, he called everyone he knew who might have an interest in the race. Shultz, a Pennsylvanian, was at the top of the list. As a friend and ultrarunning teacher, Choi thought he would be willing to help. The call came too late, but Shultz rearranged his busy summer schedule to make a visit to his brother coincide with the closest point in the course.

The man who was with him knew several of the older entrants. He said he would be with us for a few days, return home, then come back in his own car and stay as long as he could. Al Cruzado's arrival was one of many miracles; he, like Beam, Howie, and numerous others who found themselves in support roles, became an indispensable part of the mortar needed to save the crumbling event.

"There's a fantastic hotel in town," Skagerberg had told me earlier in the day as we walked slowly up the unrelenting hill. "It's a place where you can soak your worries away in mineral baths in great private rooms. When we get there, you ought to take a break and slip over there with your wife."

Even though the stage over Loveland Pass was considered one of the hardest of the race, the scenic beauty inspired solid performances from most of the group. Debladis finished last again, alone, but was an hour ahead of the cutoff for the first time in days. Laharrague still stuck by him in the evenings but had different plans for the days on the road.

With everything under control at the Recreation Center, Lisa and I decided to take Skagerberg's advice. We drove through town and asked directions to the famous Indian Springs Resort, hoping to spend a few relaxing hours in the mud baths before falling into a comfortable bed at the rustic hotel.

While waiting to inquire about rooms, we were treated to a look at the regular clientele. A Buffalo Bill look-alike, complete with buckskins and moccasins, noisily floundered his way out of the bar. On the walls hung bear skins and flintlock rifles, and in the lounge lay a pair of men, comparing tattoos. They had obviously overindulged, but both looked like they needed a drink. A hefty woman with a towel wrapped around her bosom herded whining children down the hall, leaving puddles of mineral water on the floor in their wake. The hotel was once heralded as the Saratoga of the Rocky Mountains, said the brochure, and has catered to such noteworthy travelers as Jesse James and Billy the Kid.

The only room available was in the noisy main building, next to the dripping family—and sharing their bath. We opted for a motel at the far end of town.

CBS This Morning was supposed to be on-site the next day, but they canceled at the last minute for the second time in the race.

"It's the Democratic Convention," I was told, "and they've lined up some exclusives they didn't think we could get." In a sense it was just as well. Skagerberg had been one of the runners scheduled to talk, and his mood was worse than the rest.

The moon was full and hung magically over the rustic buildings that lined the main street as the runners left town on day twenty-six. I drove ahead, scouting locations for photographs, but it was too dark to get any meaningful shots. When I returned to the start area for the banner and ladders, Linzbichler waved me down.

"I don't know what will happen here," said the bearded Austrian sternly, "but I have a problem with my crew that makes me worry even more than the mess with the race."

Since he had been injured, Linzbichler felt that his support team had been taking advantage of his position. "They no longer do their job and they think now they are tourists, not on a work trip, but I must still pay their way. I have fired them, but I am stuck with my van."

Just what we need, I thought: more strife and fewer bodies. The Cruzado advantage was neutralized before it even began.

After Linzbichler left, I dismantled the starting line and drove to the local 7-Eleven to load up on supplies. Dale Beam was there with Howie, so we had a good bitch session over coffee. Beam filled me in on his latest economic report. He had been keeping a tally

For the uncrewed runners, a yellow Ryder van meant welcome relief. Dale Beam, standing, was injured on day two and became the backbone of the support effort for those who remained in the race. He set out for the course shortly after the 5 A.M. start each day and drove back and forth until the slowest runner was in. Stefan Schlett, left, and John Surdyk often took Beam's offer of a chair and a chance to relax.

sheet of the payments he received from various runners, and with the food fund collection Rogozinski had instituted at the runners' suggestion in Utah, he was finally in the black.

"It won't last for long, though," Beam said while he filled up with gas. "It's unbelievable how much all this stuff costs."

The back of the yellow van was organized chaos, with athletes' rain gear, socks, and shirts jammed into the rails on the side. Beam had the Gatorade jugs full of water and electrolyte replacement stacked alongside huge buckets of ice. A case of Coke was wedged between a pair of coolers holding cold cuts, cheese, mustard, and several loaves of bread. Another bucket was loaded with half-full bags of potato chips, pretzels, Doritos, crackers, and cookies—the cheapest Beam could find.

"We sure need a big city like Denver," he mumbled as he took inventory, "so I can get some decent prices and really stock up."

Howie was still furious about the reported attitude toward his running, and no matter how much we tried, we couldn't bring a smile to his face.

"You should be out there doing what you were born for," said Beam, "and everyone but a jealous few agreed. Running like a gazelle, that's Al Howie—not riding in a van."

Even with shredded heels, the tiny Scotsman had been able to joke. It saddened me to see him hurting again, and I felt powerless to help. Time will repair this, I told myself, just as it had done for his feet.

When Lisa rode with me, we talked about the multitude of problems that plagued the Trans America, but as I listened to myself rehashing what had happened so far, I realized how important it was to look for solutions rather than dwell on the past. Another revelation hit me as I spoke with my wife: When Howie had been back running with the leaders, he was much more positive in his general approach. During his recovery period, he had developed a great understanding of the complex structure that lay behind the event, and while he ran he relayed feelings to the others on a whole different plane.

Even though I had come to care for the tiny Scotsman dearly, I began to recognize that dealing with the psychology of his injury and troubles with Riley had been a drain on us both. We didn't exactly start out every morning with an anti-Jesse chant, but as problems persisted, we worked each other into an angst-filled frenzy more often than not. With Lisa as my passenger, the negative spiral came to a long-overdue end. My mood was decidedly brighter, though we never did get to soak in any of Colorado's recuperative springs.

Though the athletes pretended to look forward to big cities for the potential recognition, facilities, and variety of diversions that supposedly lay in store, Denver was a rude awakening after so much time in relative isolation. It was almost 18 miles from the western side of town to the finish in the eastern suburbs. That much city running isn't pleasant at the best of times, let alone at the end of a hot, 45-mile stage.

Even though Kenney had written that the course was a straight shot through town, congestion, lights, bike paths, and traffic circles without police supervision made for a difficult run. John Wallis was almost knocked over three times—twice by cars and once in a dispute with a drunk.

"This guy jumps out of nowhere," Wallis said later with comical mimicry, "and starts yelling, 'You buggers ought to keep off of the streets. You freaks should run in the park.' I told him I'd love to be running in the park. He came after me. I guess he thought I was trying to be smart."

Wallis had spent plenty of time putting people to the mat in his youth as a wrestler and had coached his favorite sport for many years since. When the drunk's words turned into slow-motion movement, Wallis reacted automatically. He dodged a clumsy swing aimed at his head and gave his aggressor a counterblow to the crotch. He laughed as he told the story, but I knew he must have been weary at the time and far from steady on his feet.

Wallis looked much like Colonel Blake in the *M*A*S*H* TV series and had the gentle, gregarious demeanor to match. He spoke slowly but with the type of passion for his subject that forced the listener to take notice of every word. He often wore long nylon pants to protect his pale skin from the sun; his hat was the cotton fishing type on which Blake carried his lures. To look at Wallis, you would never peg him as a tough-as-nails ultrarunner. Then again, he didn't look much like a wrestler, either.

"I started running in 1978," the fifty-five-year-old, semiretired teacher from Michigan told me, "because as a single parent raising three young daughters, it was about the only thing I could afford to do."

A year after his debut in a 10-kilometer race, Wallis ran his first 50-miler. He had always loved baseball and wrestling, but it took only one ultramarathon for him to know he was hooked. In the years that followed, Wallis captured age-group records for 100K, 100-mile, 48-hour, and six-day races. Going into the Trans America, he held the World Veterans' record for 1,000 miles. He ran the distance in 14 days, 9 hours, and 45 minutes on a loop course in New York.

Multiday racing is the supreme test, said Wallis before the Trans America, because it is not a solely physical ordeal. "It's really difficult when somebody goes out on the first day and takes a three- or four-hour lead. Your natural reaction as a competitor is to go after him. You want to lead, but patience is key. You have to constantly monitor your body and stay within your own limits. Otherwise you're sunk."

The desert had come close to taking Wallis out of the race, but I didn't realize until long afterward just how close. The afternoon he passed out at the abandoned train station was only the first of his scares.

"I was alone out there the next day," he told me later, "and I was out of it. I collapsed right there, in the middle of the road." Another runner came along and helped him, but by then the sun had been burning him raw. Brutally blistered hands were the most visible result.

The hands healed slowly, but at about the same time Skagerberg was approaching the height of his trouble, Wallis also decided he was so badly injured he had to pull out of the race. After the climb over Vail Pass, his ankle was so sore and swollen from tendinitis that it wouldn't bear any weight at all. The Austrian crew provided some massage and medication, and Volk, the German medical student, spent an hour taping the badly inflamed foot. A visiting doctor recommended immediate withdrawal and bedrest, but in the morning, Wallis realized he had come too far to simply quit.

The tape provided his ankle with much-needed support, and the spectacular mountain views somehow got him over Loveland Pass and through to the end of the day. Shultz and Cruzado's subsequent appearance inspired him onward. He cruised to the finish on the west side of Denver, weary but with a contented look on his face. The altercation with the drunk had rekindled the light.

"Maybe I should call work and tell them I'm stranded," said Lisa as I dropped her at the airport that afternoon. "That way I can stay and help on the course."

Our farewell was short, and though I knew I would miss her incredibly, I was in far better spirits now than when my wife had arrived. She understood how strong my commitment to helping the group achieve its goal had become, and she too was filled with genuine concern.

Warady led the way into Denver, passing Mile High Stadium, the U.S. Mint, and the state capitol building well ahead of the rest. He clocked 6:58 for the 45-mile stage from Idaho Springs to the front of the Beck Recreation Center in the suburb of Aurora, and increased his lead over Rogozinski to 6 hours and 3 minutes in overall time.

The visitors to the finish area included newspaper reporters, owners of a Blimpies sandwich shop, and several runners who had heard of the race. One of the local athletes, fifty-seven-year-old Ted Epstein, was a prominent lawyer who had become involved in ultradistance events more than a decade earlier. He had also taken part in the running event with Riley and me in Siberia, and though it may have been a disorganized mess, he loved the people so much that he returned the following year. The mission he accomplished in 1990 was somewhat different: He became the first man to swim across Lake Baikal. At 30.5 miles, it was no minor feat.

"I'm slow," he told me when we first met. "I'm really slow, so I like to go long. For me, regular Ironman triathlons are too much of a sprint."

Epstein had competed in a Double Ironman Triathlon with Schlett a month before the Trans America began. He invited me to join him and his German friend for an afternoon away from the group, but I had to decline. Yasso, Czechowski, and I had scheduled a meeting for the third time in as many days.

"The way we have to handle this thing," insisted Yasso, "is to convince Jesse and Michael that they have to take control and respect *Runners World*'s input as a sponsor— or we get the hell out. If they can get it together, there's no need for all these hassles. We should be able to work together to make it come out in the end."

He said he would approach Kenney and Riley to see if they were willing to undergo the necessary attitude shift. Czechowski borrowed my portable computer so that he could print out the duties of a fictional person we called the technical coordinator. We had hopes that this being would arrive out of nowhere to help with the race.

The help from the *Runner's World* representatives was appreciated, but all their questions had put the runners on a three-siren alert. Kenney and Riley told the athletes they were under a great deal of pressure but were trying to negotiate for additional help. By the end of stage twenty-seven, rumors were rampant. Tensions were rapidly approaching another uncomfortable peak.

Byers, Colorado, was little but a series of grain silos, a gas station, a restaurant, and a well- appointed school. The stage from Denver was only thirty two miles, but it covered a narrow stretch of Route 36. Westbrook won the stage and moved within 50 minutes of Rogozinski, but the overall positions remained exactly the same.

Sprengelmeyer spoke about his expectations before the start of the day: "We'll be trekking over the high plains. I'm going to feel like Clint Eastwood, but I don't have a horse. All I have is my shoes."

Daily patch-and-repair jobs had been holding Sprengelmeyer's Nikes together. He was pleased when another package arrived with two sparkling new pairs, but the heels were worn off both sets by the end of the week.

Footwear was put to a supreme test during the two-month ordeal. Sprengelmeyer repaired his soles daily; others customized the uppers to accommodate blisters, hot spots, and swelling feet. Helmut Schieke seemed the easiest on his shoes, using only six pairs. David Warady rotated often, going through twenty-three sets, but they didn't go completely to waste: Hodson retrieved the race leader's discards and used them himself.

"The Great Plains," said author Ian Frazier in a talk about his book on the subject, "have had an unusually lively imaginary existence for the past two hundred years . . .

"First we called them the Great American Desert, when early explorers happened to go west through the sandhills along the Arkansas and the Platte Rivers and extended those sandhills indefinitely north and south in their minds. Then the Plains were the Wild West, and people went there in search of an adventurous life which their very presence caused to disappear. Thousands of buffalo hunters made millions of dollars hunting themselves out of a job. Then the Plains became a cattle kingdom; that lasted for a few years until there were more cattle than the range could hold . . .

"Then came the homesteader boom. The railroads sold the Plains as a garden spot, 'The Garden in the Grasslands.' Then WWI came along and the Plains were supposed to win the war with wheat. The war ended, the sod cover was gone from the prairie, drought hit, the wind blew, and suddenly the Great Plains were the Dust Bowl. During the energy crisis fifteen years ago, people were drilling and digging the Plains, which by then had become part of the New Energy Frontier.

"The lesson of the Great Plains is that it's a place that does what it wants . . ."

The runners' first experiences on the Great Plains were terrifying. There were no shoulders on Route 36, and the entire road was dampened by a dangerous fog. Trucks appeared from nowhere out of the thick, soupy mist, reminding us all of the quantity of roadkill we had seen since leaving the coast.

Thirty-five miles into stage twenty-eight lay a Texaco station, a disorderly collection of mailboxes, and a small general store. Howie and a journey runner named Celine Mercier rode with me, helping to supply the athletes spread out on the course. I had an hour's worth of phone calls and faxing to take care of, so they dropped me at the general store and continued ahead. The rotary phone outside was broken. I stepped inside the little store to see what the manager could recommend.

"Come on in," she said, "and make yourself at home. Your friends told us to expect you. In fact, the mayor is off printing a sign."

Shultz and Cruzado had interrupted a coffee klatch in the store when they had stopped in earlier to gas up their car. In the middle of a rolling, rural farming area, the general store also served as video shop, post office, social club, and dwelling place for homegrown advice. I didn't even know I was in a town, but the residents of Last Chance introduced themselves as I poured myself a coffee and pulled out my wallet to pay.

"Keep your money," said Dennis Everheart. "This is your last chance to have a cuppa on us." I joined in the laughter, as the gathering of ten rocked in their chairs.

Everheart's wife pointed to the telephone jack when I asked if there was anywhere to hook up my fax so I could send a report. "Help yourself," she said, "so long as you don't charge us for long-distance calls."

Mayor Ed Miller arrived with a computer-generated banner welcoming the Trans America runners to his peculiar little domain. Last Chance, he told me while taping the homemade billboard to the front of the store, was exactly what its named implied: "If they're running to Byers," they'd better stock up here. Ain't nothin' in any direction for at least 20 more miles."

Route 36 is a common throughway for cross-country travelers, and the church where we would stay in Anton had been used by many groups before. As the runners arrived at the finish line in front of Masters Excavating and Cafe, I informed them of the full-scale meeting scheduled for after dinner that night. Even Warady, who came in third in the 55-mile stage, was expected to attend.

Elvah Masters allowed the runners to shower in her home while she prepared the evening meal in the cafe below. The $8 dinner was an elaborate affair, held in a giant tin-walled garage at the back of the house. Chicken, lasagna, salads, garlic bread, apple crisp, rice pudding, jello, soda, iced tea, and beer were on the menu. Fortunately there was something for everyone; the Masters Cafe was the only facility in the place they called town.

Beam and I shuttled late-arriving runners from the finish line by the Cafe to where gear had been unloaded outside of the church, and then back for the meal. I was last to the food table but managed to load a plate with salad and find a spot in the middle of one of the long tables, just as Czechowski distributed papers to everyone in the room.

Riley started in with a brief preamble about how negative he had been about *Runner's World* in the past.

"We've had some discussions," he continued, "and Bart and Eric came up with some ways to solve the problems you always bitch about. Michael and I said we should see what you think, then maybe give them a try."

As he turned the floor over to Yasso, I sensed disaster. The concept of solidarity that Yasso had spoken so much about did not seem to have made an impression on the race director. The picture Riley was trying to paint would only widen the gap.

"What you have in front of you is a new set of rules," stated Yasso with authority. "They're designed to enhance the quality of the race. Jesse and Michael have put a ton of work into this thing, and they're getting nothing but hassle for all they have done."

Murmurs changed to vocal protests when the athletes were asked to focus attention on the pages they held in their hands.

Czechowski's draft of the Official Race Rules were based on the discussions with Riley and Kenney, but no one had been given them for potential review before the meeting. The way they were written was abrupt, and seemed to me almost tyrannical in tone. Rather than explaining the reasoning behind them, or that they were meant to be the start of a two-way dialog, Yasso presented the rules in the same voice in which they were written: Here is the law. He became flustered and angry when denouncements started coming from the tired and weary crowd.

Laharrague was the most vocal. He never held back, and he shouted his reaction as soon as it came into his mind.

"We are not children and we can decide for ourselves if we want to carry water bottles or not! This is outrageous. We are the ones who are running! You come here to watch for three days and make up these ridiculous rules."

Riley sat back and smiled, while Kenney looked on blandly, showing no reaction at all. I tried to intercede, but Yasso was yelling back at the Frenchman in a futile show of force.

"What is this!" screamed John Kim in a violent burst of rage. "You expect me to wash toilets and clean up after these superstar runners, as though I am a dog! I have three times more education than all you young fools! I am not a janitor, I come here to run!"

The Korean-born journey runner spat in Yasso's direction and jumped up and down. He swore he would call his lawyer and file a lawsuit the very next day.

Fifty-six-year-old Kim was married with two children and taught business and computer technology at a university in Maine. He had only started running in 1988, completed his first marathon a year later, and had averaged one every month since.

"Running to me is like meditation," he wrote in a letter that accompanied his Trans

America entry. "As a Taoist, I have struggled to cope with human weaknesses such as excessive greed and vanity." Through running, he said, he feels closer to nature and more able to cope with his own weaknesses.

He never finished stage one, but averaged 30 miles a day for the first week of the race. Since then he had frequently been injured and often rode with Beam to the finish, ahead of the rest. He rarely socialized with the other athletes and preferred eating ramen noodles from the tiny stove he carried with him to whatever else was prepared.

After listening to his raving for several minutes, the other runners told Kim to sit down and relax. He threw his chair to the ground and stomped off for the church, far from meditative and still in a state.

Since Riley had started the proceedings, and we had all planned for me to stay in the background, I whispered to him that he should try to get things under control.

"Remember, Jesse, you agreed to these rules—and you want to get more support for the road. Explain that this came from you and Michael, not *Runner's World*. Tell the runners that they have a chance to offer feedback and to vote on the rules." The race director stood up slowly and yelled for attention.

"I'm going to go around the room," he said in a dramatic voice, smiling in his usual, detached sort of way. "I'm going to ask each of you if you think you can make it all the way to New York if things stay the same as they are."

No one understood the question at first, but when he repeated it, it seemed to me that he was saying, Back me, I can do this without sponsors or anyone else, much as he had when the runners had approached him in Utah with their string of complaints.

His question didn't exactly cause a rally of support. Most of the athletes were more concerned about getting assurance that *Runner's World* would stay involved with the race.

As soon as the meeting was over, Yasso and Czechowski hopped into their van. I knew they had left one vehicle in Denver but assumed they were just carrying out their usual evening routine and driving off in search of a motel.

"Good luck," said Yasso when I walked toward them, shaking my head. "When we get back, we'll talk to Jane and see what we can do to get you some help."

I hadn't expected them to be leaving for another day and a half, but they said they had a flight out of Denver the next afternoon. I later learned that they didn't leave Colorado until late Sunday but drove to Pikes Peak for a day of leisure instead of helping to smooth the transition to the new set of rules.

The van disappeared in the fading light, leaving me with an empty, abandoned feeling. They came, stirred up the hornet's nest, and then were gone. A thunderstorm simmered overhead as I dismantled the finish line. Discouraged, I walked to the church to look for a pew.

The basement was oppressively hot, but it housed the only usable phone. After making my regular calls, I tried to do the daily recording but was constantly interrupted by the flow of people going to the facilities. After several attempts, I recorded a series of inane messages referring to Rogozinski's habits in the toilet, Hodson's stockings, and the strange way Howie brushed his teeth. On my twentieth try, I got the proper spiel recorded, and then went outside for air.

The sky was ablaze with twisted fingers of lightning. Rain pelted down. I wandered out into the elements, hoping a good soaking would rinse my brain clean.

"They have a saying here in Colorado," Sprengelmeyer had said while watching a similar deluge the previous day. "If you don't like the weather, simply wait 5 minutes or move 5 miles and it'll almost certainly change. The gods want to be sure we know who's in charge."

I managed to laugh at the mess we were in, and then thought of Pyle's runners, sixty-odd years ago, going through things in such a similar way. This Trans America group isn't so different, I figured, and now that they're 1,200 miles in, nothing need stop them from making it to the finish in New York. I went to sleep that night feeling hopeful, anticipating the positive conversation I would be having with headquarters in a couple of days.

When I finally reached Jane on Monday morning from Atwood, Kansas, her voice sounded frail and terribly strained. After the standard hellos, she gave in to her emotions and broke down in tears. I thought she must have encountered a family crisis. My assumption, in a strange way, was right.

I reeled in confusion as I listened to her words from another lonely telephone booth on the side of the road.

"Eric and Bart came back last night," she said weakly, as if she would choke if she put any power into the words. "They recommended *Runner's World* pull out of the race."

10

The Point of No Return

Through many dangers, toils, and snares
I have already come.
'Tis grace hath brought me safe thus far
and grace will lead me home.
—John Newton, "Amazing Grace"

The stage after the meeting was a scheduled time trial. The main
pack of runners were surprisingly jovial at the starting line as they assembled for the
6 A.M. start, but that was understandable. It would be two days before any of us learned
what Yasso and Czechowski truly thought or heard of their devastating report. The athletes set after the man in the lead as usual. The new rules were to go into effect the following day.

Rogozinski found his pace early and left the other runners in pursuit of Warady. He
bore down on the straight, flat road and finished the 31-mile stage in 4 hours and 15
minutes, gaining 40 minutes on his main rival. Warady still held on to the overall lead.

"The altitude definitely got me," said Rogozinski, as he relaxed on the grass in front
of the Maranatha Cafe in Joes, Colorado, "but now I feel like it's time to rock 'n roll."

It's ironic to think that Rogozinski had never intended to make running his sport.
He went out for cross-country as a freshman in high school just to pass the time until
baseball season began.

"I loved to run from the first time I entered the trails," he recalls, "and I just kept
on with it, having a ball."

Fun turned into obsession, and by the time he finished high school, the youngster
was competing in road races, up to twenty a year. Rogozinski acknowledges that he raced
tired a lot and his performances probably suffered as a result, but he didn't know any better.
His overtraining helped him make the transition to a college running career.

In 1989, Rogozinski led the Division II team from the Indiana University of
Pennsylvania through the National Cross-Country qualifier. He finished twenty-eighth
at the championships, missing All American by 2 seconds flat.

His entry into ultrarunning came the following year as the result of a dispute with an overassertive coach. Rogozinski qualified for the 1990 Penn Relays but figured he knew exactly how much training he could handle leading up to the race. His coach had a vastly different philosophy; when the pair butted heads, the runner quit the team.

While his teammates tackled the famous Franklin Field track in Philadelphia, the twenty-two-year-old took on a new challenge. Ten thousand meters be damned—he headed to Virginia and ran a 50-mile race. In what was the first of many ultras, Rogozinski finished fifth in a very qualified field.

"I found it pretty amazing that I was out there after 5 or 6 hours and still running," he says of that initial experience. "But when the race was over, I seized up bad. I couldn't move for days."

Ever since that day, his running has been constant experimentation, steeped in mystery, pain, and joyous revelation of what the human body can do.

Rogozinski tried a variety of distances, including a six-day race, before heading into the Trans America, but at the starting line he still considered himself very much green.

Warady, for his part, saw himself as a steeled veteran who had been preparing for a race like the Trans America since the day he was born. When it came right down to it, Rogozinski and the leader were very different people—and their divergent personalities were reflected in the way each ran in the race.

Rogozinski could hardly deny that he loved the competitive aspect, but he was there to experience the camp life that was such a big part of the continuous event. Watching him, it became obvious that he valued every detail he could extract from the road. If there was something to see, he wanted it to register in vivid color; if a friend wanted to share a beer and a story, he was always willing to listen, laugh, or help with advice. He spoke with locals whenever he could. There wasn't a person in the group he didn't make an effort to know. Even with Riley and Kenney he tried to be nice.

As far as running the Trans America, Rogozinski was the first to admit he had come in with no preconceived scheme. "My only plan," he said early on in the race, "is to make sure that whatever I do, I can get up and run the next day."

His daily performances were erratic, somewhat like Edmonson's had been: If he felt good, there was nothing that could stop him from hammering the course to register a win.

Warady, on the other hand, was content to run the race on his own terms and rely on his wife for all of his needs. His routine had altered little from the early stages, with Kelley stopping every 1 to 2 miles to replenish his bottles and give him food. Peanut butter and banana sandwiches kept him going on the course, and a double-decker of cold cuts on whole wheat was always waiting when he finished a stage.

The isolationist behavior of the leader was still pretty much as it had been at the start of the race, although he did spend a little more time now at the finish area before disappearing for the night. Most of his socializing was with Kenney and Riley, for whom he continued to have almost nothing but praise. Warady did become rattled while running alone through Denver, however, and expressed some anger at Riley for the poor markings on the course.

"The best thing about this sport," said Howie during one of his many interviews after being withdrawn from the race, "is that you're not racin' against the other competitors, you're racin' with them. I look at it as though the other runners are there to help me do better, to push me along at a faster-than-usual pace. If I beat them to the finish line, it just means I've 'ad a better day. That's why these guys are runnin' so great."

Rogozinski agreed with the grizzled veteran, but as the Trans America prepared to leave Colorado, he started thinking about his position. Despite the win into Joes, he was still 6 hours and 8 minutes out of the lead.

"There's plenty of time," he confided. "I can't wait until we get to the hills in western Pennsylvania. That's when we'll see what that bastard Warady can do . . ."

It was strange to hear the twenty-four-year-old say that, because winning had been the farthest thing from his mind when he started the race. He had already demonstrated that he was one of the most talented runners in the field, but it seemed that his rival's serious attitude was edging him closer to thoughts of the win. He was tired of hearing Warady talk about all the money he had saved to bring his wife as his crew, and how he was just taking it easy, a twentieth-century gladiator, cruising according to plan.

Few runners actually cared too much who won, but when asked, they seemed almost unanimous that Warady was the one person they did not want to enter New York at the head of the field.

Westbrook, like Warady, was a study in consistency and was only 45 minutes back of Rogozinski when he finished the twenty-ninth stage.

Ed Kelley was 9 hours behind Westbrook in the standings, struggling through good days and bad. He ran hard when he was feeling healthy, but his body was like a loan shark: It always came collecting the next day, with interest attached. Schieke was in fifth, another 12 hours back of Kelley in overall time. The German had yet to fully recover from the hamstring trouble he had developed in the desert, but he continued cheerfully on. Of the runners left, he alone knew what it would take to reach the finish in New York.

On the stopovers in Joes, although a church had been secured ½ mile away, the Maranatha Motel and Cafe offered the accommodations of choice for most of the group. Showers had become of paramount importance again: Washing in basins or under spigots didn't cut it if there was an opportunity for rooms.

"Amazin', id'n it," Hodson had laughed when he crossed the line first the previous day. "I'll prolly finish last t'morrow, but that dudn' ma'her one littul bit."

The Alien Warrior's prediction almost came true: Into Joes, he finished thirteenth out of the fourteen left in the competitive race.

Howie tended the finish with his usual enthusiasm and made a loud announcement when he learned that two of the journey runners were nearing the line. Everyone within earshot gathered at the roadside as the figures approached, more than 8½ hours after their 6 A.M. start. Ransom finished his fourth complete stage, while Bruno Fioretti managed the full distance for the first time, 3 minutes back. Both broke into uncharacteristic strides upon seeing the assembly waiting for them. Wide grins told their stories far better than words.

Fioretti was a retired postal worker who described himself as the fittest fat man in America, a fifty-year-old who had started running in 1980 after a completely sedentary life. He quickly realized that speed was not in his body's vocabulary.

"Whether I'm running 10 kilometers, 10 miles, a marathon, or more," he told me on the beach in California, "it's all the same. My pace is a steady 10 minutes per mile."

Going into the Trans America, Fioretti had competed in sixty-five races from the marathon distance to six days, but like several others, he didn't meet the cutoff on stage one.

Hodson was in the shower when Fioretti crossed the finish line, but he made a point of seeking out the rotund journey runner later in the day.

"I've bin one of the blokes who've bin runnin' ya down," Hodson said in as stern a tone as he could muster while shaking Fioretti's hand. "Now I know ya kin do wot ya say. Congratulations on yer good run."

The leisurely last day in Colorado should have been upbeat, but as usual, the high points were countered by disproportionate lows. A flare-up over donated lasagna amused the customers inside the Cafe, but it was embarrassing for the rest of us to see a pair of men in their midforties come close to blows over the distribution of food.

A well-known local ultrarunner had brought the pasta from his home in Fort Collins, Colorado, the previous day, but since dinner was already organized, we saved it for our arrival in Joes. The owner of the Maranatha heated the food for an afternoon snack; as the athletes trickled over the finish line, they were told a free meal was waiting inside.

"Leave some for the other runners!" screamed Celine Mercier at Laharrague when he dove in for a second helping.

Laharrague is not the type of person you want to get into a dispute with, as the meeting with Yasso had proven so well. When his back goes up, rational argument becomes futile and the words that come from his mouth tend toward the explicit and foul. He and Edmonson had been a tough pair to contend with in the early part of the race, but the Frenchman was focusing more on his running since Echo went home. This time, though, he caught a full frontal assault unexpectedly. Hardened in the laws of self protection, he immediately went on the attack as a natural defense.

Donated food seemed to create controversy whenever it turned up. Whether cookies, pizza, or candy bars, there was always trouble with the allotment of goods. If we happened upon a generous region and received contributions for several days in a row, there were always complaints when the pattern came to an end. Laharrague made no bones about where he stood on the issue: He felt that freebies should go to the competitive athletes first; leftovers, if they existed, could be divided among the volunteers and journey runners.

"We run so hard every day," he said, "and these tourists get driven to the finish or ride their bicycles and then go off to sleep. It's not fair that they get half of the little that comes in. These things people give, they are meant for us."

Mercier was a teacher from Quebec who was used to running a maximum of 5 miles a day. She had entered the Trans America in the journey division, hoping to eventually work her way up to a half marathon. Her main goal was to help her boyfriend, Paul Soyka, but things changed when he dropped out of the race.

I happened into the Maranatha just as the argument reached the boiling point. Soyka and other observers had lept to Mercier's defense, siding with the athletes who were still out on the road. I led Laharrague away before the shouting escalated into a physical clash.

"All these petty problems are a complete waste of energy," the Frenchman told me later that night. "We are runners here, and that is all we should be doing. We shouldn't have to worry about fighting for food, about whether there is a shower, or where we will sleep. We need to put every ounce of ourselves into running; these other distractions have no role in the race."

Dinner was à la carte from Herman Juarez's Tex-Mex menu at the Maranatha Cafe. Many of the Europeans enjoyed burritos and enchiladas for the first time in their lives. I can't recall when Mexican food ever tasted so good.

The new rules became law the next morning, but the journey runners had no intention of following the items that applied specifically to them. Instead of being driven ahead to a predetermined point, dropped off, and then required to finish the rest of a stage, they felt they deserved to start with the competitive runners and spend the full allotted time on the course. The point of the proposed change was to avoid the constant shuttling that was wearing out Beam and demoralizing the competitive runners, but none of the journey runners seemed to care about anyone else.

Kim screamed as he had at the meeting, and when Carter and Fioretti joined in, the noise drew Herman Juarez from the kitchen to the parking lot to see what the commotion was about. The whining, shouting, and crying didn't stop until Beam agreed to go back to the old system. Kenney breathed a sigh of relief as the obstinate trio shuffled out from the start at their usual pace.

As the Trans America group closed in on the halfway point of the transcontinental crossing, the athletes began to reassess goals and strategies for the rest of the race. Warady and Rogozinski appeared to be locked in a battle for the winning spot, but with five weeks still to go, nothing was sure.

Laharrague wasn't the only one who was making a charge through the ranks. He now sat 50 hours back of Warady in total time, but 14 hours ahead of the Frenchman, Milanovic, the Swiss, was making a move of his own.

"When I came to the Trans Am," the gentle thirty-two-year-old computer engineer confided, "I was not thinking I can finish every stage. Oh no, I thought it would be too difficult. My biggest worry was about some injury, like an ankle, that would get me and take me out of the race."

In the early stages, Milanovic discovered that attitude was the most important ingredient in overcoming the effort and pain.

"So much I have learned from everybody. Marvin told me about keeping running, when I thought this was not possible, not to walk every day. And Marty, from his shin splints and tendinitis. It was hard for him, but he does move better than he did. Helmut teaches me too, and from all these runners, I know now: I can come all the way to New York."

The question for Milanovic was no longer whether he could finish the race, but how fast. His early injuries had healed, and he found himself running more quickly and consistently than at any time in the previous month.

Eight years before the Trans America began, Milanovic was a smoker who had not exercised in a number of years. About the time his doctor suggested he become a little more active, a friend asked him to run a marathon. He took the challenge, finished in 4 hours and 38 minutes, and was stiff and sick for more than a week.

"This," he says, "was the start of my run."

Running took time away from other interests such as reading and chess, but it didn't take long for Milanovic to leave his mark on the sport. He had been involved with ultras for four years before the Trans America, with some impressive results: Besides a variety of mountain races, he had competed in the Greek Spartathlon twice, setting a Swiss record in 1991.

For his first six-day race, Milanovic traveled to America. He led through 24, 48, and 72 hours before encountering severe tendinitis, but he took the advice of more-experienced athletes and gutted his way to the end. He finished third with more than 400 miles. Another landmark performance came at the Barkley Marathon, a grueling race that goes through some of the least-accessible terrain in Frozen Head State Natural Area in Tennessee.

"This race is not fair," reads the last section of the entry form. "It is not reasonable. We will treat you like shit. And we don't give a tinker's damn. The old Soviet Union sent ten handpicked champions to the Barkley. Two finished. One of them summed up this race better than anyone. He said: 'This is not man against man,' with a dramatic sweep of his arm at the surrounding mountains. 'It is man against . . . against that!'"

"Those who tried to do this event," said Milanovic after completing the 55-mile course in 1991, "know it needs all your strength. I was completely alone, fell into a river, sprained an ankle, and lost my compass. I was not giving up and was able to finish, but there I saw my limits, both in my body and mind."

Thirty-seven miles out of Joes, the runners left Colorado and entered their sixth state of the race. A tailwind helped them along, but the fast times into the finish at St. Francis, Kansas, were inspired more by conditioning and a renewed sense of competition than by the weather. The thermometer hit 96 degrees, giving the group a sampling of the hot, humid conditions that typifyed summer in the Great Plains.

Three hours after the start, while riding with Mercier, I came upon the other journey runners, bunched up in a group. As usual, Ransom didn't acknowledge our presence as we offered him food. Carter said she had just been supplied by Beam's ever-popular van. She gave the thumbs-up: She was under control; no need to stop.

Fioretti was a short way ahead, walking along with his backpack-style water container, the long plastic straw dangling under his arm. He waved us on as we approached, but I noticed his stride was a little bit off. Then, in the side mirror, I saw him bend over and motion frantically. It looked as though he was about to collapse.

I spun a sudden 180, throwing my passenger and gear all over the van. When I approached Fioretti, he looked as though he was gagging, like a cat with a fur ball lodged in its throat. Convulsions racked his body. I grabbed a water bottle and ran to his side. He wasn't choking, I realized; he was having some sort of fit. Mercier was oblivious, walking back down the road to Carter, so I helped Bruno into the van. He put his head back and tried to get himself under control, but he broke into a strange combination of sobbing and laughter every minute or two. I held his hand, scared senseless; I had absolutely no idea what I should do.

When the convulsions stopped, Fioretti told me he had been retired from the Postal Service because of his epilepsy, but that running helped keep the seizures under control. This was his third such attack during the race, however, and by far the worst. No one but Carter knew about his condition—and he had brought no medication with him from home.

"Just give me a minute," he said, "and everything will be fine." He spoke about getting out of the van and continuing, as if he were merely taking a stroll in the park.

Ten minutes later, though, he admitted his feet were feeling numb. "That happens sometimes," he said quietly, "but only when I have a bad one. It may go away in an hour, or it might take the rest of the day."

Fioretti eventually agreed to accept a ride to the school where we were scheduled to stay. When we arrived, he borrowed my sleeping pad and tucked himself into a shady corner. As soon as the school was opened, he took his gear inside and fell immediately asleep.

I contacted McKeigue that night for advice. We both felt that Fioretti should wait until regular medical help was available before he continued his run. The journey runner was every bit as stubborn as Laharrague, and the thought of sitting out for a week didn't go over well. Even as he argued so vehemently, however, he admitted how terrible he felt. In the morning, he wasn't much better, and he finally decided it was time to abandon the race.

The 51-mile stage into St. Francis had gone to Warady, in a remarkable time of 7 hours and 31 minutes—his tenth win of the race.

"These times are insane," said Rogozinski when he crossed under the banner 13 minutes behind Warady, "but it was so comfortable the entire way, I couldn't slow down."

Milanovic came in third alongside Laharrague. They were followed by Westbrook, Kelley, and Hodson. Ed Williams finished last for the fifth day in a row, slipping in the standings to the rear of the pack.

The state of Kansas marked significant change for the Trans America. Fioretti made his decision to go home as the competitive runners started day thirty-one. Less than an hour later, Kim left for the bus station, fed up with the new rules and their supposed effect on his race. Our last words were civil enough, but he was still talking about lawsuits as Cruzado drove him away: "You can be sure of one thing. I'm taking *Runner's World* to court, and all the papers will know."

Carter also spoke of leaving. She was sick of the bitterness the competitive athletes displayed toward the journey runners and felt that her group was being all but forced to drop from the field. She planned to visit friends during the next stopover. How she felt after that would help her decide.

Howie, Beam, and I talked over our 7-Eleven coffees after the stage got under way. We came to the conclusion that the negative attitudes of two or three runners led to conflict almost as often as the lack of management on the course. Like overripe bananas in a fruit basket, the problem spread from a few and infected the rest. Howie suggested we start the daily awards presentations again, reinjecting the spirit of enthusiasm and levity that had disappeared from the race.

The Scotsman had a point. Besides offering an incredible challenge, the Trans America was supposed to be fun. The few who were absorbed in backbiting and bitching constantly dampened the spirits of the others, and those who wanted to avoid the problems withdrew into their own little shells. Rogozinski and Milanovic spent an inordinate amount of time listening to their Walkmans when the mood was bad; Schieke and Schlett joked with Volk in their own native tongue.

The new rule that the competitive runners opposed most strenuously was the one requiring them to carry water bottles. It was adopted in an attempt to do something about the unsanitary conditions that were rampant out on the course. Not only were the jugs of water and Gatorade Kenney had been placing on the roadside getting warm, but lids were being left off after the athletes guzzled fluids directly from the spout. Ants and flies were often bathing in the warm Gatorade by the time the later runners arrived. The various epidemics of diarrhea and vomiting were probably the result of the problems surrounding these jugs.

Westbrook turned up at the starting line in St. Francis with a tiny vial of water but was informed that an 8-ounce bottle was required by the rule. He threw the vial down and grabbed a regulation-size bottle from Tyler. Schlett didn't care about the penalty for noncompliance. The sentence was ¼ hour tacked on to the athlete's time for the stage.

"Fifteen minutes does not matter to me," he said. "You will haf to gif a penalty for effery day."

The stage started miserably, with a cold rain dropping temperatures into the forties. Visibility on the narrow highway was made even worse by a dull, hanging fog.

Fioretti and Kim were now gone, but Linzbichler had returned. After our conversation in Idaho Springs, the Austrian had decided to drive his rented van back to Los Angeles, drop it off, and return to the course. The rest obviously had done him some good: He was the first across the line in Atwood, Kansas, covering the 41 miles from St. Francis in 6:12.

After the fuss they had raised about Howie, neither Riley nor Kenney were at all concerned this time that a noncompetitive runner crossed under the banner ahead of the rest. Then again, it didn't remain an issue because the majority of Linzbichler's energy after this stage win went not into his running, but into vocalizing complaints.

"If he doesn't like it and can do nothing but criticize," said Michael Hansmann, the remaining member of the Austrian crew, "what is the point of continuing? Helmut's not even in the competitive race."

Hansmann was the perfect foil for the grumbling mountaineer: He always smiled and saw the bright side. Hansmann rode a bicycle as support to Linzbichler when the Austrian chose to run. When his man sat out, the rosy-cheeked architecture student would accompany others, supplying them from the back of his bike.

Milanovic finished 8 minutes after Linzbichler, followed by Rogozinski, Warady, and Laharrague. The other athletes ran strongly, but there was a great deal of commentary about the early-morning fog and the difficulty of sharing a narrow strip of pavement with commercial traffic and cars.

"Today was my worst day," said Sprengelmeyer after asking me to make his newspaper call. "I had to jump off the road every 5 minutes to avoid the oncoming trucks."

Once the athletes had showered, they were shuttled from the high school to the American Legion Hall. Twenty locals were gathered there, waiting to join the runners in a feast from a well-stocked buffet. When everyone was settled, I introduced each

France's Serge Debladis, said Lovy, should never have run in such a prolonged event. He was constantly injured, and to make matters worse, he spoke no English at the start of the race. He struggled through each stage, fighting tendinitis, shin splints, and blisters, and often let fly with tirades in his native tongue, expressing disappointment. "Organization zero," he would often yell. This day Debladis was happy: He finished fifth in the stage. Ed Kelley looks on.

member of the group, giving a rundown of background, accomplishments, and position in the race. Then the head of the Chamber of Commerce took the floor for a special award.

"We all think this is great," said Sheila Longcass with sincerity, "and admire everyone who takes part in something like this. You ought to be proud, especially the person who took the most time enjoying the beautiful Kansas scenery on the way into Atwood."

Debladis had the distinction of having arrived at the tail end of the competitive group, and he laughed his way to the stage after Laharrague translated the words. The chanting began as he clasped his hands above his head in a victory salute. Amburger, Amburger, Amburger! The words echoed off the walls until they filled the room.

Debladis had been known as Monsieur Amburger ever since the day he staggered into the Bagdad Cafe. It was still one of the few English words he knew, although his vocabulary had expanded to include ice cream, french fry, and team medical.

Carter brought her friends to the dinner and divvied up a special cake as the group belted out a belated happy birthday song. She grinned from ear to ear, and then announced that she wouldn't be running in the morning: She'd be manning an aid station with her friend Valarie instead. They'd be waiting on the course with sandwiches, potato salad, cookies, and an assortment of drinks. At just over 60 miles, the next stage, between Atwood and Norton, was the longest of the race.

After dinner, the athletes filed a formal grievance according to the method laid out in the rules.

"July 20, '92," began the paper they handed Kenney. "This serves as protest of the water bottle rule in the Runner's World Trans America Footrace. I propose that A) each runner have the choice to carry a water bottle, or B) crewed runners have to carry water bottles only if they are over two aid stations away from their crew." Eleven signatures appeared under the column marked A.

We came up with a compromise that everyone agreed upon: Let the runners do what they felt was necessary to avoid drinking directly from the jugs. Carry nothing and refuel at the trucks or, if bottles are a problem, carry a reusable cup.

The announcement was greeted by applause, and in the weeks that followed, the settlement was carried to ridiculous extremes. Several times a day, I refilled soggy, worn-out Gatorade cups that held water about as well as a sieve. I often saw Laharrague holding a jug over his head and pouring, without making physical contact. More than once he reached for the cup he kept tucked into his shorts only to find it had actually dissolved.

Besides the lack of leadership, another major problem the *Runner's World* representatives had had with the Trans America was the attitude of many of the athletes. "They expect everything," Yasso told Serues, "and they never thank you. I received nothing but grief."

The uproar at the meeting over the new rules had obviously influenced the pair from *Runner's World*, but the way I saw it, the runners' reactions that night had been more because of Yasso's style of presentation than anything else.

It wasn't until I spoke to Jane from Atwood that I learned the gravity of the report from the field. I immediately determined to fight for all I was worth to try to bring the sponsorship back from the brink. I explained to Jane the chaotic meeting, keying on the tone of presentation and the aggressive reactions from both sides of the fence.

"Bart wasn't exactly diplomatic," I said, "and Jesse pulled his usual shit. If there was any message to come across, it was that the athletes believe *Runner's World* is a crucial part of the race."

*Food and fluids were in
constant demand by the
athletes as they covered
between 28 and 60 miles a
day, and the runners were
thankful to the dozens of
volunteers who came to lend
a hand at different points in
the race. The author's wife,
Lisa, visited the course
several times. Here she
supplies homemade cookies
to Helmut Schieke. The
humble German runner never
accepted a thing without
expressing gratitude and
flashing a smile.*

My enthusiasm was genuine, thanks to a pair of relatively cool days, the departure of the most difficult journey runners, and Cruzado's still being there to help on the course. I told Serues that things had settled down since the meeting and weren't nearly as bad as the visitors had perceived.

"What about the organizers' attitudes?" she asked. "Michael seems to be okay most of the time, but Jesse is such a wild card. He can be charming one minute and totally irrational the next."

It was true, and it had been proven time and again. I felt that Riley had not yet come to understand what his actual role on the course needed to be, and Jane and I agreed that someone else had to take charge.

Jane felt better after our conversation, but my biggest sales pitch came later that day. In a conference call with five *Runner's World* people, they made it clear to me that the sponsorship was on the verge of collapse.

"We'll give it one more shot," said George Hirsch, the publisher, "because we owe it to the runners to give it our best. If I get Jesse's word that he agrees to work with us, we'll send a technical coordinator to help with the race."

I floated through the rest of the conversation, the nervous sweat on my palms turning to nectar as if I had been blessed by the gods. Jane admitted later that she was disappointed at how quickly Czechowski had decided the plug should be pulled on the difficult event. Yasso also had let her down: She thought he would have been a positive influence—and he was her first choice for the new coordinator role.

"No way I would do that job," said Yasso, "not to save my life, or the life of a friend. I wouldn't send my worst enemy out there to face that constant abuse."

In asking Hirsch for backup, Jane was taking a big gamble. As she considered the latest development, we both hoped my assessment was correct, that things weren't as bad as they seemed. She wasn't sending her worst enemy. Quite the opposite—her husband was going to be the person joining the battle. Bill Serues was scheduled to arrive in less than a week.

11

Down Home

I expect to pass through the world but once; any good thing
therefore that I can do, or any kindness that I can
show to any fellow-creature, let me do it now;
let me not defer or neglect it, for I shall not pass this way again.
—Stephen Grellet

Riley's pronouncement about the reaffirmation of support was done
with his usual flaire.

"I just got off the phone with George Hirsch," he said after the water bottle situation
was resolved, "and his reps suggested they back out of the race. I knew they wouldn't
bail out, and I got them to send one of their people to help coordinate things on the course."

"What about food?" someone shouted.

"And prize money?" yelled another.

"There are plenty of things we need as much as another person at this point in the
race."

I could hardly believe what I was hearing, but human nature is often that way. Perhaps
Kenney had been right when he refused to do anything about the problems early on.

"Give them one thing," he had said, "and they'll always want more."

Give them nothing, and they know exactly what they've got, that's what Kenney
believed. News of the negative report had been circulating for several days, I later learned,
and contingency plans were already in the works. Wallis, Rogozinski, and Sprengelmeyer
had put their heads together and determined that if worst came to worst, they could
probably string together enough friends to man one of their own vehicles as roving
support. They knew that if *Runner's World* pulled up stakes, the vans that Beam and I
drove would be gone. As much as they wanted to see the race organizers smooth things
over with the sponsors, the athletes had come too far to see the Trans America fold.

I didn't even allow myself to project down that particular path of thought. I was torn
enough as it was.

If people had been skeptical when C. C. Pyle first announced his transcontinental
race, it didn't keep the curious among them from hitting the roads. Half a million onlookers

lined the highway when the gun went off, and the athletes rose to the occasion. They covered the first 17 miles between Los Angeles and Puente at a blistering pace. Reporters selected three certain winners in the first seven days, but their predictions seemed to be a kiss of death. By the time the eighty-four-day race was three weeks old, half of the field had succumbed to the climb over the Cajon Pass, the burning sands of the Mojave, and the frostbitten Santa Fe Mountains. The remainder struggled on, fighting valiantly under the eyes of the world.

Pyle's greatest moments of brilliance revolved around his never-ending quest for the payoff, and with his big race he left nothing to chance. Besides placing tariffs on stopover points, he set up the daily finishes in an admission-only arena, hoping people would flock to see the runners as they arrived into town. As an alternate method of income, he developed an entertainment extravaganza, complete with hawkers, freak shows, and games of chance. See the Piu-Poison Girl, his people yelled, and Wo-Kah, the most intelligent dog in the world. The attractions ranged from Embalmed Outlaw to Five-legged Pig.

The race became a traveling carnival in more ways than one: The cook quit, the circus performers walked out, and the road crew went on strike when they didn't get paid. Although betting was rampant all along the course, the athletes were the only ones who saw the true value of the race.

The Trans America was far from a spectator sport, especially when one considered that the field was spread such a great distance apart. The leaders ran at almost 7 miles an hour on the short stages, but those at the back of the pack still struggled with the cutoff schedule, moving along at half that pace. The first runner across the line could easily be 1 hour ahead of the next finisher; the last, as many as 7 hours behind. Floods of people may not have come to watch the athletes as they fought their way along the rural countryside in northern Kansas, but they did turn out at the end of the day.

The hospitality seemed to agree with Rogozinski. On the stage between Atwood and Norton, he was in his absolute prime. Even Howie was awestruck watching the youngster click off steady 9-minute miles. He completed the 60-mile stage in 9 hours and 5 minutes, finishing 1 hour ahead of second-place Westbrook. Milanovic ran strongly again, finishing third, followed by Laharrague, another 20 minutes back. Warady came in fifth, losing more than 2 hours to Rogozinski. The Californian still held the overall lead, but his win going into St. Francis had cost him dearly. He had strained a tendon at the back of his knee.

"Norton is one of those towns where everyone knows everything about everybody," said Janet Bruce from the Chamber of Commerce as she readied cookies and chips for the runners outside the newly finished gymnasium. "That gets a little tedious at times, because there's no way to keep a secret." Indiscretions, she continued, were not exactly common, but when they happened, they were the talk of the town. It was the kind of place where people never locked their houses. And all but out-of-towners left the keys in their cars.

The length of the stage left Debladis and Williams on the road for close to 16 hours, so we packed food for them from the roast beef dinner at the local Legion hall and took it back to the school. Debladis wolfed his straight down as usual, but Williams took time to debate.

"What do I need more?" he asked aloud while struggling to keep his eyes open. "Food or sleep?" The memory of an earlier experience helped him decide.

The day after Edmonson had left the race, Rogozinski injured his knee. He effected a recovery by walking with Williams the entire next stage. That day, according to Williams, was one of his worst.

"Tom is so aerobically fit, and he moves at such a steady pace. It was all I could do just to keep with him, but I did—and wore myself out."

Then, as in Norton, Williams arrived late and on the verge of collapse. He was too worn out to be bothered to eat. "The next day, I was so depleted, I had to stop for a nap after 7 lousy miles."

Gutdayzke and Williams had become a cohesive team by then, and the runner remembers how hard his support man worked to keep him on the road. "I was 45 minutes behind the cutoff schedule, but G-Man monitored my progress every stop of the day."

Armed with a homemade fanny pack loaded with water bottles, Williams plodded on, eating a piece of Power Bar or peanut butter sandwich every 2 miles, while Gutdayzke announced the time he had gained—2 minutes became 4 minutes, then 10, 20, and so on, until the determined walker made it to the finish line, the end of the stage.

There was time to spare, and Williams had been moving well every day since. He wasn't about to repeat the mistake he had made on his way into Utah. He knew that forward motion was tough when he was overly tired, but it was almost impossible if he didn't replenish his fuel.

"I wasn't much of an adventurer as a kid," Williams told me as we walked together on the road leading out of Norton the following morning, "but I do remember getting stuck up Mount Rushmore in a snowstorm when I was in the Boy Scouts."

Six-foot-three, lean, and with a powerful stride, the sixty-three-year old rarely ran during the Trans America, but he walked at a speed that was impossible for me to maintain. Our conversation was constantly being broken; I was always falling behind.

Williams remembers watching track meets during his college years at Penn State, where he had completed his undergraduate and master's degrees, but baseball was always his sport. He pursued a career into the pros, pitching in the Cincinnati Reds chain at Olean, New York, for three years before moving on to his doctorate work.

He ran his first marathon in 1969, and he kept on with the distance until injuries occurred. His ultra debut came at a 50-miler in Iowa. It was there that he found he liked the longer distances because they forced him to slow down; less injury and faster recovery was the noticeable result. In 1980 he entered the Western States One Hundred Mile Endurance Run, admitting he had no idea of the trauma ahead. He finished, barely, returned in 1983 and '84, and then graduated to Leadville, where he completed the tough, high-altitude 100-miler seven times in a row.

His claim to fame, Williams said with a laugh, came at Leadville in 1987. "My daughter was twenty-nine, getting into running, and chose Leadville as her very first race."

The pair ran together, and they were shown on television as they reached the end.

"It was quite a story, because prior to that, only four women had ever completed the race. Now we're the only father-daughter team to complete the Grand Slam of ultras."

Although he had hoped to be fully prepared for the Trans America, Williams had been on the waiting list until two months before the start. "My training wasn't too motivated until I was in for sure," he told me shortly after hearing he had become a certain starter, "but I'm getting into it now. The joints just aren't accustomed to these kind of miles, and it's going to be difficult getting the walking muscles properly prepared."

When I finally got the chance to walk with and chase after Williams, he was suffering from the very problem he had thought might occur. On top of the inflamed tendons and sore muscles, sleep deprivation had become a constant concern.

"I'm resigned to the possibility of failure today," he confided as we were pelted with rain. "I've actually been rehearsing the calls home. I've run them through in my head. I feel sort of like the guy who goes in for surgery and is given a fifty-fifty chance of survival. He says, 'I've had a good life. If I've gotta go, I've gotta go.' There's nothing to do but hope for the best."

The rain and wind was frustrating for the local farmers, who needed to make their summer harvest soon or risk losing their crops. For the runners, however, the cool weather was almost ideal—for all but Ed Kelley, that is. His stomach and bowel problems slowed him so much that he was getting the chills.

"I'd rather be in the desert again," he said as he shivered through the damp morning, "than out here freezing and catching a cold."

The 47-mile stage between Norton and Kensington, Kansas, was dominated by Rogozinski for the second day in a row. Warady struggled to maintain contact but managed to place second, 31 minutes back. Westbrook came next, followed by Milanovic and Hodson, who ran the final part of the stage together and finished side by side.

One week earlier, Milanovic had been 13 hours behind Schieke, but a string of top-five finishes moved him ahead of the German into fifth place overall. Kelley held on to fourth, more than 15 hours ahead.

James N. Kusel had been postmaster in Kensington for close to 30 years, and when he read the logo on my T-shirt he told me we were expected in town.

"You people sure have some gumption," he said, "running as far as ya do. And in the middle of summer, though it seems this year you've been blessed. Normally it's hotter 'n a booger out here; 110 plus, with winds tearing outta the southwest."

Kensington, population 640, was a pretty place. I admired the small row of shops that made up the center of town.

"I guess you'd say we're out in the sticks, but we like it a lot." Waites Sundries, Kusel said, was a must visit for the runners when they arrived into town. It was straight out of the Archie comic books: a genuine old-time soda fountain, one of the few left in the world.

Organizationally, it seemed as though the Trans America had finally stumbled upon a system that was beginning to work. Kenney still toiled with his turn sheets and was never more than a day ahead, but he did provide me with stopover contacts, and I passed these on to Jane as often as I could. She called ahead to confirm the arrangements and get information, which I then relayed back to the runners. If meals were prearranged, I asked the athletes for commitments ahead of time, then called ahead with numbers so that the local organizers would know just what to expect.

The morning we left for Kensington, everyone agreed to attend the postrace barbecue and ice cream social, which was to be held at Riverside Park. When the coordinator told me that a pair of local businesses had donated money to pay for the meal, a burst of inspiration suddenly hit.

The runners seemed to eat a decent morning meal only if it was readily available or free. The biggest issue was time: Although a special breakfast at a diner or Legion hall was a wonderful concept, few of the athletes wanted to be shuttled off-site before the day's running began. They had to pack gear, tend to injuries, lubricate problem areas, and determine what clothing was appropriate for the conditions ahead. Sleeping time was always at a premium, and every wasted minute seemed to add an hour to the day.

Collecting money for breakfast supplies was another problem: If nothing was organized, the athletes grumbled and then ran off, knowing Dale would be waiting down the road, adequately stocked. Even though he had developed a reasonably effective system of voodoo economics, Beam still struggled daily to finance purchases for distribution on the course.

Although Kenney gave him no money for food, the volunteer did have use of a credit card, which Riley's mother had provided, to get gasoline for the van. Beam added supplies to the bill every time he filled up, which helped, but even though he shopped at discount supermarkets the rest of the time, money was constantly low. Some of the runners were generous to a fault; others were tighter than Ebenezer Scrooge.

In Kensington, I began to orchestrate a series of deceptions aimed at making sure the runners ate well in the mornings—but designed so that those of us in support roles wouldn't go broke. Instead of the $5 everyone expected to pay for the steak dinner, I told them it was a bargain at $2 a head. I collected the money before we arrived at the park and purchased a shopping cart full of breakfast foods. Then I announced that the dinner had been underwritten by the local bank, and as an added bonus, locals were putting on breakfast for free.

The turnout at the barbecue was extraordinary, and the locals were fascinated by the athletes' tales of the road.

"It feels good to be 'ere," commented Howie when I turned the presentation over to him, the color man, to introduce the athletes and announce their positions in the race. He had written the day's results along with the overall standings and time differentials on a new flip chart, but before getting into that, he expressed our appreciation at the local support.

"To have people acknowledge what these guys are doin' is somethin' special," he said, "and it's really neat to see people who actually care." The socializing continued until dark.

The next day was a 44-miler, and it belonged to Hodson from beginning to end. He was out front when Howie and I pulled alongside, our radio tuned to KKAN Phillipsburg in hopes of catching the Trans America report recorded the previous day.

"The Senior Citizens Center is having baked ham on the menu today," said the bulletin board announcer. "The driver's license examiner will be in Phillipsburg from 8 A.M. until 6 . . ." The day before it had been soybean and pork belly futures and the outlook for wheat. The Alien chuckled between sips of Coke and then ran off, his arm dangling as he shuffled comically away.

Marvin Loomis was in charge of the National Guard armory in Mankato, Kansas, our next stopover. He pointed me to the telephone in his office. My list of messages from headquarters was growing longer every day. The rest of the country suddenly seemed to have heard about the Trans America; requests for interviews were coming from nearly all of the states.

Hodson's winning time of 6:43 put him into Mankato 20 minutes ahead of second-place Milanovic. Westbrook followed the Swiss, while Laharrague was another 22 minutes back. Rogozinski and Warady had run together throughout the day and tied for fifth, as if they had declared an uneasy truce. Rogozinski told me he was taking it easy to relieve pain in his shin.

I asked him how he got along with the race leader. "David may be a jerk to the other guys," he replied, "but to me he's actually become fairly nice. It could be that he worries I may kick his butt, and he wants to build a foundation of mutual respect."

Warady told his wife that she could help Rogozinski if they were together, a drastic change from his early approach.

"One of the hardest parts for me," Kelley said later, "was when David told me I couldn't help anyone else, no matter what. I understood his focus and knew what we had gone through to get me to the race, but it was incredibly difficult to have to say no."

The local Lions Club cooked hamburgers for dinner, and a cheerful crew from the United Methodist Church Women's Auxiliary prepared breakfast in the armory at 4 the following morning.

Some attributed it to the food, others to the cool weather, and still others to the challenge presented by the unexpectedly hilly terrain. Whatever the reason, the pace at the front of the pack got faster as the group crossed Kansas. Competition became increasingly fierce. High spirits seemed to translate into a physical force that propelled the runners forward more quickly than in the previous states. Most appeared stronger than ever before.

It was dark and cloudy when the group left Mankato for the 41-mile stage to Cuba, Kansas. Milanovic quickly broke away from the pack, setting a blistering pace as he passed the endless stretches of cornfields that lined both sides of the road. Rogozinski held with the main bunch for the first 2 hours, then put on a series of bursts in pursuit of the Swiss. The young American caught him at the 30-mile mark. They continued together, laughing at the effect Rogozinski's determined running had had on the Swiss.

"I thought you were the Red Devil," said Milanovic, referring to Laharrague. Like most of the runners, the Frenchman's nickname had gone through several transitions. The original, El Diablo, had been based on his attitude, wry grin, and pointed goatee. "I don't want him to catch me," Milanovic continued. "This is something I have told me to push and make me run all the more fast." He looked back while he spoke, keeping an eye out for any sign of his foe.

The pair arrived at the Cuba High School together in less than 6 hours. With aid stops included, they had been running better than 9 minutes per mile.

Warady made it to town more than 2 hours later. Rogozinski thus moved within 1 hour and 7 minutes of the overall lead.

Stefan Schlett reflected on the Kansan hospitality during the 41-mile stage from Mankato to Cuba. For the first time ever, he had refused food on the course.

"I weighed myself last night," he said with a serious face, "and discovered I am the same size as thirty-five days before. I planned to lose some pounds in this race, so I must not eat so much for some while of time."

Schlett was as lean as any of the others and had the type of build where the veins popped from his legs. Warady was the only one who had what one reporter called "excess baggage," but he insisted that that was part of his strategy going into the race: "Fat is a much more efficient source of energy for endurance races. That's why I have peanut butter and banana sandwiches all day long. Sometimes Kelley adds cashews, because I need all the extra calories I can get."

Each of the runners had his or her own dietary preferences. The Frenchmen were the most obvious lovers of meat. "Serge and Emile ask me every day for hamburgers or Egg McMuffins," said Dale, "and they have loved Kansas because of all the beef."

Hodson ate jelly sandwiches when he stopped at Beam's truck, and from my van he always took salty chips and a cup of Coke. "The Alien isn't fussy at all," Beam told me one night when we discussed supplies, "except, like all the foreign runners, he won't eat peanut butter. I think it scares them, the way it sticks to the walls of their stomach on the way down."

Cuba was another friendly outpost in the Plains, and the local Booster Club showed up to prepare dinner for the Trans America group. When I inquired about breakfast, they offered to provide a spread of pancakes, toast, fruit, and danish—along with sandwich supplies for the road. We worked another cross-subsidy deal.

The most significant development of the day was the arrival of new volunteers. Baker had gone home to tend to his overgrown grass, but a couple from Missouri, Bob and Sara Risser, whom Riley knew from his first scouting effort, turned up as replacements.

On day thirty-six, Warady and Riley headed off alone, beginning another time trial. When the rest started, Milanovic and Laharrague took the lead in a rain-soaked pursuit. Westbrook and Rogozinski kept contact for several miles, until Westbrook backed off and bid the youngster to go on his own.

"This pace is ludicrous," he said. "Those guys are running better than 8-minute miles."

Rogozinski passed the dueling Europeans as they settled in to a more reasonable

Twenty-four-year-old Tom Rogozinski entered the Trans America, he said, to see the country up close and personal, as well as to "test the limits within." He soaked up every moment of the experience—and impressed everyone with his running talent and inner strength. Six stage wins over a seven-day period moved him into the overall lead during a period of unseasonably cool weather in the Great Plains.

speed and continued alone after the man in the lead. At the 25-mile mark, he overtook Warady.

The stage ended in Marysville, Kansas, 44 miles east of the little town where it had begun. Rogozinski crossed the finish line still looking fresh in 6:05. Westbrook finished the stage second, ½ hour back. Warady was another 5 minutes behind, and even before Howie calculated the time differentials, we all knew the result: The Californian had been bumped from the lead he had held for the previous twenty-five days.

Entering Marysville from the west, we had passed a bronze sculpture of a Pony Express horse and rider. The town had begun as the first civilian post office in Kansas Territory in 1854.

"Wanted: young, skinny, wiry fellows," said the ad in a San Francisco newspaper, "not over 18. Must be expert riders, willing to risk death daily. Orphans preferred. Wages $25.00 a week."

A trio with many years of transportation experience saw the necessity of getting mail through to the new western territories. To carry out their mission, they required 400 strong horses and 100 such men. Their Pony Express venture began in St. Joseph, Missouri, (the westernmost point of the railroad from the East) and ran nearly two thousand miles to Sacramento, California.

The inauguration took place on the afternoon of April 3, 1860, from the railhead in St. Joe. After a barge ride across the river they called The Big Muddy, Johny Frey rode like the wind until 11 p.m. He blasted his bugle as he entered the relay station in Marysville, jumped from his saddle, and threw the leather saddlebags to the waiting Jack Keetley. Keetley put the mail pouch over his fresh steed's saddle, mounted, and galloped into the night. The mythical mail service was on its way.

During its 18 months of operation, the Express never lost a single packet of mail. Lightning, snowstorms, scorpions, rattlesnakes, warring Indians, and hostile outlaws were all overcome. A museum in Marysville told the story, and I felt a true sense of wonder upon reading that the old stone barn was the only station on the Pony Express Trail still standing on its original site.

"Runners must run facing traffic and on shoulder of road or on sidewalks, when available," said one of the new race rules. "Penalty time for infraction: 15 minutes."

The intention had been there from the very beginning: Running on the left side of the road facing traffic was an absolute must. After the rules were outlined in Anton, Colorado, the warnings began. The camber on the left side of the road was creating problems for some of the runners, but the policy, of necessity, became an enforcable rule.

Driving out of Cuba, the roads had been wet and dark. The countryside rolled. I had the fright of my life when a tall silhouette leaped off the road at the last second of my approach. With the rash of long stages we had just been through, Ed Williams was extremely weary. He was hurting. And worst of all, his reactions were slow. When I thought of all the times I had seen him in the middle or on the far right of the roadway— and of all the trucks that appeared from nowhere at the crests of hills—I feared for the worst. I warned Williams, Kelley, and Schlett about penalties if they didn't stay to the proper side of the road.

As we left Marysville on another damp, dreary morning, I thought nothing more about it; everyone was more than aware.

Debladis was still struggling daily, but knowing there was medical help on-site gave him a tremendous psychological boost. His sense of isolation was a constant problem, however, because he couldn't communicate with any of the athletes around him at the back of the pack. I decided to spend some time with him on the long stage into Hiawatha, Kansas. He fought to keep moving while I battled my French.

"Serge should never have run beyond a thousand miles," said Andy Lovy, the psychiatrist, later. "We had to work on him for at least an hour every day. But then, he wasn't the type of person to accept a nonfinish." The same, evidently, could be said for the rest of the field.

Debladis stayed ahead of Williams for the entire thirty-seventh day. I looked back several times and saw the elderly walker hovering in the middle of the road. The next time Beam happened along, I asked him to inform Williams that he was being penalized for ignoring the rules. A short while later, Mercier arrived with my van. I had walked and jogged with Debladis for 3 hours. Tired and hungry, I drove up ahead. Rogozinski was in control again, at the front of the pack.

"I like to go hard early, while the weather is cool," he told me when I pulled alongside. "Especially if it's a long stage. I can hammer until it gets hot, and then settle into a cruise."

He didn't settle down that day, pushing through 25 miles in 3 hours and 30 minutes, then picking up his pace, hitting 50 miles in 6 hours and 50 minutes, a personal best. Rogozinski finished the 59-mile stage at 1:08 P.M. Warady managed to place second but came in nearly 1½ hours behind the new leader of the race.

"I'm totally psyched," said Rogozinski. "It's all there, and I'm not pushing, just running how I feel."

It looked as though the kid from Steel City had been out for an easy afternoon jog, and seemed like nothing was going to keep him from widening the gap.

Debladis came in late and wolfed down pizza and ice cream while the medics worked on his swollen legs. Williams arrived in last place, limping painfully. Even with penalty time added on, he had almost 2 hours to spare.

The principal of Hiawatha High School was awake before the rest of us the next morning, mixing eggs and flipping sausages in the kitchen, a chef's hat hanging over the side of his face. By the time the runners assembled in the parking lot to begin their final stage in Kansas, they were well fed and spirits were high. Someone dubbed the school the Hiawatha Hilton for the principal's excellent service and the sparkling decor.

Everyone signed in, with Westbrook, as usual, waiting till last.

"What's this?" he asked, pointing to Williams's name on the sign-in sheet. Where the sixty-three-year-old normally scrawled a tiny Ed Wms., there was a notation scrawled: Withdrew Sunday P.M.

I couldn't believe it. We had thirty-seven days behind us; only twenty-seven to go. Williams had been hobbling badly, but the stage ahead was only 36 miles.

"What's the deal, Ed?" I asked when I found the soft-spoken geography professor slowly packing his van. "It's not that long a day. You can do it with your eyes closed. Or better still, take a 7-mile nap."

"I've made up my mind. Gutdayzke and I will swing out of here as soon as we're done."

The day ahead had the potential to be one of the best of the trip, but my announcement brought everyone down with a crash: Big Eddy was out of the race. The field was down to thirteen competitors. New York, all of a sudden, seemed an impossible goal.

While helping Dale, I caught wind of Williams's real reason for pulling out. When

I went to speak to the runner about it, he confirmed the fact that I was actually to blame. "I had 10 hours out there yesterday worrying about the 15 minutes being tacked on to my time, and I knew that the only way my knee would get better was by keeping away from that side of the road."

"Shit, Ed, I'm sorry. I didn't even think about that part of it, but it's so dangerous in the middle of the road when you're tired and dragging your feet. How long can we cry wolf with the rules?"

"You can't, but you should be able to use some discretion. Sending Dale with the message was rather poor form, and the whole thing devastated me psychologically. I couldn't go on in face of the rule."

But it's there for your safety, I wanted to scream, angry that I had been forced to make the hard choice, that my decision was the thing that had pushed him over the edge. Better out of the race than out of the world, I felt like yelling. One mistake on the narrow road when a truck was coming meant certain disaster.

I fluctuated from anger to sadness to attempts at justifying my actions. I told myself I was giving Williams an honorable way out, a point of departure before his knee injury forced him to abandon the race. Then there was the heat we were getting from highway patrols for running in the roadway; they could shut the whole operation down at the turn of a hat.

None of it worked. I still feel badly for Williams and will always wonder if I should have let that penalty go.

12

The Price You Pay

Like one, that on a lonesome road
Doth walk in fear and dread,
And having once turned round walks on,
And turns no more his head;
Because he knows a frightful fiend
Doth close behind him tread.
—Samuel Taylor Coleridge

While Rogozinski and Westbrook vied on the flat roads that led
eastward from Hiawatha, I set up the finish at Elwood High School, commandeered the
telephone in the administrative office, and started making my calls. The talk with
headquarters sent me into a spin. The oft-altered live television appearance had been
rescheduled again, for the following day.

A grand reception awaited us in the cafeteria: an all-afternoon buffet, with an
abundance of food. Meats, cheese, fish, salads, spaghetti, breads, and desserts were
available from the moment the runners arrived until they were ready for bed.

Besides coordinating the volunteer effort, Mayor Sue Bartley cooked a mean fish
stick. When everyone had assembled for dinner, she gave us an official welcome,
complete with a blessing, speech, and declaration in the tradition of the Pony Express.

"Our nation is based on people that have the courage to face great challenges," she
read from a specially prepared certificate, "and in running across the United States, you
exemplify courage with your determination, dedication, and will to succeed no matter
what the elements."

The entire evening was charged with emotion and underlined the fact that the runners
had become united in their drive toward the ultimate goal. Westbrook and Rogozinski
had crossed the finish line together that afternoon, one on either side of Tyler. All three
had been holding hands, and they had embraced as Howie recorded their time. Now, when
the day's winners were presented with T-shirts for their efforts, they called for silence.

Rogozinski spoke quietly from the front of the room. "We ran for someone special
out there today—someone who has shown us all what is possible when you dig deep and
come from the heart. Big Eddy, this one's for you."

Applause erupted as Williams stood up. Towering over Rogozinski, he accepted the shirt and then recited a poem he had told me while we walked in the rain several days before. It was about the hardship of going on when all seemed hopeless, and of the bright light that shone at the end of the trail. It captured a feeling we had all known from past ultradistance experiences, but it took on even more meaning when applied to a Trans America scale.

"The next thing on the agenda," I choked out when he finished, "is to introduce somebody new. Bill Serues, the technical coordinator, is here to help us, all the way to New York."

Boos, hisses, and catcalls filled the cafeteria when I uttered the words.

"Oh, oh, it's the heavy."

"The enforcer has arrived."

"We'd better shake in our boots."

Serues was 6-foot-1, rail thin, and tan. He had a calm, comforting way about him that put everyone instantly at ease. He stood up, took a bow, and deflected the heat.

"My wife sent me here to get me out of the house," he said when the jeering died down. "I've been a tennis pro for a couple of decades, I've done a few marathons, I'm the president of my running club, and I've directed a bunch of short races over the last dozen years. The most important thing, though, is that I love a few beers after a hot day on the road."

Serues had turned up in the afternoon and helped Howie man the finish line as though it was his natural job. He drove out along the course, checking on the late finishers while gaining a sense of the race and the field. The Trans America, Jane had said months before, would be the perfect adventure for Bill.

Born and raised outside of Boston, Bill was the son of a tennis pro. He ran in high school and loved watching the Boston Marathon, but he and his brother were raised on tennis and squash. Serues went to the University of Massachussets in Amherst and the Naval Academy in Annapolis before doing three years of service during the Vietnam War.

"Tennis, believe it not," he said, "kept me out of Nam." He left the navy in 1972 and lived in Tacoma and Portland before settling in Pennsylvania's Lehigh Valley. By that time he had played in a few pro tennis tournaments. "I did so well, I decided to teach."

A secure position in a local country club followed his move east, as did an increased interest in running as a fitness and recreational pursuit. Serues set himself the goal of running the famous Boston Marathon and qualified in his first race at the distance in 1982. He had seventeen marathons behind him when he joined the Trans America, but he knew little about ultras—or what to expect.

Bill Serues was immediately recognized by the runners for the kind of person he was: no-nonsense, caring, and willing to do whatever it took to do a job well. As he settled down on the floor in one of the classrooms that night, he seemed to fit right in. It was almost as though he had been along from the start.

The live shoot the next morning was nerve-racking, particularly since the timing of the broadcast meant that the runners being interviewed had to be brought back to the school 2 hours after the start of the race. Rogozinski and Wallis may have appeared nervous as they struggled to hear Paula Zahn's questions through their tiny earphones, but I was a total basket case off-camera.

Like Rogozinski, Milanovic, and Laharrague, Westbrook seemed to have decided to pick up his pace after leaving the mountains behind. With Rogozinski out for the

After tense deliberations, Runner's World, *the main sponsor, sent a technical coordinator to help sort out the management problems that had plagued the race from the start. Unemployed tennis pro Bill Serues, left, was the ideal choice for the demanding role. Here he advises local volunteers on their duties for day fifty-one.*

interview, the Georgian took the lead early in the stage and held it through to Hamilton, Missouri. In spite of temperatures in the low nineties, he clocked 7 hours and 27 minutes for the 48 miles. Milanovic was only 7 minutes back, with Warady and Laharrague not far behind.

When Rogozinski and Wallis finished their interviews, Bill took them back to where they had been picked up on the road. Rogozinski took off immediately, like a starved greyhound in pursuit of its prey. He passed the slowest runners within an hour and arrived at the finish line just after Hodson had crossed. When the time differentials were sorted out, he was clocked in at 7:13. The effort was good enough for Rogozinski's fifth consecutive stage win, and increased his lead over Warady to 3 hours and 11 minutes in overall time.

Our entry into Missouri was smooth, thanks to the assistance Serues offered—and the reappearance of Choi. The ultrarunning postman had scheduled time off from his job to take part in a long-distance bicycle race but canceled his plans to return to the Trans America and provide support for his friends. He flew to St. Louis, rented a car, loaded it with supplies, and caught the runners partway through their day on the course.

The media excitement had worn me out, but when Hodson asked for a ride from the high school into town, I was glad to oblige. He wanted to do laundry, pick up some supplies, and get a haircut, if there was a cheap barber in town.

Main Street wasn't much, but there were at least half a dozen options when it came to coiffing one's hair. I went to check out a couple of the places while the Alien put in his wash. My first choice was a western apparel shop, full of jeans, cowboy boots, saddles, and bridles. In the back corner was an old-fashioned barber's chair, where an ancient little man busily clipped the mustache of a friend.

"Sorry, son," he said when I inquired if there was any chance to fit in a couple of quick cuts, "I've got one more waitin' and then I'm done fer the day. Try back tomorrow. Say around 10?"

The nearby barber shop was already closed, as were the two salons that lay at the corners on the other side of Main. Tuesday wasn't big in the grooming business, I decided, although it struck me that the number of facilities seemed disproportionate to the size of the town.

"Wot about that one?" asked Hodson when I told him the news. One beauty shop remained, and when we entered, the proprietress was getting ready to close. She took a quick look at Hodson, listened to his plea, and agreed to give us both trims before finishing up for the day.

The Alien told her about the Trans America runners and invited her to the dinner being held by the Hamilton Booster Club at the Methodist church.

"Where's a good spot to pick up some nylons?" he asked in the next breath. "I'm running a bit low."

Halfway through the next day's 50-mile stage, the group came upon an aid station that was far more than abandoned jugs and Power Bars on the side of the road. "Welcome to Chillicothe," read the sign on the front of a car. It flanked a table laden with watermelon, bananas, ice, soft drinks, cookies, and an assortment of goods.

"We read about you guys in the magazine," said Doug Long, the organizer, "and collected supplies from a few local stores to show you we care." After 3 hours of running with Laharrague, I appreciated any refreshment I could get.

"The head," the fiery little Frenchman had said as we plodded along Route 36 near the front of the pack. "That is where the race really takes place, as much as the road."

Laharrague loved to lose himself in reflections on his wilderness travels, and on this occasion told of his preparations for a transcontinental race in the early '80s. He had entered the million-dollar event, but it had never gotten off the ground.

"I went to the mountains of Chihuahua," he related, "to train with the Tarahumara Indians. Do you know about them?"

I had first heard of the Tarahumaras in the fictitious rendition of Pyle's race, but research showed that they did actually exist. Seeking refuge in the harsh canyonlands of Mexico's Sierra Madre Occidental in the days when Spanish conquistadores forced many Indians into servitude, the Tarahumara made running an important part of their lives. To subsist in the wild region of deep gorges and high mountains, the reclusive people hunted by chasing their prey. When the animals grew tired, often days later, the Indians moved in for the kill.

Adapting their endurance skills to recreation, the Tarahumaras developed a game: Teams kicked a wooden ball along the rough trails from noon until sundown, or in longer contests, for one or two days. Participants ran continuously, pausing only for brief drinks of water or corn gruel, and often covered more than 200 miles before a winner was declared.

Laharrague spent two months in the mountains, living with the Indians in caves and crude huts and learning their ways. When he returned to the United States for the transcontinental race, he was completely prepared. The organizers were not, however, and the event was canceled.

The Frenchman then went south through Mexico and Central America. At the Panama end of the Darien Gap, he chose to continue on by foot rather than take the sea route around.

"It was so difficult there," he said, "but that is what appealed to me. People in modern society have become so feeble, so soft. A nice house, money, these things have come to mean far too much."

The jungle was so thick that Laharrague had to use a machete to chop his way through. When his supplies ran low, he hunted monkeys and dug for edible roots. He strung himself up in a hammock at night to avoid leeches and snakes, but in Columbia he was bitten by a rabid bat. How he made it out of the jungle once the fevers started, he cannot quite figure out, but somehow he managed to get to an army hospital in Ecuador. He received treatment for nearly a month.

Laharrague overtook Hodson just before reaching Chillicothe, and 10 miles the other side of town, he surged past Westbrook, who had been running in the lead. The Frenchman raced in to the finish at Brookfield High School in 7 hours and 33 minutes. He took a beer from Howie and told me another story, in a serious voice.

"I use voodoo," he said, "and you see how my spell on Warady has helped the young boy. They'd better be careful, or I'll get out the chicken. You will see what can happen from here."

Whatever the stocky adventurer's assertion, Rogozinski had a flat day, struggling with a sore shin and finishing eighth. Warady ran well, coming in 35 minutes behind Laharrague—and picking up almost 2 hours in his fight back toward the lead.

The next day, the runners followed the rolling terrain along Route 36 through a series of small towns before turning in to Clarence, Missouri, population 1,026. By 9 that morning the sky had cleared, and the day had turned stifling hot. Brookfield High School the night before had been a luxurious stopover by our standards, but the veterans hall that waited at the end of stage forty-one was one of the worst. Bob Farmer was there to open the hall before the first runners arrived, but when he gave me a tour, I became instantly depressed.

There was one bathroom in the back, with no shower. The single room was dirty and stuffy. Keep the door closed, Farmer said, or the place will be swarming with flies. At least there is a fair amount of room, I told myself, trying to look for a bright side. And a dark section with a divider where the tired early arrivals can go for a sleep.

Luckily, Kenney had arranged for Rose Shuck from the chamber of commerce to prepare a lasagna dinner for $6 a head. For an extra dollar, she volunteered to provide cinnamon rolls, coffee, and juice for breakfast. Apart from the convenience store back on the highway, she was the only source of food in town.

Milanovic had taken control of the running early in the day and finished first in 6:51. Warady came in ½ hour behind him. Warady was still down 1 hour and 15 minutes in overall time, but it was his turn to appear fresh at the end of the stage. Rogozinski came in 6 minutes later, looking weary. He took off one of his shoes and asked for ice, just as he had on the previous day.

The next morning, within an hour of leaving the veterans hall, Milanovic opened a substantial lead on the rest of the group. Warady, Westbrook, and Laharrague jockeyed for position within range of one another, while Rogozinski ran steadily a short distance back. By the 10-mile mark, the Swiss was out of sight. Rogozinski was slowing, battling stomach problems that had been with him since the 5 A.M. start. Hodson and Schieke followed him, and the others were strung out over a several-mile stretch.

Kelley was still running inconsistently, as he was battling sickness and diarrhea, but he caught up with Rogozinski near the midpoint of the stage. Seeing that the younger runner was in trouble, Kelley backed off his pace and stuck by the race leader's side for the rest of the stage.

Day forty-two ended in Hannibal, Missouri, in front of the old Admiral Coontz

Armory building at the not-so-pleasant far end of town. A few kids from a summer activity program wandered over to see what was going on as Howie and I waited for the first finisher to approach.

"We've got a bunch of really great fellahs comin' here soon," said Howie. "They're runnin' from California all the way ta New York."

The youngsters were amazed by Howie's accent as much as by what he said, and after taking turns breaking the finish tape, they agreed to hold it when Milanovic came into view. The winner's time was 7 hours and 16 minutes for the 51-mile stage.

"Nobody wants to run today," said Milanovic, "so I ran fast to make them pick up the pace. They did not come with me, so I must continue to go on my own."

Westbrook arrived 43 minutes later, just ahead of Laharrague and Warady, who were only 1 minute apart.

Local media people were intrigued by the battle that was shaping up at the front of the pack. The big question related to Rogozinski: How far back was he? Would he hold on to the overall lead?

At 2:18 P.M., we knew the answer. Rogozinski hadn't yet arrived; Warady regained his former position in the number one spot. He would start the next morning's time trial as he had the previous four: at 5 A.M. with Riley, ahead of the rest.

It was another 49 minutes before Rogozinski staggered in beside Kelley, looking feverish and barely awake. He was pale and drawn and shivered in spite of the heat.

"I'm just going to lie down in a corner," Rogozinski said with the hint of a smile.

The Trans America was not a huge spectator event, but media interest and local turnouts increased as the race moved toward the East. In Hannibal, Missouri, young recruits from a summer recreation program held the tape for Milan Milanovic and Paul Soyka as they finished the stage.

"I might even die." He grabbed his sleeping roll from the pile of gear at the side of the building and curled up on the cold cement floor.

Surdyk may have taken 11 hours and 7 minutes to get from Clarence to Hannibal and finished last of the thirteen competitors, but to him it didn't matter a bit. He had still come in 3½ hours ahead of the cutoff, the armory had a shower, and he'd received an update on the Cubs. Best of all, his doctor friends were scheduled to arrive sometime soon and remain with the Trans America through the entire Midwest. For the Illinois native, that was the most perfect homecoming he could imagine, not only for himself, but for everyone involved in the race.

Hannibal was crawling with tourists intent on seeing Mark Twain's boyhood home and the scenes that had inspired the author's best-known works. More than the historic sites, however, the people are what I recall. The residents made all of us feel like heroes the night we spent in the riverfront town. Linda Rex-Dobson, director of a local revitalization effort, put together an evening of hospitality to rival the best we had seen.

The first order of business was a dinner prepared by a slew of volunteers, which once again included the mayor. Next came one of Howie's flavorful talks, and then local ambassadors "Tom Sawyer" and "Becky Thatcher" gave Milanovic and Rogozinski the keys to the town. After presenting a Trans America cake, the mayor invited us to his home for a party, but only Riley's cycling friends and Linzbichler's crew member, Michael, took the offer. They were shuttled by local trolley and had cocktails in the pool.

Various people arrived at the armory and offered the runners real beds in their homes, but the athletes didn't want to interrupt their established routine. They were used to sleeping close to their friends and the start of the race. Amid all the excitement, Surdyk's saviors appeared. Cheers echoed off the walls of the old armory building as Andy Lovy and Jordan Ross unloaded their equipment and got down to work.

The Mississippi was shrouded in mist the next morning when Warady left the armory. His wife led the way through the darkness, Riley and the runner silhouetted against the streetlamps as they headed up the road toward the bridge that would take them into Illinois.

Rogozinski left 49 minutes later. His fever had broken just before dinner the previous night, and he had actually managed to eat a decent amount at the meal. His foot was still sore, but the padding Lovy had put in his shoe helped relieve some of the pain. Amazingly, his spirits were good, considering the ordeal of the previous day.

The others had been promised a police escort, but it was late, so when the group crossed the narrow bridge over the mighty Mississippi, they were on their own in the thick morning fog. Hodson led the way, followed closely by Milanovic and Laharrague. The rest were bunched together, engaged in congenial morning conversation, happy to know the stage was a short 34 miles. At the tail end came Westbrook, walking with a pained expression, almost as though he had been stabbed in the leg.

"I can't believe it," he said as he stepped from the bridge and into the eighth state of the race. "Yesterday I was running great, with no problems at all. My leg got sore last night, and when I woke up this morning, I was barely able to stand."

The medics had worked on Debladis, Surdyk, and Rogozinski for an hour before the start, then examined the newest patient. "It's definitely shin splints," Ross informed me, "but he can make it through if he just takes it slow." Muscular manipulation and taping were essential to Westbrook's survival, cautioned the student from the Chicago College of Osteopathic Medicine. With patience, the Georgian could recover inside of a week.

A bigger worry was Ed Kelley: The man Howie called "Hollywood" for his Omar Sharif looks had a severely inflamed liver. He was in serious danger of long-term complications if he kept on with the race. Kelley said he felt fine when he woke up in the morning but agreed to run easy and check with the medics at the end of the day.

Rogozinski's illness was somewhat of a mystery. It almost seemed to be a reaction to whatever distress was taking place in his foot. The area Rogozinski had been icing had ballooned as a result of the long, slow day into Hannibal, and the preliminary diagnosis was not too good. "The foot is where his main problem lies," Lovy reported after examining the young runner. "I'd be surprised if he hasn't done some real damage in there. It looks like a stress fracture more than anything else."

It seemed like it had been ages since Lisa's first visit, but when she flew into Decatur that afternoon, I realized it had been only three weeks and three states before. Her flight from Chicago to Decatur was late, and by the time she arrived, she was in worse shape than I.

"This is the last time you're doing this," she said as she had a dozen times during her first visit. It wasn't just the problems with the planes and the race, but all the cases of Murphy's Law that had occurred back home in my absence.

Two days after the start of the race, the car had packed it in, so Lisa had traded it in on a comparable heap. Not long after, the alarm on the condominium had been triggered by a power failure; it hadn't been rearmed for a number of weeks. The latest episode was the death of the washing machine, a cheap under-the-counter job that had always been more trouble than it was worth. My wife was determined not to spend her nights in a seedy laundromat on 10th Street, so she called a handyman friend for advice and effected a cure. She dismantled a spare that lay abandoned in the basement, replaced the faulty part, and the machine actually worked. Life thus went on while we were out on the road.

Lisa had been following my recorded updates and knew of Rogozinski's charge to the front, but when I told her the news from the medical team, she cursed out loud.

"Tom's such a great guy," she said, "and an incredible runner. He's the person who really should win." My wife always said what was on her mind and her words reflected the feelings of many involved in the race. Warady, the calculating tactician, may have planned, prepared, and piled up every advantage he could, but Rogozinski was infinitely more likable, the exuberant youth following his passion with everything he had. The two represented an interesting dichotomy within the ever-tightening group.

Warady seemed to have recovered from his injuries and ran in comfort alongside Riley. Milanovic and Laharrague, meanwhile, intensified their quest to outdo one another. Pushing the pace through growing humidity, the Swiss pulled away from his rival and took the stage win for the second day in a row. Milanovic's time of 4 hours and 45 minutes moved him within 2 hours of Kelley and to fourth place overall, but he was still 29 hours back of Warady, who held on to the lead. Laharrague finished 18 minutes behind the stage winner, which put him only 29 minutes behind sixth-place Schieke in overall time.

Rogozinski placed fifth, dropping only 7 minutes to Warady, but he looked weary and sore. When not running, he moved with a disheartening limp. Westbrook suffered immensely throughout the day, alternating walking and light jogging while Ross kept tabs on his progress from the medical truck. The student doctor stopped to massage and retape his patient's shins at different points in the day.

For one of the most consistent and focused competitors in the race, the slow pace was frustrating, yet there was nothing else Westbrook could do. It was shuffle, risk further injury, or drop from the race. With a seventeen-year streak of running at least a mile every day, the Georgian decided to listen to advice and move more slowly than he was used to to stay in the race. Never even close to the cutoff before, he came in 90 minutes behind the next-slowest finisher. He made the time limit with less than 1 hour to spare.

Day forty-four began in front of the Church of the Nazarene in Pittsfield, Illinois. It was one of those still, small-town mornings with neon signs and a red-rimmed horizon casting a strange glow, lighting nothing, but throwing everything into dark silhouette.

As the athletes and volunteers assembled in the parking lot, I noticed that we had built into quite an impressive entourage. Warady's wife and Westbrook's handler, Tyler, were there, as were Beam and Serues in their vans. Sprengelmeyer's sister, Rita, had driven down from her home in Palatine, Illinois, to crew for the weekend and waited in her car. Choi left from Hannibal, but Cruzado had returned. Ross was there, advising Westbrook, Kelley, and Rogozinski on their best strategy for surviving the stage. Lovy was preparing to run, picking up from where he had left off on the previous day.

"This way I'm out there and the runners know I know what they're going through," said Lovy of his plan to run each day as we crossed the Midwest. "But my first priority is helping the athletes, and I'm available for whatever situations come up on the road."

They say that timing is everything. For the Trans America group, the arrival of the medical team couldn't have been timed better. It was almost as if the onslaught of injuries had waited until help was at hand.

The Trans America was about challenge, hardship, and surviving with a little help from your friends. When Al Howie, left, was pulled from the field on day eight, he put aside personal disappointment to be an advocate and morale booster for the rest of the group. Andy Lovy, right, was a key member of the medical staff, and as an ultrarunning psychologist, he provided insight into the mind games that were an inevitable part of the seemingly endless event.

13

Galaxy of Terror

We are not now that strength which in old days
Moved earth and heaven; that which we are, we are;
One equal temper of heroic hearts,
Made weak by time and fate, but strong in will.
To strive, to seek, to find, and not to yield.
—Alfred Lord Tennyson

John Surdyk, like Wallis, had had an extremely close call in the desert. Like Debladis, he had struggled to make the daily cutoffs through the mountains and the Plains. When the race entered the Midwest, he was still at the tail end of the field on most days, but he no longer had trouble keeping ahead of schedule. The underdog wasn't exactly tearing things up at the front of the pack, but he was starting to feel as though he at least had a chance of making it all the way to New York.

He knew that even with all the vitamin therapy, anti-inflammatories, and determination in the world, he wouldn't have come far without the unflagging support of the rest of the Trans America group. Swollen shins, dehydration, exhaustion, and a constant rash of blisters threatened to take him out of the race time and again.

"I would have been dead meat if Dale hadn't turned up when he did," Surdyk said about the day he had overheated in the Mojave and was on the verge of collapse. Of a particularly brutal stretch in Utah: "I was totally shot. Milan, Al, Peter, Dale, and the others looked over me like mother hens. I was wasted, but felt too ashamed to quit."

Sprengelmeyer was in top form, Howie said, because he had the right kind of company along to help with his run. The man we called "Easygoing" was escorted into Hannibal by a female friend from his running club in Iowa, and from the Mississippi into Illinois by his sister and another woman from home. He thrived on the attention, and though his pace remained a steady 4½ to 5 miles an hour, his frame of mind improved with each passing day.

"The weather is not so goot for the Tank Commander," said Schlett in Kansas about the unusual cool. "I want it more hot and humit so the real pain can begin."

Schlett was known to thrive in adverse conditions and was not running as well as the other athletes in relative terms. He was having knee problems, so every time there was a weight room available, he spent at least half an hour doing leg extensions and curls. Despite his troubles, as official leader of "The Back Bunch," the German was having a ball.

"Since we go slow," he said by way of explanation, "we make our own club and form special rules." Debladis, Surdyk, Wallis, Sprengelmeyer, and Hodson were charter members; occasional invites went to front runners on their slowest of days. Most of Schlett's enrollment criteria were pornographic in nature and related in some way to the smut-filled magazines Beam carried in the back of his van. The publications kept the runners amused when their spirits were down.

"The jokes reflect a base sort of locker-room humor," acknowledged Beam, "but it keeps their minds off the enormous chore of the road."

Besides extra clothes, food, and reading materials, Beam carried several lawn chairs in his van. When the roads allowed for it, he set them up so that the runners could take a break while refueling their bodies and souls.

"Stefan and Surdyk really like to sit and read the girlie magazines. It really helps their moods. It also helps mine."

On day forty-four, Kelley took off at the head of the competitive field, but his pacing was sporadic. The moment he pushed too hard, he had to back off because of the pain in his side. His toilet stops were so frequent that he had long since given up going into the cornfields; instead, he just squatted on the side of the road. He was making a serious push for the stage win, according to some of the other runners, because the doctors were talking about pulling him out of the race.

"If Ed has to go," someone said, "he wants to do it in a blaze of glory, to seal his fate with a win."

The stage ended at the Sangamon County Fairgrounds in New Berlin, Illinois, at one of the main buildings just off the side of the road. Hodson crossed the finish line first, clocking 8 hours and 27 minutes for the 53 miles. Milanovic finished 12 minutes later, ahead of Laharrague; Kelley ran in with Schieke an hour later in a tie for fourth. An ecstatic Debladis came next, only 5 minutes back.

"Runner French," he sputtered, pointing at himself, and continued in French, "Number five! Where is Warady? I'm gaining!"

Rogozinski was a long way back, hobbling slowly and turning his foot awkwardly outward to alleviate some of the pain. Cruzado was keeping as close an eye on him as possible, but with his commitment to Wallis, Surdyk, and Sprengelmeyer, he was not as accessible as he felt he should be.

"These guys have to see you every 2 miles," he said while running toward Wallis with a selection of cookies and crackers. "They need encouragement as much as regular fuel." Cruzado was right: The runners had come to rely on a variety of junk foods in order to keep energized during their long days on the road, but morale sustenance was as important as the enormous number of calories they ate.

Cruzado had been in the marines for sixteen years before an accident took him out of the service. When he recovered, he became an official for the Athletics Congress and the NCAA, working at track and road events across the country. In the early '80s, he began to help organize ultradistance races and took his race walking to new personal goals. He found that officiating took on less meaning as he became more familiar with ultrarunners and their specific needs.

A fascination with trying to help athletes attain new levels of performance led Cruzado to what he says is his mission in life: "It gives me great pleasure helping people, and this is what I really want to do. Sure, I'd still like to see what I can do in the races, but my knees can't take it the way they used to."

In any given year, Cruzado puts more than 50,000 miles on rental cars, traveling across the nation to help race directors, friends, and athletes he doesn't even know. He is always there in the background, quietly taking care of whatever most needs to be done. He's "God's gift to ultrarunners," said Surdyk and others at many points in the race.

"This pisses me off," Rogozinski exclaimed as I walked him toward the finish at the end of the day. "If it wasn't so painful I'd be able to run faster. Then I could be done earlier and have more time to recover before it's time to do it again."

The battle with Warady obviously weighed heavily on the young runner's mind, but he seemed to be coming to grips with the fact that mere survival might have to suffice.

"What can you do? I always said I just wanted to finish the race. I'll walk the rest of the way to New York if that's what it takes."

Bill Serues called Riley, Kenney, and me together to recap what he had experienced in the week he had been with the race.

"I've got to give you guys credit for doing such an incredible job scouting the course. The turn sheets are excellent, and each time we arrive somewhere and have a roof over our heads, it amazes me." Things had gone relatively smoothly, he said, and he was happy with the way support seemed to have gelled out on the road. He mentioned several incidents that perturbed him but made a very positive assessment of the race overall.

One area of particular concern was the ongoing support. Cruzado and the other visiting volunteers were taking some of the burden from Beam, but they were only temporary help. What could we do, Bill wondered, to make the maximum use of the other people we had?

I took the bait immediately, baring my teeth and jumping right to the point. "Just what do Dean and Patricia do out there all day?" I asked Riley regarding his cycling friends. "Are they still supposed to be helping the runners? It's pretty obvious they're doing anything but."

Serues suggested that Riley speak to the pair and get them to come to him willingly and seek out a task.

"If you're nice to them," said the race director, "they'll do anything. Just ask them and they'll do whatever you want."

Springfield, Illinois, known as the Lincoln Capital of the World, was the biggest city we had encountered since leaving Denver and marked the place we bisected old Route 66. As we neared the outskirts the following day, I dug up my notes about Pyle's 1928 race. It was like entering a time tunnel; I found myself suffering a serious case of déjà vu.

When Pyle found he was unable to collect the $60,000 fee he had levied against a consortium of towns along his route, he resolved to wind up the race as quickly as he could. Between Los Angeles and Chicago, his stages varied in length, averaging 38 miles a day for the first sixty-three days. On reaching the Windy City, he set the timetable for the remaining 1,063 miles. He wanted them completed in twenty-one days. Many of the stages covered more than 60 miles, and when the runners learned of the proposed changes, they sought out the management to voice their complaints. The protests fell on deaf ears. Pyle's regard was for the health of his pocketbook, not that of the athletes.

Englishman Harry Berry wrote about the result of the promoter's action in his book *From L.A. to New York, From New York to L.A.*:

> In the face of increased pressure brought to bear on the runners, a new solidarity emerged. There had been a sadness in St. Louis when eighteen year old Nick Perisick from Long Beach had to finish due to exhaustion, but it gave way to anger when Lin Dilks left the race. At 35 he had passed his best running days, but he was still capable of extending anyone on the day and his mild mannered approach endeared him to all . . .
>
> From that point on, an invisible band linked the runners in an alliance that refused to be broken. The competitors not involved in the possibility of prize money spared no endeavors to ensure that their colleagues stayed in the race. Those not suffering from fatigue hung back to run alongside and encourage the ones who had nearly reached the breaking point.

The day the Trans America group passed through Springfield on its way to Decatur, Illinois, epitomized the spirit of camaraderie that had developed through the course of the race.

Westbrook was in agony at the start, but he was accompanied by members of the Back Bunch in the early part of the day. The Georgian's shin splints were far from healed, and the stage was long, the second of three tough days in a row.

Lovy was convinced that Rogozinski had a stress fracture. Padding in the shoe, pain relievers, and perseverance were the only things that could help. Kelley had been suspected of having hepatitis, but his test had come back negative; his liver enzymes were elevated, apparently from the overall stress.

Ross drove back and forth along the course constantly, keeping tabs on the trio of former front-runners, as well as the others who struggled with injuries and pains. On several occasions, I came upon the medical student with his table set up on the side of the road, working magic on the afflicted athletes however he could.

Every time I stopped to offer one of the runners food or drink, they would ask about the others: Is Tom on schedule? Is Richard keeping ahead of cutoff pace?

Kelley finally took the advice of the medics and enjoyed a leisurely day. He ran relatively painfree in the company of Wallis and Debladis and finished laughing, rather than suffering alone. Surdyk and Rogozinski spent a great deal of time together, running short sections when they could to break up the tedium of having to walk. Rogozinski eventually pulled ahead, though, and was accompanied at different points by Howie and Schlett. Serues ran out from the finish to bring him in the final 2 miles.

Westbrook was behind all the others, hovering dangerously near the cutoff, but he was attended by Tyler and Volk. Ross was never far away.

When the presentations took place at the dinner hosted by the Decatur Running Club that night, two athletes were noticeable in their absence. Warady had finished in just under 11 hours and gone directly to a hotel; Westbrook was still out there somewhere, fighting the clock.

As soon as Rogozinski had refueled his own broken body, he gathered an extra plate of spaghetti and a bowl of ice cream and asked Dale to give him a ride.

"There's no way I'm going to let Richard drop," he said quietly. "He's come too far to lose it now. He's finishing, if I have to carry him in."

With 56 painful miles already behind him for the day, the young runner went back to help his struggling friend. After feeding Westbrook, Rogozinski spent another 1½ hours

A network of medical professionals and students cared for the athletes along 80 percent of the course. When Georgia's Richard Westbrook, left, was hit by a severe case of shin splints, osteopathic fellow Jordan Ross watched over him like a hawk. Besides stopping to massage and treat injuries through the day, Ross and others prepared athletes in the mornings and worked on them well into the nights.

on the road, coaxing the proud cross-country coach along through 5 more torturous miles. The pair rounded the final turn to the finish line in the parking lot of Milliken University at 8:10 P.M. to the sound of applause. Westbrook finished with 50 minutes to spare.

The Running Club supplied us with muffins, bagels, and doughnuts the next morning, sending the athletes off on the forty-sixth stage in an excellent mood. Several members were there at 5 A.M. to run the first 10 miles with the Trans America group; others turned up on the road during their lunch breaks to supply the runners with Coca-Cola and moral support.

As soon as the group left the start area, the discussions began. Dr. McKeigue had arrived for the remainder of the Illinois stages and wanted to know what he could do to provide the most effective medical help. We talked about the rash of recent injuries, as well as old wounds, then began to forge ahead.

"I think one of the most important things is 'aving someone around all the time," said Howie, "just the way you guys 'ave been in the past few days."

"You're right, Al. Being able to get to people on the road or as soon as they're finished, at night, is key. That way you can get to the little problems before they run out of control."

Many of the runners had pushed themselves to the absolute limit. The six weeks of extreme mileage were having a cumulative effect.

"Jordan and Andy have eight to ten people waiting to see them every night now. That's got to tell you something about the strain of the race."

Hodson led the field into the little town of Newman, Illinois, completing the 53-mile stage in 8 hours and 45 minutes. Milanovic came in 7 minutes later, followed by Laharrague, another 6 minutes back.

Runner's World associate publisher Mike Greehan showed up at our Legion hall stopover in the early afternoon. He and Chicago area sales rep Jeff Broder had been at a trade show all weekend; the two were looking forward to seeing what the Trans America was really about. They missed the television crew that came down from Quincy, Illinois, but did arrive in time to see Kelley and Schieke finish the stage. The athletes smiled and yodeled as they crossed under the banner, holding hands in the air. They embraced and exchanged thanks for the good company, introduced themselves to the new arrivals, and went off in search of their gear.

Westbrook and Rogozinski finished together in just under 14 hours. They both looked haggard and weary but were happy to beat the cutoff, one day closer to the end of the ordeal.

The pizzas Greehan bought from the little joint on Broadway Street were absolutely superb. Washed down with cold beer, accompanied by one of Howie's better presentations, and topped off with a nice piece of coverage on the 6:30 news, they made for a heavenly night. There were no showers to be had, and the Legion hall was hot and stuffy, so many of the runners set up tents outside on the lawn. Greehan and Broder circulated among the athletes, listening to tales of the weeks on the road. The runners were friendly, open, and amazingly content.

With 2,088 miles behind them, the athletes were spread across the spectrum in overall time. Each runner had been thinking about his own position and waging battle with those around him, but several of the placings were beginning to look as though they would stay as they were.

At the tail end of the group, Surdyk was ahead of Debladis by 9 hours but acknowledged that the Frenchman was a faster runner when he wasn't injured. Debladis was on a healthy streak and had gained nearly 5 hours in the previous four days. Wallis seemed to have a lock on eleventh position, but Schlett and Sprengelmeyer were in close competition for numbers nine and ten, sitting only 1 hour apart. There was a mammoth 35-hour gap between them and Hodson in eighth. Schieke held on to seventh, another 9 hours ahead. From there, things started getting crazy, and with the current number of injuries, it seemed that only Warady's position was secure.

Laharrague sat in sixth but was gaining significant ground on Kelley every day of the race. Milanovic was only 2½ hours behind Westbrook but still an impossible 24 hours out of the lead. Rogozinski clung on to second but had slipped more than 8 hours behind Warady during his four miserable days. When the overall leader saw the state of his two closest rivals the day the group entered Illinois, he decided he must do nothing to jeopardize his own physical state.

Lisa cooked breakfast in the tiny kitchen at the Legion hall: eggs, ham, English muffins, sticky buns, orange juice, and the all-important caffeine. Broder and Greehan arrived to wish everyone well and to save my wife the terror of a prop-jet ride out of Decatur. They drove her directly to the Chicago airport, where she caught a wide-body back to the East.

Stage forty-seven should have been a scorcher: It was August 5 and we were crossing another state line into a part of the country where cool weather in the summer isn't supposed to exist. After the dark start, the sky brightened slowly, but a cloud cover and crisp breezes kept the temperature down for most of the day.

Milanovic got straight down to business, jumping into the lead right off the start. Laharrague and Hodson stayed in contact for the first half of the 41-mile stage, but when the determined Swiss reached the finish in Rockville, Indiana, he was more than 30 minutes ahead.

The first sub-50-mile stage in four days gave Westbrook some small sense of relief. He moved a little faster than he had been, encouraged by the constant reassuring presence of Tyler and Volk. For Rogozinski, on the other hand, it was a day of total breakdown, one in which he reexamined, a thousand times, the strength of his resolve.

He knew his foot was in bad shape, but the medics assured him there was no risk of lasting damage if he continued on in the race. For inspiration, he focused on the story of a world-class runner named Henry Marsh.

"He crashed into a barrier while he was training for the '83 World Championships," Rogozinski had told me the day before, "and he broke a couple of ribs. The doctor told him he could still run but that it would hurt like hell. 'Pain is pain,' said Marsh, 'That's all it is.' That's where I am. It's not getting any worse, it just aches like a son of a bitch."

Twelve miles out of Newman, however, Rogozinski believed his battle was lost. He had been guzzling ibuprofen for the better part of a week but had reached the point where

The medical team may have nursed Richard Westbrook through his most serious injury, but it was Shelley Tyler, left, who helped him from beginning to end. Besides her full-time duties as a handler, Tyler often cooked meals at the end of a stage. There were days when she ran as many as 30 miles with Westbrook, carrying water so he would not have to stop for aid.

pain relievers were having little effect. Even worse than the physical torment was the overwhelming sense of mental fatigue that engulfed him, something we had all seen develop in the injured runners who had dropped out of the race.

"Even the good days are a fight," he confided. "They begin with a terrible sense of fear about what lies ahead. I can't even acknowledge the thoughts that leap at me in my waking moments, because then I might start questioning why I am even doing this. That would be the beginning of the end."

Struggling just to keep moving—and with 29 miles still to go—Rogozinski found himself slipping into a black hole of self-pity and doubt. The inner turmoil had been bad before, but it had never continued unabated for so long, or become so terribly dark. He was gazing longingly at the thick cornfields along the road when the yellow Ryder van pulled up. Dale jumped out, set up a lawn chair, and watched with concern as the lean, young runner staggered to the seat, slumped forward, and put his head in his hands.

After clocking the early finishers through, I hopped back in my van to return to the course. Schlett and the rest of the Back Bunch were fairly close together, well attended by Cruzado and feeling cheerful. The German, Sprengelmeyer, Wallis, and Surdyk were all approaching the end of the run. Westbrook was 5 miles out but feeling far better. He gave the thumbs up and ran slowly on, cracking a smile for the first time in days.

When I came upon Rogozinski, he was 15 minutes ahead of the cutoff schedule but still 10 miles out and looking like hell. Beam was walking with him, so I turned the wheel of my van over to Mercier and joined the pair for some time on the road.

One minute with Rogozinski revealed the foul mood that had overcome his normally positive attitude. Beam's small talk indicated that the pair had been through many phases of conversation but that the energy levels were beginning to sag. I tried to divert the focus by passing on the jokes Andy Lovy had told me a short time earlier. He had been going through hardships of his own, several miles back.

"I always tell people that what they think they can't do is just a boundary in the mind," the stocky little medic had said as he shuffled along in his awkward, bow-legged style. "Look at me, I tell them. I'm a mutant stump monster. I don't exactly inhabit the body of a distance runner, but I do ultramarathons because I focus on what is possible, instead of what is not. You can always stretch your limits if you're willing to try."

Running across the midwestern states while helping the others had been Lovy's goal, but a serious chafing problem was slowing him down. He tried various lubricants, but nothing worked to relieve the pain. He resorted to crotchless shorts and moved on, behind Rogozinski, focusing on the new goals that he constantly set.

I thought back to the Lewis and Clark Trail Run and the friendship I had made with the winner of the individual race.

"What do I think about?" Adrian Crane had reflected as we ran together in the middle of the week. "Anything and everything when I'm feeling good. When I'm hurting, I think that I only have 1 mile to go before I see the van and the crew. That's as far as I go. How do you eat an elephant? One bite at a time."

Rogozinski managed to keep moving, but within 5 miles was on the verge of dropping off the critical pace. Mercier returned with another passenger: Howie, who jumped out of the van and joined us on the road. We all refilled our bottles, continuing forward with a new injection of thoughts.

Half an hour later, we were still moving and on schedule, but Rogozinski seemed to be slipping again. Then we saw my van with Ed Kelley at the wheel.

"Anybody for pizza?" he said as he pulled off the road beside us. "Or perhaps a shot of ice cream?"

Half a mile from the school, we rounded a corner by the Dairy Frost take-out, where many of the athletes had gone for sundaes and shakes. The entire European contingent stood there, clapping and chanting as Rogozinski made his way by. I ran ahead to get my cameras and inform the rest of the group. He walked across the finish line holding hands with Dale, in agony, but overwhelmed with joy. It had taken him 11½ hours to cover the distance he normally would have completed in less than 6, but he accomplished his goal for the day. He made it 20 minutes before the cutoff.

The next stage was 53 miles to Indianapolis, and once again, the runners had the good fortune of starting off with uncommonly cool temperatures. Rogozinski spent the early part of the day with the Back Bunch again, but by the time the sun burned the mist from the fields, he had moved ahead to the middle of the pack.

Westbrook hung back, as did Debladis, who had been in his element since the previous night. A trio of female French students had learned of the race and arrived at the school to give their countryman a hand. Beam and I helped them pack supplies into their VW van in the morning. One could see them laughing with their adopted runner at several stops through the heat of the day. At one point, Debladis was sitting in their van, smiling, chewing on a hamburger while one of the ladies massaged his shoulders and another rewrapped the bandage on the lower part of his leg.

Milanovic set the pace once again, stretching his lead over the next runner to nearly 4 miles by the halfway point of the stage. He slowed on reaching the outskirts of Indianapolis and glided the last 5 miles but still finished 30 minutes ahead of second-place Laharrague. Warady was third, unconcerned that the Swiss gained another 90 minutes on his overall lead.

Serues and I spoke about trying to get Beam away from the group for some rest and relaxation, but the opportunity had yet to arise. Indianapolis had the most potential, so we agreed to collect the "Guardian Angel" and rendezvous at a particular bar.

The gathering place was packed, but Dale and I found Serues and extra seats at the bar. I felt guilty: It was the first time I had been in a strip joint since my wedding a year before. Then again, I reminded myself, it was all for a cause: a mental health break, male bonding, essential relief for a cracking-up crew.

Closing on the East was a total mixed bag. On one hand, it was a positive thing, because many areas had running clubs that on hearing of the Trans America, were eager to help. Traveling through cities, on the other hand, became an increasingly dangerous prospect. We had grown used to cars and trucks on the open highways, but traffic lights, discourteous drivers, and bad parts of town presented a new series of concerns. On the leg out of Indianapolis, a rash of incidents forced urban awareness back on the athletes.

Sheriffs issued warnings to drivers of crew vehicles about stopping on the side of the road; snarling dogs chased runners from their territories; and the day's leader was struck by a car.

It wasn't as bad as it could have been: Milanovic was a heads-up runner, even when he was tired. He had taken off from the pack again and was alone at the front, when a car cut him off at a turn. Luckily he saw the vehicle just in time to get out an arm. He pushed off and only suffered a jolt. He was rattled by how close to disaster he had come, but after Lovy made some adjustments, he continued on. He took the stage win, his third in a row.

The Ohio state line wasn't far off, and when Milanovic reached it the following morning, he seemed indestructible, running away from the pack and in utter control. I couldn't help but think about Rogozinski's streak in Kansas and how it had come to such a frustrating end.

"I'm not pushing so hard to make an injury," Milanovic explained, "but I hate to see things finish without some little bit of a race."

He covered the 33 miles to Lewisburg, Ohio, in less than 5 hours, 20 minutes ahead of Warady, who held onto the overall lead. Rogozinski finished last but still managed to cover the distance in 7:13.

The basement of the Trinity Lutheran Church where we stayed that night was somewhat dingy, but the reception from the Ohio River Runners added a homegrown touch even the Hiawatha Hilton couldn't provide. There were only two tiny toilets available, but club members ran a hose to a makeshift shower outside on the lawn so that the runners could scrub themselves clean. A pair of massage therapists set up a table and worked on sore bodies until well into the night. The athletes were treated to dinner in a local restaurant and shuttled back and forth when they wanted to eat.

"This is just so amazing," said local ultrarunner Ron Hart when we got back to the church. "Seeing these guys is incredible. And to think they've made it this far and are still in one piece."

Hart was the type of person you like the instant you meet: honest, friendly, ready to give the shirt off his back. Rogozinski and I sat under the moonlight with Hart and his wife, sharing running stories, beer, and outlooks on life until we were so weary we could no longer speak.

It's people like this, I thought, that have held the Trans America together since it left California. Will I ever remember all of them—or be able to tell them what a difference they made? As tired of the whole messed-up affair as I was, it made me sad to think that the end was a mere two weeks away.

14

Close to Home

Clay lies still, but blood's a rover;
Breath's a ware that will not keep.
Up lad: When the journey's over
They'll be time enough to sleep.
—A. E. Housman

Don Shepherd was one of the first athletes in the modern era to document his transcontinental run. Even more impressive than the forty-eight-year-old's crossing was the fact that he did it completely alone. With a long history in distance racing, Shepherd had decided it was something he just had to do. In 1964, he sailed from his home in South Africa to New York City, then caught a Greyhound to the opposite coast. He planned a return trip of less than three months and budgeted $10 a day.

Carrying a small canvas bag covered in foam to prevent friction, Shepherd set out from Los Angeles, relying on his own resourcefulness to find food and a place to sleep before nightfall. Despite numerous injuries and weight loss totaling 33 pounds, he completed the 3,200-mile journey in 73 days, 8 hours, and 20 minutes.

Five years later, a British Olympian set out to better the South African's feat, but in a very different way. Bruce Tulloh organized an expedition of sorts, traveling with two cars, a trailer, and a camper-van offering total support. Backed by corporate sponsors and a publishing contract, he intended to run as hard as he could.

The difficulty of the endeavor set in on the very first day, and Tulloh was forced to alter his plan a hundred times before reaching his goal. In the end, he covered the distance from city hall in Los Angeles to city hall in New York in 64 days, 21 hours, and 50 minutes. It may have been argued that Tulloh's concept was less pure than Shepherd's and his route was less than 2,900 miles, but it didn't matter. The record was his.

Whether talking of Shepherd, Tulloh, or any one of the dozens of athletes who crossed the nation by foot before them or since, many elements of the experience remain essentially the same. The extreme stress of the transcontinental crossing almost inevitably leads to injury, but it has been amply proven that a strong mind enables the shattered body to forge forever ahead.

James Shapiro speaks of injury during his 1981 crossing in *Meditations from the Breakdown Lane*:

> Under no circumstances in my previous life would I have violated all the instincts that warn you to lay off. What could I do? It didn't feel like a one-day rest would help—it needed at least a week. Sleep was the cure. Go to sleep and wake up and get out of bed putting your weight down slowly. Newspapers and phone calls and the prattle of your children and the hope of success in your job that morning do not exist in the world of the journey runner. The world has gone about its business of daily mayhem and earthquakes, but all that matters in that empty motel room, empty except for yourself, is how the muscles will speak.

Richard Westbrook was the perfect patient. He had followed Ross's instructions to the letter, and he was regaining his form. During his fourth-place finish into Lewisburg, Ohio, he hadn't pushed himself and felt very little pain. He seemed happier as he ate his bowl of Wheaties on day fifty-one than he had for most of the trip.

"If Richard was a football player or a short-distance runner, he would have been on his back and told to rest for a couple of weeks," Ross said later. "These ultramarathoners have an incredible ability to recover from injuries. They almost seem to be able to heal themselves."

A sharp contrast was Debladis: The Frenchman never listened to advice and paid for his stubbornness almost every day of the race. He had run hard on back-to-back days in an attempt to overtake Surdyk in the standings and had awoken in the church basement as tired and sore as ever before. Ross shook his head in frustration as he taped the swollen shins and ankles in preparation for the 52 miles ahead. "I told him to take it easy, but he has no common sense."

Milanovic got down to work immediately in the heavy morning mist and took command right from the start. Riley cycled alongside, but at the 30-mile mark he erroneously led the Swiss runner north instead of continuing east. By the time the race director realized his mistake and returned to the intersection he had marked incorrectly, five others had followed the wrong path. They all turned around and ran back to the proper route, saving their thoughts until later that day.

When we reached the school in South Vienna, Ohio, that afternoon, Serues, Kenney, and I agreed to deduct 15 minutes from the times of the runners who had been led off the course by the mismarked turn. Riley had little to say about the mishap. "It's no big deal," Kenney reiterated, the same broken record repeating overused words. "It's happened before. It'll happen again . . ."

Milanovic finished first once again; Laharrague was second, only 10 minutes back. Westbrook came in 12 minutes later, running in comfort, his recovery almost complete. Kelley and Schieke finished together, followed by Hodson, Warady, and Rogozinski, all within 1½ hours of the winning time.

Rogozinski was still struggling to find the best combination of shoe padding, running stride, and thought processes, but he managed to place eighth for the day. He was testing himself out, trying to focus on Pennsylvania. He wanted to appear strong, if at all possible, when nearing his home.

Tom Possert, a well-known ultrarunner from Cincinnati, turned up to offer Sprengelmeyer and Howie a bed for the night.

"It'll do you good to get away from things for a while," he told his friends, "and my girlfriend said I'm not allowed to take no for an answer."

Howie came to me, feeling guilty about accepting, but I insisted he leave. The little Scotsman was due for a break. Possert proposed to return Howie to the race several days later, but he and Sprengelmeyer were back well before starting time the very next day.

At our stopover in South Vienna, there was no restaurant around and no meal organized for the night. The only real facility was an IGA across from the school. Some of the runners bought barbecued chicken or deli sandwiches at the store and took them back to the gym. I drove 10 miles back to Springfield, Ohio, with Serues and the rest of the group. We talked and laughed, the way good friends do, about the things that had happened during the day—and the crazy expectations we had for New York.

I knew that Jane had been working through her *Runner's World* contacts to secure permits and special permissions for the finish in Central Park, but beyond that there were no concrete plans. Riley had told me months earlier that Sri Chinmoy disciples would take care of everyone when the race ended, yet the times I had mentioned it since, the race director had been vague.

Sri Chinmoy is an eastern thinker whose philosophy includes gaining enlightenment through physical achievement, powered by the strength of the mind. A great musical, poetic, and artistic talent, the guru has been a major force in the world of ultrarunning and has established a following all over the world. His Sri Chinmoy Marathon Teams have put on challenging races ranging from 10 kilometers up to 1300 miles. Many of the Trans America athletes had taken part in the group's multiday events in New York over the years. They made friends with each other, got to know the guru's followers, and experienced the generosity he so openly shares with the rest of the world.

Howie informed me, however, that the Sri Chinmoy disciples were overwhelmed with preparations for a birthday fete and concert that involved visitors from all over the globe. They may be able to house a few close friends, he said, but there was no way they could care for the whole Trans America group.

Warady and I were talking after stage fifty-two, when the race leader asked me what was happening in New York. Riley sat beside him on a lawn chair, so I turned the question over to the race director.

"That's too far away to worry about now," Riley responded. "There're more important things to deal with than the end of the race."

Two days later, when I took a poll to determine who had accommodations arranged for the end of the race, I learned that Warady's parents were planning a luxurious reception for their son, and he in turn, had offered the race organizers a room in his suite.

Throughout the stage from South Vienna to Reynoldsburg, Ohio, Westbrook battled it out with Laharrague. Rounding the final corner that led to the finish at the United Methodist Church, the pair sprinted, elbowing each other as though they were racing for medals on a banked indoor track. They crossed under the banner together in 7:43, 13 minutes behind Milanovic, who had taken the stage for the sixth day in a row.

"I thought I should let him go," Westbrook confided later, "but everything felt good. I figured I had to test myself eventually, to give it a shot and get back into my stride."

Rogozinski sought out Wallis as company for the long, difficult day. The youngest and the oldest in the race came across the line together in 11:28. Milanovic had gained 6 hours on Rogozinski, moving him into second place in the standings. With twelve days left in the race, however, Warady was still more than 18 hours ahead.

Community involvement was always appreciated, and there were times when the Trans America became the focal point of a town. Local people reveled in the opportunity to be part of such a monumental event and always enjoyed hearing about the runners, the race standings, and tales from the road. At the United Methodist Church in Reynoldsburg, Ohio, members of the congregation hosted a dinner on the lawn.

"This really is a lot like a job," Milanovic said the next day, after he won his seventh consecutive stage. "You get up early in the morning, find some breakfast, and then run for 8 or 10 hours, maybe a little bit more. When you are done you get yourself a shower if you are lucky, buy some food, do laundry, and find a place to sleep for the night. Time is the problem: There is never enough."

Thunderstorms and rain showers had punctuated the morning for the second day in a row, but by the midpoint of the rolling 57-mile stage to New Concord, Ohio, the heat and humidity had returned. Milanovic ran to the front but was chased by Laharrague throughout the day. The Swiss came out on top once again, gaining 1 hour on Warady. The overall leader finished comfortably behind Laharrague and Westbrook. Rogozinski ran with Sprengelmeyer and Hodson, finishing another hour and 40 minutes back.

Westbrook asserted himself the following day, fighting it out with Laharrague for command of the stage, while Milanovic ran comfortably with Schieke, content not to push the pace. The leaders started off reasonably under cool, sunny skies; their pace was controlled by rough, narrow shoulders on the side of the road. Howie and I traveled back and forth on the course, tending the runners with our meager supplies. In the late morning, we debated whether to go ahead to set up the finish or take one more swing through the field. The day was heating up, and since Cruzado had left, we had no extra helpers. Support once again was critically low.

"They won't get there before 12:15," Howie said, "12 at the earliest, even if they pick up the pace."

He had been almost perfect in his estimates, and I had to agree that the leaders couldn't run much faster through the final 10 miles of the stage. We turned back, stopped to fuel Milanovic, Schieke, Kelley, Rogozinski, and Schlett, and then came upon Beam.

"Bill's got everyone covered back there," he said. "I'll hang with this bunch. You go on ahead."

It was almost noon by the time we got to the pretty town of St. Clairsville, Ohio, but we had yet to see Westbrook or Laharrague. Road construction slowed my maniacal driving as I followed Kenney's directions onto South Sugar Street and into the Belmont County Fairgrounds. I raced up the hill toward the recreation center and saw the big Ryder, the rental car with Georgia plates, and Riley with his bike. At the end of the gravel parking lot stood Laharrague. The sign above his head was ominous: "Welcome to Red Devil Stadium." He hadn't even noticed the reference to his nickname. He was too busy seething with rage.

Westbrook and Laharrague had increased their pace to sub-7-minute miles in the last part of the stage and fought it out to the absolute end. The Georgian's handler had helped him refuel without stopping, but the Frenchman had to rely on Kenney's aid stations to keep himself hydrated and fed. To add to Laharrague's frustration, Volk and Tyler had developed a system of running with Westbrook, switching roles of pacer and driver throughout the day. When Laharrague found himself unable to catch the other runner, he expressed anger at the system that allowed such disparity in a supposedly competitive event.

"This is not fair!" he yelled at Riley. "These rules make a joke of the race! I should have won today, but his crew never gave me any help. He had a pacer the whole of the way."

Howie and I spoke about it later that night. "Emile isn't so bad," said the Scotsman. "He's just so focused on doing as well as 'e can in the race."

"He's intense, all right, but at least there are no bones about where he stands. No pretense in the Red Devil. He spits out whatever's on his mind."

"David's actually not that bad either, but if I was in his position, I wouldn't be cruisin' to the finish. I'd be openin' it up, showin' that I won 'cause I'm a better runner, not just 'cause I've 'ad better luck—and money to afford support in the race."

Rogozinski came back from an outing with Tyler. There was speculation on whether their daily search for ice cream was the beginning of a romance; it had turned into a regular thing.

"I'm totally psyched," said the young runner as he joined us on the curb outside the gym. "Tomorrow we head into the best part of the race: western Pennsylvania." He sounded as though he'd forgotten about the stress fracture and hadn't a care in the world.

Several visitors had been helping Rogozinski in recent days, but for him, nothing would feel better than nearing his home. He was looking forward to sneaking away with some friends for a night on the town.

Most of the others were asleep when we stole back into the gym, and after brushing his teeth, Howie felt it was time for a practical joke.

"Three-thirty," he said, just loud enough for Serues to hear. "Time to get up."

Bill jumped out of his sleeping bag, grabbed a towel, and bolted for the bathroom without a thought. He came out a couple minutes later, exasperation giving way to laughter as he threatened to cut Howie off from the beer. It was only 9:30 at night. In the morning, we became hysterical when Riley made his regular call: "Three-thirty. Where are the lights?"

Instead of the 53 miles we had been expecting for stage fifty-five, it measured out to 60¼ miles, which made it the longest day of the race.

"How can they do that?" said Surdyk when he got the day's turn sheet. "How can they possibly make a 7-mile mistake?"

"Don't worry about it," replied Kenney with his typical unconcern. "The original mileages were only estimates. It'll probably mean the next stage is shorter than we thought, because New York is still the same distance away."

Laharrague and Riley spent the first few miles arguing about the pacing issue from the previous day.

"You're asking for it, Emile," yelled the race director as he rode ahead of the feisty Frenchman at the front of the pack. "I've told you before, and I mean it. If you don't like the rules, you're welcome to get the hell out of the race!"

Westbrook, Milanovic, Rogozinski, and Warady ran nearby, hot on their trail. Ten miles into the stage, the runners veered off the road onto a painted metal bridge. Rogozinski moved to the front as they crossed over the Ohio River and ran through Wheeling, West Virginia. Fifteen miles later, the race would enter Pennsylvania, and the local hero was determined to lead the way, no matter how badly it hurt.

Halfway through the stage, we started seeing little signs stuck in the dirt on the side of the road. "Go Rogo." "Welcome home Rogo." "Go get 'em Tom." Rogozinski pushed on, putting 2½ miles between himself and second-place Laharrague. He had been looking forward to the hilly terrain but hadn't expected to have to run it with a broken bone in his foot.

"I'm doing the best I can," he said during one of his breaks at the van. "Just keep the pain reliever flowing and forget about the foot, I tell myself. It's no longer a valid excuse."

It had been incredible to see adrenaline and desire drive the injured athlete through the preceding week, but it was almost beyond belief to watch him demolish the field during one of the most difficult stages of the race.

Monongahela, Pennsylvania, was a bustling town, the oldest in the Keystone State. The stage ended at the fire hall, where the mayor and chief of operations held the finishing tape. Rogozinski ran across the line, ecstatic, in 9½ hours. His father and aunt were there and proudly hugged him before they went off to lunch. Rogozinski returned, grabbed his gear, and disappeared for the rest of the night. He didn't learn until morning that he had regained 2½ hours on Milanovic and more than 3 on Warady—in one single day.

Although he couldn't offer showers, the fire chief, Don Devore, turned the fire hall over to the Trans America group and gave us anything he could. When he learned that there were no meals organized, he rounded up a group of volunteers and cooked dinner: hamburgers, french fries, salad, and pasta, all we could eat. He opened the bar, told us to help ourselves to the draft beer, and walked down the street to persuade the owner of a nearby diner to prepare takeout in the morning, before the athletes headed out on their run.

Lovy and Ross had longer lineups than usual that night. The runners all despaired over the fact that the medical team had to leave in the morning and wouldn't be with us for the final stretch to New York.

"They're going to be all right," said Lovy as we walked through the drugstore that evening, gathering supplies for the first-aid kits he planned to leave in each of the vans.

The departure of the medics would be hard on the group, particularly those athletes who had relied on them so heavily in the previous week. Debladis was right back where he had been early on, fighting every day just to survive. Westbrook was fine, and even

Rogozinski seemed to be on the mend, but there were still nine long days until the end of the race.

"One thing you have to remember is that there are only a couple of exceptional runners out here, if you look at them athletically," said Lovy. "Most of these guys are just ordinary people. What sets them apart is what they have in common—they all have extraordinary minds."

Lovy was right, and his words made me realize that I was concerned as much for the rest of us as for the athletes on the course. The runners were so focused they had actually become tougher as the race progressed, but those in support roles had been worn down by the constant strain of meeting the athletes' needs on the road. The medical team had been as much help psychologically as they had been in the physical sense, and I hoped we would get along without them.

Stage fifty-six also turned out to be longer than the initial estimate—by 4 miles— and the mood was decidedly dour at the start. Shortly after the runners crossed the Monongahela River, the sun should have risen, but it was obscured by a dense, murky fog. The route to Ligonier, Pennsylvania, was extremely hilly. Twisting, narrow roads with low visibility made the race a laborious, mind-numbing affair for runners and crews alike.

It was Laharrague's turn to take control and hold it through to the end of the day. The Frenchman won the demanding 43-mile stage in 6 hours and 45 minutes. Westbrook was second, only 15 minutes behind.

There always seemed to be something that added spice to the most miserable of days, and on this next to last Friday of the race, it was the appearance of a crew from the ABC evening news. They arrived in the early afternoon and conducted interviews for a story scheduled to air at the end of the race. Milanovic and Rogozinski were humble and animated on-camera, full of wonder at the team spirit that had brought them and the others so far. Warady said there were no surprises: He had expected everything to turn out as it had and was just cruising to the finish, protecting his well-deserved lead.

"I'd have to be real unlucky not to win now," he said, "either that, or get hit by a car."

My wife and Jane Serues arrived separately that night to help us through the last full weekend of the race. By this point, the whole event had become such a huge part of me that I could barely tear myself away from the armory to go with my wife in search of a motel.

When the weekend was over, I noticed that Bill had regained some of his usual spark. I hoped that the time spent with Lisa had done the same for me, but I was so tired and road worn that I had no way of knowing.

Dale told me that he had been reacting like an automaton for the past several weeks. He said he tried to think about what he was doing, but it seemed like he was merely watching himself go through a series of Pavlovian motions rather than following a logical plan. I knew exactly what he meant, yet it seemed hard to imagine it all coming to an end. Almost before we knew it, we were approaching New York.

Seventeen days before the 1928 finish, Peter Gavuzzi had appeared to be the certain victor: He led by an insurmountable gap. The spritely Englishman had been running at the front of the pack for several weeks but was concealing a serious problem: His gums were so badly infected that he was unable to eat. Fourteen days without solid food left him in such a weakened state that he could hardly see straight.

It came as a shock when Gavuzzi dropped out during a 65-mile stage, leaving a twenty-year-old farm boy from Oklahoma named Andy Payne in control of the race. Johny Salo was 24 hours behind Payne and launched a full frontal attack, but he was still 15 hours out of the lead by the time the race came to an end. Payne took the $25,000 first prize, paid off the family mortgage, and put himself through college. His life was never the same.

Besides Payne and Salo, fifty-three other members of Pyle's entourage made it to the finish in New York. When the all-consuming event was over, many went through a period of anticlimax; they suddenly felt a great void in their lives.

"I believe in tapering off," said one. "When you've been through torture like this, it's dangerous to stop the agony all at once. When the misery's gone, you feel kind of lonesome and lost. A lot of the boys are feeling terrible and don't know what's the matter with them. The thing they are suffering from is a lack of pain."

The opportunity to relive the test of the road presented itself when Pyle announced his second race the following year. Starting at Columbus Circle on the southwest corner of Central Park, it went back toward Los Angeles. In a seesaw battle that took 78 days and covered more than 3,600 miles, Salo beat Gavuzzi by 2 minutes and 47 seconds. Long before the race ended, Pyle was totally broke. The promoter had borrowed heavily to pay off the money earners the first year, but in 1929, he left a trail of debts leading all the way back to New York. Not one of the winners received so much as a cent.

As in Pyle's day, the Trans America athletes' moods and running performances were often dictated by the standard of food and rest they received at the end of a stage. The final week was far different from the desert, but it offered some of the harshest conditions since the desolate West. Rain, hills, and treacherous roads made the running far from pleasant, and most of the stopovers were dismal, with cold showers or none at all. The Trans America entourage resembled Pyle's by the time it reached New Jersey: a beaten-down mass of humanity, merely struggling to survive. Anticipation of the finish was long gone. We had all worked long enough. It was time for it all to be over.

In keeping with the fickle nature of the race, the last stopover was one of the worst. The day was much like the rest of the week had been: cool and crisp, more reminiscent of fall on the Pacific Coast than summer in the East. When the runners began to arrive at St. Andrews Episcopal Church in South Orange, New Jersey, the caretaker bent over backward to accommodate them. Sadly, the only shower he could offer was a hose out in back.

The setup was certainly cause for grumbling, but as the athletes unloaded their gear from Kenney's truck, there was a sort of melancholy calm. On the one hand, there was the palpable elation of finishing an almost impossible task; on the other, existence had become so ephemeral that it was difficult to even think beyond the next day.

Every one of the Trans America group was delirious at the prospect of returning to normalcy: of waking at a sane hour, enjoying a leisurely breakfast with the family, reading the paper, and going off to a less painful day on the job. Still, we could not quite imagine leaving one another and the strange, unsanitized life of the road.

"This is not a temporary episode you're involved in," wrote Shapiro, in *Meditations from the Breakdown Lane*, "it's your life. In a rational way you know that it just goes on for two and a half months, but in the middle there is nothing else. Past life is gone, future life will never come, so there is only the doing. I could talk for ten thousand years, but it would not carry me an inch closer."

A pair of German television crews turned up to interview the Europeans, and one of the editors of *Ultrarunning* distributed the latest issue of his magazine, hot off the press.

Pizza and beer were supplied by Patrick Taylor, the *Runner's World* public-relations man. He congratulated the group, and then invited them to the pub to join him and his wife for a drink. There were a few takers, but most of the athletes tended to their affairs back at the church. Small groups formed to share conversation, jokes, and thoughts about what lay ahead. Surveying the Trans America entourage in the stuffy church lobby that night, I felt their closeness as never before.

Kenney, Jane, and a New York ultra organizer named Rich Innamorato had set out in the afternoon to reconnoiter the route from South Orange to Central Park. Jane and Innamorato coordinated their efforts with the New York Road Runner's Club (NYRRC) to ensure a more impressive finish than the lonely banner and two wooden ladders I had been using since leaving the California coast. When they returned at 10 P.M. Jane, Bill, Kenney, and I went over the plan. When we were done, Kenney rewrote the last day's four-page turn sheet and went in search of a copy machine. The rest of us rolled out our sleeping bags and settled down on the floor.

At 7:00 the next morning, Warady started out alone on the final stage of the race, another time trial. His closest rival was almost 6 hours back in overall time.

15

The Big Apple—and Beyond

To the Victor go the spoils.
In the eyes of Newberry Springs—
You are all Victors.
May the Saints bless you.
—Dick Devlin and the gang from the Bagdad Cafe

Although most of the positions had been settled early in the final week, Rogozinski had still wanted to improve his time as much as he could. He mounted an impressive charge and won two more stages in spite of his foot, moving within 1½ hours of Milanovic and solidifying his place in third. The only other spot that had been in question was number five: Neither Laharrague nor Kelley would relent. Three consecutive victories in Pennsylvania, however, moved the Frenchman ahead, and even though Kelley mounted a comeback attempt in New Jersey, the Red Devil proved too strong. Laharrague locked his position in fifth with the stage win on the second-to-last day.

Throughout the week, talk had revolved around the final stage. The leader would leave early, in a regular time trial start, but the rest of the athletes planned to run together, taking it easy and enjoying one another's company on their way into New York. Then, ½ mile from the finish, they would split up and fall into their positions, giving each a private moment of glory while passing under the Trans America banner for the very last time.

Laharrague and Debladis broke rank early, however, unmoved by the concept of such a finish. The Red Devil found his way through Newark, New Jersey, and over the George Washington Bridge, but Monsieur Amburger couldn't keep up. Unused to following turn sheets on his own, Debladis became frightened and ran back to the rest of the pack.

Laharrague had argued that along with prize money comes credibility—and that without it the endeavor was for fruitcakes or nuts—but still he chased after the leader, even though he knew there was nothing waiting at the end of the line.

Ridicule had come early and often to the Trans America athletes, but they were committed to their difficult task. The coverage in the *Denver Post* was typical of the commentary the race received from some of the press. An article ran alongside a piece about the Tour de France bicycle race: The cyclists drew raves akin to hero worship, but it was suggested that the Trans Americans had taken "insanity leave." The writer, presumably, would have had the authorities round the group up as they had done with Wise in Washington state. With us, they'd go the extra step and throw away the key.

The majority of radio talk show hosts were little better, although they did express amazement at the mettle of the participants before searching for laughs by running them down. My second interview with WTEM in the nation's capital occurred just before the end of the race.

"So tell me," said the jock at Harris-in-the-Morning, "what's the payoff for these guys when they get to New York?"

"The knowledge that they have become a part of history," I said in a far too serious tone, "and an intrinsic satisfaction that very few will ever know . . ."

"Now hold on a minute!" said a sidekick, while laughter from the studio gushed into the telephone receiver—and erupted over the air. "You mean these people are busting their chops for two months, and they're going to get to the finish line and there will be Barry, waiting with a handshake and a pat on the back? Such a deal!"

"Well, you have to understand, this is a great challenge . . ."

"I understand money, that's what I understand! It ranks way up there on my list of motivators. Knowledge and pride I can do without!"

When the Trans America runners made the final turn of their 2,836-mile ordeal, they were less than 20 meters from the statue of Christopher Columbus that sits at the intersection of Broadway and Central Park West. The sight ahead of them in the nation's most famous and elaborate park was worth every one of their four million steps.

Friends and family were there, along with a vast cross section of the New York curious, waiting to see the epic ending unfold. Half a dozen *Runner's World* people rushed about, taking care of a million tiny details, while a surprisingly large number from the press prepared for their shots. When the announcement came that a runner was approaching, George Hirsch and Ted Corbitt stretched a tape across the finishing chute. I scrambled among the other photographers but had difficulty focusing as I fought back the conflicting emotions that had plagued me through the last days of the endless ordeal.

The first vehicle around the corner was a white Pontiac with a road-worn Trans America sign on its side, driven by the woman whose sole focus of the summer was to help her husband accomplish his dream. Then came Kenney in my filthy brown van. A large timing clock sat atop the wooden ladders that had been carried so far. The vehicles motored past the impressive finishing structure that had been erected by volunteers from the NYRRC some hours before.

Howie sat on the curb beside the line in the exact same position he had assumed so many times before, his eyes on the wristwatch and his pen poised above the clipboard. Fred Lebow, race director of the New York Marathon, stood beside the Scotsman, looking out at the approaching runner and then up at the banner and the large overhead clock. The hours, minutes, and seconds were calibrated to the winner's overall time.

Jogging slowly, David Warady ran toward the crowd with a smile on his face. Holding a water bottle in his left hand, he raised his arms in the air and ran through the tape. He embraced his wife and family, accepted a bundle of roses, and was mobbed by the press. The man who lived where the Trans America had begun sixty-four days earlier was in control when it came to an end.

It was almost an hour before another athlete arrived. Despite the spotters posted on

Victory in the race with no prizes, said some, came for David Warady at too high a price. The winner had stayed away from most of the community experiences that were such an appealing part of the event; by sleeping in motels and eating on his own, he missed out on the camaraderie of evenings spent with the rest of the group.

the far side of the final turn, Laharrague slipped in unnoticed, sprinting through the crowd and over the line before he was even announced. The intense Frenchman had beaten Warady's time for the stage, but his effort left the standings unaffected and caused little stir at the finishing area. Laharrague did, at least, have the satisfaction of running the leg into his adopted hometown faster than anyone else.

One of the most notable of the many onlookers at the finish was also one of the most excited. Eighty- five-year-old Harry Abrahms hovered around while Warady spoke with reporters, reveling in the opportunity to shake hands and share his tale with a young man he considered a peer. The resident of Briercliffe, New York, is the last surviving veteran of Pyle's events. He had run in both directions, and he talked about the 1929 start as though it hadn't happened sixty-three years earlier, but the day before.

"That's where we started," Abrahms said in a gravelly voice, pointing to where the likeness of Columbus stood, out in the street. "Right there. I remember it well . . ."

Of those gathered for the culmination of the Trans America, several had firsthand knowledge of crossing the nation by foot. Bill Shultz and Skagerberg were there to share the elation of the finish. Tom McGrath was also on hand, keeping scavengers away from the VIP area and making certain that everyone was aware of his plans for later that night. McGrath had not only joined the athletes as a stage runner in western Pennsylvania, he also helped with the finish by organizing access to showers, accommodations, and a party at his restaurant to celebrate the end of the race. He knew what it was like to come in from the road: In 1977, the scrappy little Irishman had run from San Francisco to New York. It took him fifty-three days and one hour.

Corbitt had dreamt about it and had been at the New York finish nearly every time it was done. Innamorato had trained with James Shapiro and helped him in planning his run. Shultz and McGrath had done it themselves. And yet apart from Skagerberg, Abrahms was the only one who had gone from coast to coast as part of a race.

Milanovic took second, finishing 5 hours and 40 minutes back of Warady in overall time. When the Swiss crossed the line, he threw his cap in the air, embraced Warady, then turned to watch Rogozinski run his final few yards. The young Pittsburgh native punched the air, gave Milanovic a high five, and hugged Westbrook as he, too, came over the line. Kelley came in 15 seconds later, followed by Schieke and Wallis, 10 seconds apart.

"They asked me to run with them up in that group," said Wallis later, "and that was the greatest honor I could have asked for in this race."

Wallis managed eighth for the stage and eleventh in the standings of the overall race. Journey runner Linzbichler came in 1 second after Wallis. He was every bit as elated as those who had completed the competitive event.

Stefan Schlett was known for his showmanship, and although he didn't go quite as far as he would have liked—he had spoken of hiring a plane in Newark and parachuting into Central Park—he did end the run with his typical flair. He stopped at the final corner, had Volk unfurl an enormous Bavarian flag, and dropped to the ground. He did twenty-five perfect pushups, grabbed the flag, and ran to the finish, where he was doused in German champagne. He fell to his knees, threw his head back, and waved peace signs above his bubbling head.

Debladis finished alone, almost 1 hour later, staggering and falling, and then kissing the ground. The Frenchman sobbed in an agonized ecstasy, overwhelmed by emotion and tears. Lovy, McKeigue, and Ross had flown to New York for the finish, and they helped Debladis to the table where they had been checking over the others. My wife, Lisa, was there, helping to take pulses, pressure readings, and final samples of blood. Sprengelmeyer, Surdyk, and Hodson finished in just less than 7 hours, crossing under the banner together—and glad to be done. By the time Carter and Ransom arrived at the finish, everyone had packed up and left.

Tulloh had written of the final miles of his run:

I ran faster and faster. The lights were stopped for us, people in the streets stopped to look; gusts of steam blew up from the manhole covers. The hundreds of weary hours dropped from my feet as I covered the last quarter of a mile, veered across the square on my left, and jogged up the steps of City Hall . . .

It was a day I shall never forget, memorable not so much for the events it contained as for what it signified—the successful conclusion of a lengthy undertaking. When I had finished and stood on the steps of City Hall, they asked me: How does it feel to have done this? and I replied: It feels grand, because that was the answer they expected of me. It was impossible then to explain in a word or two how I felt about this thing that had been an obsession for so long. . .

Tape recorders, electronic flashes, and videocameras may have captured Warady's image and thoughts, but as with Tulloh, his initial words did little to capture the true spirit of the event.

"I feel great," said Warady, sounding almost bored when the first question was asked. "If I had the time, I'd do it again."

Even though Surdyk finished 147 hours behind the leader in cumulative time, the sentiments he expressed later were surprisingly similar.

"Physically, I could probably turn around and run right back. Almost any one of us could. But mentally the effect is devastating. I couldn't get myself to push every day. It's just too much to be able to ask."

McGrath's Irish hospitality that night proved the perfect reentry after the trials of the road. Even though the group that packed his restaurant swelled toward fifty, no one was allowed to buy so much as a beer. Howie's presentation was his best of the race; the applause that echoed from the Trans America section drowned out the Saturday night noise from the bar. Several runners called their newspapers from the kitchen during the festivities, the pride of achievement evident in their tone of voice.

I knew that without the contributions of Beam and Howie, many of the athletes never would have accomplished their goal, just as I knew that Lovy, McKeigue, and Ross were responsible for pulling many of the finishers through to the end. Cruzado, Bill, and Jane had all played significant roles.

I felt overwhelming joy for every one of the athletes, and yet I was oddly detached. I was happy to see my wife; I was delighted the wearying event was over; and yet I was an empty desert compared with the rest. It was as if the experience had drained from me the essence of life. I had no sense of accomplishment and took no pride in the tiny things I had done.

David Warady, his wife, and Riley went to Atlantic City on Monday, wielding copies of the *New York Times* article about the race in an attempt to get a discounted room. Within a week, the winner of the Trans America was in Florida visiting his in-laws, preparing for a leisurely drive back across the country. He eventually headed for home.

Warady's postrace reflections were similar in attitude to the words he had used from beginning to end: "Everything I looked forward to learning in this race, I've known all along. Just how to achieve incredible human performance? It's a matter of having the mind to get out and do it. It's in all of us. The things you've done in your life that have been the hardest—they are usually the best."

Even though he had talked during the Trans America about trying for North American ultra records in distances he considered soft, few believed that Warady had the speed to back up his words. The event ended in late August, yet in December he said his legs were still feeling the effect. Donations from his running club helped offset some of his race expenses, as did an advertising campaign for ASICS and fees from motivational talks. Warady returned to his job but struggled to regain balance in his life—and his form on the road.

The first thing Milan Milanovic did was to count the coins he had gathered on the way between California and New York. His 538 outnumbered Schieke's in sheer volume, but the German was the winner in a strict financial sense. "I found a $10 bill in California," said the gaunt Schieke, "but since then only little coins. They must be rich in the West."

Milanovic returned to Switzerland with little fanfare and for several months after the race was somewhat morose. He resumed his prerunning habits: smoking, drinking, and doing no exercise at all. He went to watch a 24-hour race early in 1993 and was reunited with Schieke.

The German said that once the media hype had died down, he too had felt very blasé. The reunion served as a motivator for both athletes and got them back on the run.

Milanovic and Schieke both resumed training and before the summer was over the German was running competitions on the track. In August, the Swiss went to Japan for a three-day nonstop 455-kilometer race. He completed the distance in extreme heat, humidity, and unbearable smog.

"I have no idea how I was able to finish," he said afterwards. "There were six of us who started in Hiroshima and only two made it to Nagasaki. I did not win, only against myself, and I did not quit."

Tom Rogozinski had resigned from his job at Boonsboro Middle School with two weeks left in the race.

"It's not fair to teach without enthusiasm," he told me the day he borrowed my computer to write his letter of resignation, "and I know I've lost my interest, at least for now."

An offer to pursue a graduate degree at IUP kept him busy during the fall months, but even living near his old cross-country house and slowly returning to speed training had little appeal. He left his coursework before it was completed.

"There's something very hard about returning to a day-to-day existence after the intense focus of the race. The little things are like distractions, nothing but noise."

In January, Rogozinski took a teaching job at another school in the same Maryland district he had left, but that lasted less than three months. He constantly weighed the need to have his life revolve around running and the narrowness that he feared would result.

By July, Rogozinski's recovery was complete: He won a grueling 50-mile trail race in the Pacific Northwest. Ten days later, he flew to Guam on a two-year teaching contract. If the times of the island's top competitors were any indication, he said, there was a good chance he'd be running for the national team. It didn't work out, however: By late November he was back in the States.

Richard Westbrook and Shelley Tyler left McGrath's restaurant before the others to begin their long drive home. The cross-country coach was back teaching on Tuesday, tired and almost unhappy that the Trans America experience had come to an end.

Westbrook's shin splints were completely healed, and as his team's season got under way, his speed slowly returned. He said he would do the race again someday if it followed a different course. For him, seeing the beauty of America so intimately had been the very best part.

Tyler returned to college and kept in touch with Rogozinski for several months after the race came to an end. The two talked vaguely about an ultra liaison, but they soon found that a long-distance relationship between two highly independent souls was untenable after the closeness of their time on the road.

Laharrague and Debladis lost contact shortly after reaching New York. Their friendship had always had an edge to it, as Debladis claimed to be the number one French runner in the Trans America because Laharrague resided in New York. The last-place finisher returned to Toulouse and the hero's welcome he had hoped for; Laharrague sought refuge in a friend's apartment and continued to search for sponsorship in the ivory towers that surrounded his home.

Intent on competing in a second race if it offered prize money, Laharrague contacted Kenney several months later about the status of the advertised 1993 event.

"After speaking with you the other day," wrote Kenney in response, "I talked to David Warady and Jesse. They both expressed the importance of maintaining an atmosphere of camaraderie and cooperation during our race, and for that reason both were opposed to extending you an invitation to run. They cited your generally combative attitude, as well as incidents such as your hoarding of food meant for the group, and the threat of voodoo curses on others. This, of course, is in addition to your numerous shouting matches with us, and the many reports of how you ridiculed us behind our backs . . ."

The last time I spoke to the Frenchman, he told me he was giving up ultrarunning. He planned to return to jungle explorations and life among primitive tribes rather than continue with such an unprofessional sport.

Debladis's most recent letter said he hoped to return to the Trans America in 1993 or 1994, if he could get sponsorship again.

"I will return for the tenth anniversary of the Trans America in 2002," he wrote in French. "I hope that this fantastic race will have great success throughout the world."

Edward Kelley went to his mother's home in Sacramento to overcome the physical effects of the race before returning to Los Angeles and his search for a job. In spite of an extremely slow recovery, the concept of running as a lifestyle became an obsession he was unable to shake. Late in 1992, he tried to pull together a record-breaking transcontinental attempt of his own.

The idea was to follow a team approach, with himself, Howie, and Rogozinski blitzing the country in fifty-two days. He contacted me for help with proposals and pursued a national educational organization for fund-raising support. His notion was a good one, but he packaged it vaguely and never got the backing he needed to get it off the ground. Although he had vowed that if Riley was involved he would have nothing to do with another Trans America race, Kelley entered the second edition two weeks before it began. He finished fifth of the six who completed the low-key 1993 event and immediately began making plans to run again the following year.

Peter Hodson went back to a regular work and training routine as soon as he returned to England. His performance at a 24-hour event two weeks later was less than impressive under normal circumstances, but it saved him from the depressing withdrawal many others suffered after their two months on the run.

"What comes next?" he said about his future goals. "Why not an around-the-world run? This has proven to be just the sort of thing that I'm able to do."

By completing the Trans America, the Alien beat Tulloh's British record by more than a day. He was back in New York running a Sri Chinmoy multiday race the following fall.

Five days after Stefan Schlett reached New York, he joined his disciple friends for the 47-mile Sri Chinmoy Birthday Race. A week and a half later, he ran 50.4 miles across the Trans-Panama Highway from Colón on the Atlantic coast to Panama City on the Pacific, finishing fourth in the race. Seven days after that, he was in Switzerland for a 200-mile stage race that traversed the country from north to south; a week later, he took part in a multiday trail race in Wales.

The biggest event for the German "ultraman" came in November, when he competed in the eighteen-day Dekka-Ironman Triathlon in Mexico. He completed 24 miles of swimming, 1,120 miles of cycling, and 262 miles of running well within the time limit, and then took a climbing vacation among the volcanoes of the south. His schedule in 1993 was just as busy. The head of the Back Bunch did not let up.

Marty Sprengelmeyer called his sports editor from McGrath's restaurant and was asked about a statement he had made two weeks before.

"You said that you probably wouldn't enter again if there was another race," said Don Doxie of the *Quad City Times*. "How do you feel now?"

"There are no probablies about it: Never again. Once is an adventure. Twice is stupid."

Sprengelmeyer returned to job, family, and regular training, but when talk of a second event persisted, he worked hard at keeping informed. When he heard that *Runner's World* might be involved, he called me to confirm the rumors. Things were still up in the air, I told him, but he went ahead and sent Kenney his check.

"With sponsorship and good organization," he said by way of justification, "this can be a real race. It can be enjoyable, instead of the farce that last year's became."

Two days later, he learned that negotiations with *Runner's World* had come to an end. He immediately withdrew his name from the race.

John Wallis was surprised to see his wife and daughter at the finish, yet like most participants, he had mixed feelings about the end of the competition that had been his whole world for the previous two months: "It was definitely hard for us to go our own separate ways, but I don't know anyone who wasn't happy to see that final finish line in New York."

Getting back to his teaching job, spending time with his wife and new granddaughter, and preparing for new challenges kept the oldest finisher occupied for the rest of the fall. His positive outlook remains, even when thinking back to the near disasters that occurred throughout the course of the race.

"We grumbled a lot, but I've formed friendships and bonds with people that will last the rest of my life. A race like this is a test of survival, not really running ability. There were times when most of us wanted to call it quits, but we picked each other up and pushed on to New York."

John Surdyk returned to Chicago, kept in touch with many of the runners, and continued to take part in marathons and ultradistance runs. He inspired Ross to try a 50-

miler later that year and a 24-hour the following spring. He moved in July to study for an environmental engineering degree.

"Before this race, Al Howie was my hero as a runner," wrote Surdyk in one of his many letters in the months following the race, "but after, he was my hero as a person. To be such a great athlete and still be warm, funny, humble, and kind, even after all the bad breaks and abuse he took. This is something beyond greatness—it's pure goodness."

Howie himself wrote early in 1993, "My misfortunes and misadventures in the summer of '92 left me physically and mentally out of shape. During the months of September and October, I barely ran a step, my enthusiasm for ultrarunning and racing at an all-time low since I stumbled on the sport more than a decade before."

Working a series of jobs that included construction and net repair at an oyster farm, Howie's interest in doing what he does best slowly returned. At the end of November, with three weeks of weight training behind him, he set out from his home at Qualicum Beach for a typical Howie-style long-distance run. His destination was a race site in Sacramento, 1,200 miles to the south.

Supported by his wife from a van, he weathered a series of miserable storms and arrived in Sacramento on December 28. He was gleeful in anticipation of three days of rest before the start of the six-day race. He won but was disappointed with his 463 miles. He had hoped to run over 500 miles, but terrible conditions prevailed. Nevertheless, he was glad to be reunited with Schlett, Kelley, Cruzado, and others who had become so close the summer before.

Dale Beam felt good about his role in the race for a long period of time, knowing he had been an indispensable element in helping the struggling participants reach their incredible goal. Even though the "Dial" chanting took place every time we held a presentation, it was on day sixty-one that he gained a true sense of how strongly the athletes felt.

The stopover in Kutztown, Pennsylvania, was the closest the course came to the *Runner's World* headquarters. The sponsors put on a party that none of us will ever forget.

"This is our night to show the athletes how much we appreciate their efforts," Jane said when planning the festivities. "As runners ourselves, we are all amazed by what they have done."

In addition to an afternoon of refreshments and snacks, the Trans America athletes had the benefit of podiatrists and massage therapists until a wonderfully catered dinner began. After Howie's presentation, specially labeled T-shirts were handed out to Riley and Kenney for conceiving the race; Maria Farnon for being my lifeline back at the office; Bill for performing like a champion in a sticky situation; Jane for holding all the disparate elements together; and Howie for his morale boosting and constant support.

Beam, the Guardian Angel, received far more than a shirt. John Wallis's wife had made a custom teddy bear and dressed it up in a Trans America T-shirt and *Runner's World* cap, the garb Beam had worn often since the start of the race. The Big Man received a certificate of excellence for going above and beyond the call of duty, signed by the runners, along with the lovingly stitched bear.

It was 5 minutes before the applause subsided and the gentle, bearded man was able to speak.

"In his own way, everyone cares about each other," he said, choked with emotion. "Everyone has been tenacious and trapped in the ordeal. Nobody has wimped out. Even

Dale Beam, the Guardian Angel, was seen as a savior by most of the runners. Though he still struggles to find meaning in the chaotic event, he says that he is lucky: "To accomplish something good is a miracle, and the road to miracles is the road for all those that won a special place in my heart. I would be a fool to lose, by some sleight of hand of my overactive brain, the sweet hope of these most wonderful friends."

though we get mad at each other, I think later we will realize what warriors we all are. The thirteen survivors are true American heroes, even if some of them are from countries other than the States."

Like many of us, Beam still grapples to find meaning in the Trans America endeavor—what lessons had we learned from our lives on the road?

"Outside of the commitment, curiosity, and challenge," he said the last time we spoke, "I would say we were surely caught in a mire. We had race directors who could not communicate, journey runners who were lost in their neuroses, and competitive runners who really had no choice but to suffer through, however they could . . .

"People overdo things. They should understand what they are about to do. I would warn anyone contemplating running such a race that they are embarking on a voyage they will not come back from. Their life will never, ever, be exactly the same."

A great triathlete once said that it is necessary to view the deepest, darkest parts of yourself in order to break through fear and uncertainty and perform at your ultimate best. We all came to grips with our personal demons that summer and gained new insight into human possibility as a final result. John Surdyk, of all the finishers, may be the one who came closest to realizing his full potential. He was the man who had expected to be out of the race in less than a week.

"It's amazing that people can actually get through something like this," he observed. "It just shows what is possible when you focus the mind. I guess you have to believe in the unbelievable—and then be willing to give it a try . . ."

Final Results:

The 1992 Runner's World *Trans America Footrace, June 20–August 22, 1992.*
2935.8 miles in sixty-four stages.

Competitive Division

1. David Warady, 35	Huntington Beach, CA	521:35:57
2. Milan Milanovic, 32	Switzerland	527:16:21
3. Tom Rogozinski, 24	Pittsburgh, PA	528:48:54
4. Richard Westbrook, 45	Jonesboro, GA	537:33:04
5. Emile Laharrague, 45	France	542:38:03
6. Edward Kelley, 34	Hollywood, CA	545:09:45
7. Helmut Schieke, 53	Germany	563:05:40
8. Peter Hodson, 37	Great Britian	596:20:01
9. Stefan Schlett, 30	Germany	619:28:22
10. Marty Sprengelmeyer, 46	Davenport, IA	640:56:30
11. John Wallis, 55	Ludington, MI	653:14:37
12. John Surdyk, 37	Cicero, IL	695:30:41
13. Serge Debladis, 44	France	704:09:10

Journey Division

Helmut Linzbichler, 51	Austria	2,615 miles
Leon Ransom, 55	San Diego, CA	1,924 miles
Carol Carter, 44	San Diego, CA	1,306 miles
Paul Soyka, 43	North Bergen, NJ	1,071 miles
Celine Mercier, 44	Canada	403 miles